Dancing With Spies

A Memoir by Andrei Ostalski

Copyright © 2025 Andrei Ostalski

ISBN: 9781918264531

All rights reserved, including the right to reproduce this book, or portions thereof in any form. No part of this text may be reproduced, transmitted, downloaded, decompiled, reverse engineered, or stored, in any form or introduced into any information storage and retrieval system, in any form or by any means, whether electronic or mechanical without the express written permission of the author.

Part One

IN SEARCH OF A DESTINY

Chapter One

The Wrong Choice

On a warm, dark Thursday night, on 10 January 1991, three limousines with diplomatic number plates were parked near the arrival terminal of Abu Dhabi International Airport. All three had been sent to meet me, and I had to decide which one to choose. I made the wrong choice and landed myself in horrendous trouble. The consequences of that spur-of-the-moment decision were profound and far-reaching, not only for me personally, but also for my family, and some other people too. Looking back, it is extraordinary to think how much can hang on such accidental choices – how they can take life down unexpected byways, through unforeseen twists and turns, and shape its outcome. Had I known at the time how extensively that incident would affect my life, I would have thought long and hard before choosing which car would take me into town. As it was, I acted impulsively, without a clue about the calamity that would befall me.

That evening, I had come to Abu Dhabi on an Aeroflot flight from Moscow. My newspaper, *Izvestia*, had sent me to cover the war which, everyone knew, was about to break out in the Gulf. I had hoped to be met by a colleague from the local TASS office. I was astonished to be greeted by three people instead.

More than a quarter of a century later, if I close my eyes, I can still clearly see the three serious-looking 'comrades' waiting for me in the arrivals hall of the airport. Two were standing together, chatting; the third, a rather thickset man with greying hair, of a vaguely eastern appearance, stood aside, keeping his distance from the other two.

He was the only one of the three I knew by sight, but seeing him there came as a bolt from the blue. I was stunned, as the last time I had been face-to-face with him had been over ten years earlier. I hadn't expected to see him again, let alone find him greeting me at Abu Dhabi airport. Known to me as 'Comrade S.', he was a member of that powerful and sinister organisation that I, like most other Soviet citizens, had feared all my life. One day in the early 80s, I was summoned by my bosses at the Soviet TASS News Agency, where I worked at the time, and ordered to train him as a journalist. In the end, during the brief period, two or three weeks we spent together, I couldn't help warming to him a bit. He was a very likeable man.

Can someone learn to be a professional journalist in such an absurdly short time? Probably not, but I did my best to teach him, and he was a quick learner. I guessed he was a spy who, for some reason, didn't have time to build a plausible 'cover', with the necessary training period. We never talked about his real job, and I never heard from him again after he disappeared. I certainly never saw his byline in the press. I rightly assumed he hadn't needed to use his journalistic cover for long, if at all, and the training I had given him had been a waste of time. I didn't know what had become of him, nor did I care: I was sure he had left my life forever.

And yet there he was, older and greyer but immediately recognisable, grinning at me slyly as if taking pleasure from the shock he had given me. 'A remarkable coincidence,' I thought, 'but surely, he must be meeting someone else.'. There were plenty of other Russians on that plane from Moscow. I was wrong. 'Comrade S.' took a step towards me.

'Nice to see you again, Andrei,' he said, shaking my hand.

'Nice to see you too,' I managed to say.

I looked at him in astonishment, still trying to figure out what he was doing there and what it had to do with me. Ten years earlier, though considered a high-flyer at TASS, I was still young and politically naïve. The Communist Party's hold on power seemed absolute and unshakeable. And the KGB was its fearsome instrument.

Now, ten years on, we lived in a different world. Gorbachev's *Perestroika* had opened the floodgates and broken the Communist Party's monopoly on power. I had enjoyed a spectacular career at *Izvestia*, a liberal newspaper at the forefront of the fight for press freedom and democratic reforms. Its daily circulation exceeded 11 million copies. It was widely respected both within Russia and beyond the country's borders, having sidelined the Communist Party's Pravda, which was still extremely conservative and simply outdated. Being a senior journalist at *Izvestia* was an enviable position, an honour, the pinnacle of a Russian journalist's career. I was part of a radical anti-communist faction among the newspaper's staff. We were no longer afraid of the KGB (or so we liked to think).

'Let me introduce you to these two gentlemen,' said 'Comrade S.', directing me towards the other two members of the reception party: 'This is Alexander, first secretary of our embassy here.'

The diplomat, who was formally dressed in a jacket and tie, shook my hand, a serious expression on his face.

'And this youngster is Sergei, chief of *Novosti News Agency*'s Abu Dhabi bureau.'

At least Sergei had a nice smile. I had heard good things about him from a common friend in Moscow who said he was kind and friendly and would certainly be willing to help.

'Look how many people have come to meet you, Andrei,' said 'Comrade S.'. 'You must choose one of us to take you to the embassy. The ambassador is eagerly awaiting you, even at this late hour.'

He sounded serious, but his tone had a note of hidden irony. But why on Earth were there three of them? How had that come about? That was what I was trying to fathom.

My editor at *Izvestia* had decided that I should try to gain access to Saudi Arabia to report on the impending war, as that country would be the closest to the military action. I thought it was a brilliant idea, but the only problem was that the USSR didn't have diplomatic relations with the country at the time. So I had to go somewhere else to get a Saudi visa. Mr Vladimir Petrovsky, deputy Soviet foreign minister, with whom we had been on friendly terms, suggested that I try the United Arab Emirates, as Riyadh and Abu Dhabi were allies.

'Also, don't forget that our ambassador there is Konstantin Kharchev; he is one of us and will be happy to help. I will send him a telegram asking him to help you as much as he can,' Petrovsky said.

I knew perfectly well what he had meant by saying that the Soviet ambassador to Abu Dhabi was 'one of us'. Mr Kharchev was talked about a lot in Moscow. An obscure Party apparatchik, he had been accidentally appointed head of the Religious Affairs Council on the eve of Gorbachev's *Perestroika*. His predecessor, KGB general Vladimir Kuroyedov, had been a sworn enemy of the Russian Orthodox church, as well as all other faiths, and had bragged that his life's dream was to show the last Russian priest on TV. Alexander Yakovlev, Gorbachev's ideology tsar and the father of *Glasnost*, had encouraged Kharchev to change all that and try to give the church as much freedom as possible, freeing it from the KGB's control. Kharchev had appeared to try to achieve those goals but had probably lacked the political cunning to succeed. Perhaps, it had just been an impossible mission to start with. In the end, hardliners within the KGB and the Communist Party Central Committee set in motion a complex plot against Kharchev, accusing him of all sorts of mistakes and faults, both real and imaginary. Yakovlev had failed to defend him, and he was dismissed. The Russian liberals saw him as a courageous reformer who had fallen victim to a reactionary conspiracy.

In Soviet tradition, officials who lost their jobs for committing a political faux pas or who had been found lacking in some way would be given a consolation prize: another position, perhaps less important and prominent, but still retaining some prestige. Such official appointees belonged to a privileged caste known as the 'nomenklatura' in Soviet bureaucratic jargon. Kharchev was one of them; he had been a sailor and later trained and worked as a marine engineer, but, taking a party career route under Brezhnev, managed to get into the diplomatic service and was appointed an ambassador, serving in that capacity in Guyana for a few years. Then, after being sacked from his nearly ministerial position at the Religious Affairs Council, he returned to the Foreign Ministry. The first ambassadorial posting to become vacant then was in the UAE, which was why it had been offered to him. It was a short-sighted appointment, as an experienced and accomplished diplomat, preferably an Arabic speaker, was needed in Abu Dhabi at that critical time to navigate the region's complexities. Mr Kharchev hadn't demonstrated any noteworthy diplomatic talents. Such skills were not required in Guyana, a country on the farthest edge of great powers' interests. It had been a pure sinecure.

Such appointees would often be a burden on other embassy diplomats, who would end up doing all the work while the big chief delivered official speeches to show off their importance. But even in that, they weren't always successful. Often, they didn't speak any foreign languages. When meeting local officials or other diplomats, they would have to rely on an interpreter, usually the embassy's first secretary. The latter would not only have to act as a translator but also watch over his boss, stopping him from making foolish remarks, correcting his factual mistakes, helping him to ask properly formulated questions and give reasonable answers to queries. Later, the same diplomat would also have to draft an account of the conversation to be forwarded to the Foreign Ministry in Moscow. Ambassadors were officially required to edit this text, but this requirement did not always lead to improvement. It was a way to confirm their importance to themselves and their subordinates.

There were, however, some notable and rare exceptions. Anatoly Dobrynin, who served as the USSR's Ambassador to the USA for 24 years, was a professional, talented diplomat of the highest calibre, winning the respect of American presidents and other officials. Another brilliant Soviet ambassador was Sergei Vinogradov. Largely thanks to him, Moscow and Paris enjoyed a very special relationship in the 1960s. To be sure, Soviet courtship of Paris had been made possible by De Gaulle's burning desire to demonstrate France's independence from Washington. Still, I doubt that it would have happened without Vinogradov. Not only did he have to work his charm on de Gaulle and his ministers, but he also had to keep his own government in line, stopping it from making shocking mistakes and idiotic faux pas. Take, for example, the incredible story of the outstanding Russian ballet dancer, Rudolf Nureyev, who was granted political asylum in France in 1961. If Ambassador Vinogradov hadn't prevailed over the KGB, which had suggested punishing 'the traitor' by breaking his legs, that special relationship would have had no chance to survive, and European history might have taken a slightly different course.

Even under the most competent ambassadors, first secretaries often played a crucial role. Alexander Smirnov, who held that position at the Soviet Embassy in Mozambique in the early 1980s and later became the USSR's Ambassador to Portugal, is the hero of my favourite anecdote from the Soviet days. He served as an official interpreter at the Kremlin talks between Brezhnev and the Mozambican leader Samora Machel. While the African guest passionately orated about his country's enormous potential, Brezhnev fell asleep. He then woke up abruptly, astonished and apparently somewhat blindsided, to see an inky black face on the other side of the negotiating table. Shocked, Brezhnev interrupted Machel's speech, asking in an unsteady voice: 'Who are you? And where are you from?' Without hesitation, the interpreter asked a very different question in Portuguese, making a polite, to-the-point observation that seemed to demonstrate how attentively the head of the Soviet state had been following his interlocutor's narration. Then, translating the Mozambican's answer, Smirnov said: 'Comrade Brezhnev, comrade Machel says that his country, Mozambique, is quite rich in…'

A possibly disastrous incident was averted, and the talks and Brezhnev's reputation were saved. I heard the story directly from the then-Soviet Ambassador to Mozambique, Valentin Vdovin, who had been present at the talks. (And who also happened to be my father-in-law). He was delighted by his first secretary's sang-froid and later did his utmost to support his career.

Still, good ambassadors were a rarity in the Soviet Union, and there was no reason to expect Konstantin Kharchev to be one of the happy exceptions. I had heard rumours of his typical party-boss rudeness and tales of the mistreatment his subordinates allegedly suffered at his hands; his embassy management was said to involve humiliating dressing-downs of diplomats in front of their colleagues for perceived faults or mistakes. Nevertheless, Petrovsky's calling him 'one of us' rang in my ears and had made me give Mr Kharchev the benefit of the doubt, allowing for the possibility that the rumours had been greatly exaggerated. Malign gossip was not uncommon within and around the Soviet diplomatic service. It was not unheard of that someone, especially an outsider, would become the subject of unfounded bad-mouthing. I wondered whether his liberal reputation had been the real reason for his unpopularity among the Foreign Ministry conservatives. After all, it wasn't very likely that a major player and political heavyweight like Petrovsky would so badly misjudge someone.

I failed to foresee how an ambassador might react to a telegram from the Deputy Foreign Minister curtly demanding that he 'render all possible assistance' to a visiting journalist. That was not what typically happened, unless the said journalist was on some state business and an unusually important one, for that. Or unless his journalistic position was just a cover for something else entirely. That short telegram might have contained some wording that would have made it clear to an experienced diplomat that it didn't necessarily reflect some secret decree coming from high above, but was essentially just a personal favour to a friendly journalist. But Kharchev's experience in those matters was limited. He could have easily mistaken Petrovsky's missive for a request from a very high authority, if not the Politburo itself. As a result, the ambassador ordered a senior diplomat to meet me at the airport and insisted on seeing me right away – at whatever hour.

Sergei, the second member of the 'reception party', was there, I guessed, as a result of the well-intended stubbornness of my good friend Dmitry Osipov, who worked for *Novosti News Agency* and who had insisted on asking his colleague to go to the airport too, just in case. But what about 'Comrade S.'? How did he come into the equation? He explained it himself: 'You see, Victor couldn't meet you as his wife unexpectedly had to fly to Moscow and he had to accompany her to the airport, so at the last moment I decided to step in'.

Victor Lebedev was precisely the person I expected to see meeting me – he was a former colleague of mine who happened to be the TASS news agency's Abu Dhabi correspondent. Not anticipating the hype Petrovsky's telegram would create, I asked Lebedev to pick me up at the airport, and he kindly agreed. So, 'Comrade S.' was supposed to be a last-minute substitute for Lebedev. That seemed to explain the surprising appearance of my old mysterious 'trainee', although I was not entirely sure I should fully believe that narrative.

One of the minor, yet telling, symptoms of the Soviet system's decay was the way spies operating under journalistic cover were positioned in relation to ordinary, genuine journalists — known as 'the clean' — like myself. We were expected not to notice the oddity of the situation when these men — many of them with clear signs of military bearing — would suddenly and inexplicably appear among us, only to be dispatched abroad a few months later to serve as 'correspondents'. About half of all journalistic positions abroad were 'reserved' for intelligence services. Usually, they would replace men of a similar type — in other words, other spies — which really didn't make much sense, as it made the task of watching them far easier for local counter-intelligence. They would know that whoever comes to replace the previous TASS correspondent in, say, Kuwait, would practically invariably belong to the same organisation, be it the KGB or the GRU (Military intelligence service). There were exceptions when something went wrong, such as when a spy was caught red-handed and ordered to leave the country. In such cases, a 'clean' journalist could be chosen to take up the compromised post for a while – as happened to me once.

It was impossible not to guess the function and special status of those strangers amongst us. They mainly kept to themselves, often talking to each other in low voices, falling suddenly silent when one of us approached. In our turn, we often discussed them behind their backs. Somehow, it was common knowledge who among them was '*blizhniy*' – literally meaning 'the near one', the coded designation for the KGB, and who was '*dalniy*', 'the distant one', which stood for military intelligence, or the GRU. Some of the spies didn't try too hard to conceal what their real job was. It seemed they couldn't resist bragging about their special position. Nevertheless, everybody had to play the game and pretend the whole charade remained a secret. We, 'the clean ones', were not supposed to know anything about it; thus, we were not even sworn to secrecy. These fake journalists had much in common, but they were still different. Some were highly intelligent, others were less so; a few seemed charming, while most were dull. Nearly all of them shared a common trait of hauteur and carried themselves as if they couldn't for a moment forget that they belonged to a superior caste.

'Comrade S.' was actually a rare exception. He seemed a pleasant, civil and entertaining interlocutor. Devoid of any arrogance, he clearly possessed a sense of humour and even self-irony, which is not a very typical characteristic of his profession, to put it mildly. We almost made friends, as much as was possible in such a peculiar situation. He was also a diligent student, although it was clear that he would never win any prizes in journalism; extraordinary talents were not required of him for the elementary maintenance of a plausible cover. In fact, not all of my 'clean' colleagues shone particularly in terms of stylistic skills. He did not disclose any secrets of his real profession, and I was careful not to ask. Then he disappeared, and I thought I would most likely never see him again.

And suddenly I found myself in this encounter, many years later, in another country, in an entirely different political situation in the world and in our homeland. I had a superb career at *Izvestia*. I had joined the most liberal faction in the newspaper, whose unofficial leader was Igor Golembiovsky. They were bright, talented people, great masters, and I felt flattered that they accepted me as one of their own. I was also asked to do some moonlighting in Yakovlev's section of the propaganda department of the Central Committee, participating informally and without any remuneration or recognition in the preparation of speeches and documents. Alexander Yakovlev was the architect of *Glasnost* and the informal leader of the liberal wing inside the Party apparatus. He was also a hate figure for hardliners. Out of mischief, I gave occasional interviews to Radio Liberty and the BBC. For the KGB, I became an enemy. And, deep in my heart, I still harboured some fear: I was still afraid of this organisation, though not to the same extent as before.

The devil made me do it: against my better judgment, I decided to get in the car with 'Comrade S.'. Some strange, sentimental feeling overcame me; after all, we parted company in a friendly way, and I had never seen the two others, who were total strangers to me. Curiosity also played a part — I wanted to find out what had become of my 'apprentice', and how he had ended up in the Emirates. It was clear that he was no longer merely 'a correspondent', but someone of considerably higher standing within the Soviet hierarchy. Of course, I had no idea exactly what position he held. Had I known, I would have kept well away from him.

'Do you know, Andrei, who I am?' 'Comrade S.' asked, as soon as we drove from the airport.

'I've got no idea.'

'Well, fancy that: I am the resident here.'

In Soviet parlance, the word 'resident' referred to the Chief of the Station, the main representative of the KGB or military intelligence in the country. The rest of its employees, working under the cover of various Soviet offices, were entirely subordinated to him. (There is no gender issue here: there hadn't been a woman resident ever.) Typically, the official diplomatic rank of the resident would be that of an Embassy counsellor, but in many respects, he would feel almost equal to the ambassador. In Soviet times, the resident's clout was great. It was in his power to break a career and brand anyone who would cross his path 'nevyezdnoy' (not allowed to travel abroad). And that would be a huge blow, as a foreign posting was the only chance for an average Soviet citizen to legitimately improve their living standard and gain some semblance of relative prosperity. The ambassadors were usually wary of residents, though in post-Stalin times they were considered the nomenclature of the Politburo and thus officially classified as untouchables. In Yemen, the KGB dug up dirt on the Ambassador - he was a great ladies' man - but when the so-called 'security officer' sent the compromising evidence to the Centre, he was recalled to Moscow and sacked (I will tell this story in more detail in one of the following chapters). I have known several cases where the ambassadors were at odds with the residents, but it often ended in tears for both.

My father-in-law, who was experienced in all such matters, taught me that the resident or his people might one day try to involve me in their risky machinations, and that in these cases, it was vital never to refuse directly. Play it dumb, telling them that one was ready to help: 'I am a Soviet patriot, after all! But I must go to the ambassador and ask for his permission. At the Communist Party Central Committee, I was told that in all delicate situations, the ambassador must be consulted and that, as the representative of the Politburo, he is my ultimate boss in the host country. From him, there can be no secrets.' In the overwhelming majority of cases, the request would be immediately withdrawn, my father-in-law said, because KGB operatives would not want the ambassador to be aware of their activities. I followed my father-in-law's advice, and it worked.

In the *Perestroika* years, KGB men were forced to tread more cautiously. Their power was on the wane. And after the fall of the USSR, in the first post-Soviet years, it came to the point that some embassies tried to get rid of 'diplomats in uniform'. An example of this was in London, where the Russian ambassador to the UK, Boris Pankin, sent nearly all of them home. In my last *Izvestia* years before I left for London, the intelligence chiefs of the KGB were almost fawning on me, and once it came to the point that the very head of Soviet intelligence had asked me, in a half-whisper, the incredible question: whom I would advise him to put a stake on: Gorbachev or Yeltsin! (This happened during the short period of dual power in late 1991).

Fortunately, I have not had any relations with the Russian state system for many years now, but rumours reach me that the old times seem to be back. There is no Politburo, though. The intelligence services, especially the political police, are all-powerful, and ambassadors are increasingly forced to kowtow to residents.

On that hot, murky, humid evening in Abu Dhabi, I was still stuck in no man's land, mired in limbo. In part, I remained a Soviet journalist. A shiver ran down my spine — and not because of the powerful air conditioner in the smart car carrying me smoothly to the Soviet Embassy. I was shocked to realise that I was being driven around the city by the KGB resident in person. 'Is it a good thing?' I was asking myself. And I knew that it wasn't. Firstly, what will local security services think about me? They would, no doubt, exchange information with their colleagues in the West. And secondly...

'Comrade S.' was kindness itself: he wanted to hear the latest Moscow news and political gossip, and made it clear that I had nothing to fear from him, that he generally felt indebted to me and would be happy to help. And, intuitively, I believed him.

'It's all very well,' I said, 'but you know what bothers me? You are going to take me to the ambassador now, are you not?'

'Oh, yes, he is keenly awaiting you, sitting in his office even at this late hour. Shows off how hard he works.'

'Don't you think he can misinterpret the situation? What would he think of me if you, of all people, were to introduce me to him? Please, I beg you, explain to him clearly and right away that we are not colleagues, are not involved in any common enterprises, that it just so happened that we became friends, on a strictly personal level.'

'Not to worry. I'll make it absolutely clear to him.'

I calmed down and spent what was left of the short journey to the Embassy staring out of the window, marvelling at this miracle of miracles – a breath-taking mirage that had grown in the middle of the desert.

Ambassador Kharchev was really waiting for me in his office. A cosy table lamp projected soft light on his desk, where an apparently important document lay in front of him. It was with some possibly slightly exaggerated difficulty that he took his eyes off it when we entered. But for some reason, he did not turn the paper face down, as was the rule when you were dealing with secret information.

'Comrade S.', aka the KGB resident in the UAE, loudly and clearly reported, as we had agreed, that we had known each other from our days in TASS, that we didn't work for the same organisation and that the only thing that tied us together was shared memories of a short period when life had brought us into contact. Andrei, he said, is a well-known journalist who holds a prominent position at *Izvestia* and is here on behalf of that newspaper.

I felt everything was stated clearly and correctly. The ambassador, though, seemed to be in a strange mood. He listened absent-mindedly, as if it were of no interest to him. He nodded dreamily, as if his thoughts were hovering somewhere far away.

'May I leave you alone with Andrei? 'Comrade S.' said. 'I have some urgent business to attend to.'

'Go,' allowed Kharchev. And the chief of the spies bowed out.

I felt relieved. Now the situation has been clarified, I thought with relief. The ambassador understands that I have nothing to do with the *Kontora* (one of the somewhat outdated Russian terms for the KGB, literally meaning 'The Office'). Otherwise, why would the resident leave me alone with the ambassador? After all, when someone important is coming from, say, the Ministry of Foreign Trade, the trade representative in the host country is necessarily present during the conversation with the embassy bosses. A newspaper or news agency correspondent will surely participate in any embassy's conversation with an important guest from the Moscow headquarters of that media organisation, and so on. The same applies to visits by any other significant figures from Soviet departments. After exchanging a few pleasantries, Ambassador Kharchev took the bull by the horns.

'Moscow has set me the task of rendering you every possible assistance,' he said. 'In what way exactly can I help?'

'If you could assist me in getting a Saudi visa, I would be very grateful to you,' I replied.

'Of course. Tomorrow I will arrange to meet with the Saudi ambassador. I have a great relationship with him. I think that you will get your visa. But, perhaps, he will have to refer your request to Riyadh. It may take several days or even a couple of weeks. What would you like to do in the meantime?'

'Oh, I'll find something to do, this is a fascinating country. I have only been to Dubai, and then just passing through. Maybe I can gather enough material for a feature article,' I said.

And then... To this day, when I remember what happened next, I still feel the shock I experienced. I was totally dumbfounded and couldn't believe my own ears.

Kharchev suddenly said:

'You may be interested to know that I have a meeting with the Emirates' Chief of Staff in the coming days. I can probably persuade him to grant you an interview. Would you like that?'

I was taken aback.

'Thank you, Konstantin Mikhailovich, it's very kind of you, but I ... I do not know ... it's so unexpected ... I have to think and consult with my editors,' I muttered.

I thought to myself: as a journalist, shouldn't I seize any opportunity to interview an important official, especially somebody who usually does not give any interviews? But on the other hand, it is a weird proposition. Why on earth should *Izvestia* be interested in running this kind of material? Even if the local general, against all odds, agrees to an interview, he wouldn't probably say anything interesting; he would only repeat the official statements of his government and the Foreign Ministry - and this is the best we can hope for. And we will then have to print it all, because otherwise, it would cause embarrassment. No, my hunch was: do not mess with it.

Kharchev, laughing in an odd way, continued:

'By all means, of course, consult the editors, ha-ha... But my advice is: don't miss this opportunity, the local Chief of Staff is an interesting person.'

And after a pause, he added, as if hammering a nail:

'And then you could turn him at the same time.'

The ambassador used the term '*zaverbuyete*', which is widely known in Russia thanks to spy thrillers and popular films. It meant recruiting, turning somebody into your 'asset'. The noun derived from this word is '*verbovka*' (the recruitment of an agent), and from very early childhood every Soviet citizen was taught to dread sneaky and treacherous Western spies, who, of course, were everywhere, trying to make you betray your motherland, by way of this frightful '*verbovka*'. The unavoidable punishment for this crime was a disgraceful death. The KGB, probably, had some other terms for it, but all the laymen knew by heart those scary words.

'Excuse me, what?!'

I thought I had misheard. Surely, he couldn't be suggesting that he wanted me to '*zaverbovat*' the Chief of Staff of the

Emirates' armed forces! Who was the ambassador taking me for if he thought I could do such an unthinkable thing?

Kharchev met my eye and gave a curious, almost unsettling smile, his gaze turning unnervingly glassy as if something inside him had briefly switched off. I was looking at him and thinking: *No, it can't be real! It must be a joke, albeit a stupid one. Even if he still thinks I'm some incredibly important boss from the KGB, he can't be a complete idiot.*

He surely understands, I thought, that an attempt to turn such a high-ranking military figure of a relatively friendly (but not allied) country can only end in one thing: a monstrous scandal with dire consequences for a cretin capable of such an idiotic act. In 2018, Matthew Hedges, a researcher from Durham University, was sentenced to life imprisonment in the UAE simply for asking a local senior official a security-related question. It is hard to imagine why the Soviet spy acting in a much more brazen way would have been treated any more compassionately. Inevitably, it would have meant horrendous trouble for the Russian embassy too, and for His Excellency personally, especially if it were the ambassador himself who had introduced such a hapless 'recruiter of spies' to the general!

Even less audacious steps may end in disaster. For example, in one country where I worked, a KGB officer had only started to develop approaches to the president's brother when he was immediately expelled. Then the Soviet embassy got a dressing-down from the local authorities. No, I thought, it was a joke, Kharchev can't be serious, he is taking the mickey. I honestly did not know how to respond to that kind of humour, if humour it was.

Meanwhile, the ambassador changed the subject. But in what way!

'Andrei Vsevolodovich,' he said in sotto voce, 'May I in my turn ask a favour of you. I want to pick your brains and seek your advice on something.'

'But of course, Konstantin Mikhailovich! I will do whatever I can... Though I cannot imagine what that might be. But by all means, I will be delighted to be of help.'

'As you can see, I have stayed up late, struggling with a telegram, which I must send urgently to Moscow – it concerns military affairs... There is an unexpected opportunity to sell a large batch of equipment to the Emirates, which could generate significant revenue in hard currency for our country and strengthen our position here. Could you please review what I have written here? My experience in such matters is minimal. I am not always sure how it should be formulated and what kind of reaction to expect from particular government agencies.'

I could not believe my ears and eyes, either: the ambassador was trying to pass me the draft of that telegram.

I recoiled in horror. Clearly, it was a top-secret document that the ambassador would soon give to the cypher clerk for encoding. And he, the ambassador, was about to commit a criminal offence, punishable by a long term of imprisonment. It equated to disclosing state secrets of a very high category. And I, too, could have been accused of violating the law if I read a word of it!

'No, Konstantin Mikhailovich,' I cried out, 'I beg you, do not do it, I'm not going to read this.'

But the ambassador persisted, holding out the ill-fated document to me more resolutely. I pushed my chair away from the table and turned away. I even closed my eyes, just in case.

And then it hit me! That's probably how he understood the KGB resident's assurances that we were not colleagues and did not work together. He imagined that I was from the other major intelligence service of the USSR, the military one, the so-called GRU, which stands for *Glavnoye Razvedyvatel'noye Upravlenie* (The Chief Directorate of the Military Intelligence!). That would explain the emphasis on military affairs, and that's where the stupid (still stupid!) idea to recruit the Chief of Staff came from. God, why didn't 'Comrade S.' and I think of the possibility that the ambassador could interpret the situation this way! On the other hand, in this scenario, why wasn't the GRU resident present at our meeting? No, it still didn't make any sense.

'Konstantin Mikhailovich', I tried to bring the ambassador to his senses. 'Please understand, I am a journalist of *Izvestia*, I came here to get to Saudi Arabia so that I could cover the coming war from there...'

'Yes, I know about Saudi Arabia. I told you that everything would be done, so do not worry,' he answered, but I couldn't help but notice a trace of irritation in his voice now.

Finally, he took the ill-fated paper away from me, even turning it face down.

'Thank God, I am safe!' I thought with relief.

But then the conversation took a new, and again unpleasant, turn.

'What I completely fail to understand,' said the ambassador with righteous indignation in his voice, 'is why you, in your organisation, allow attacks on the most sacred pillars of our country – against the Communist Party itself! Why are you so indifferent? Why do you tolerate these despicable anti-Soviet actions? These outrageous, vile intrigues that play into the hands of our enemies?'

And he even started to beat out a rhythm with his hand as an accompaniment for his invective.

I need to get out of here — now, I thought, as I sprang to my feet, mumbling:

'Konstantin Mikhailovich, this is a misunderstanding, I'm from the newspaper *Izvestia*, which, on the contrary...'

I wanted to say that our newspaper itself, in a sense, was involved in those vile attacks, i.e. dared to publish acute criticism of the Communist Party's policies, but the words stuck in my throat. I was clearly in shock. Contrary to all logic and all my hopes, Ambassador Kharchev clearly took me for an incredibly important boss of the KGB, or a super-agent, some kind of James Bond, capable of magically recruiting anyone, be it Chiefs of Staff or anybody else. In his view, my mission must have been so secret that even the resident could not know its details. Utter nonsense, of course, but how else could I interpret the ambassador's words and behaviour? Vladimir Petrovsky must have made a big mistake, I thought. Comrade Kharchev was not 'one of us'. Far from it: he was the flesh and blood of the party bureaucracy, viciously snapping at *Glasnost*, the openness to the world and the freedom of speech we were fighting for.

Muttering at the door some incoherent thanks, I popped out of the ambassador's office like a bullet.

'Comrade S.' must have been waiting for me somewhere close by, because he appeared in the hallway almost immediately.

'So how did it go? Everything is fine, I hope?' he asked.

'You wish! It has been a complete disaster! He either didn't listen to you or didn't believe you... I beg you, do speak to him alone as soon as possible, explaining the situation, but please be tactful. Tell him it was just a silly misunderstanding.'

'Ok, will do. You shouldn't be so worked up about it.'

'How can I not? He will hate me to death now. He will feel he behaved like a complete idiot and almost betrayed state secrets to a hack.'

'Comrade S.' tried to assuage my anxiety as much as he could, but I decided there and then to stay away from the embassy and from my old acquaintance and his colleagues, too. Sergei Kanayev, a pleasant friend of my soul mate Dima Osipov, and therefore, by definition, a 'clean journalist', will surely help me, as well as the TASS correspondent Victor Lebedev. With his legendary contacts among locals, including highly influential people, he might even get me the treasured Saudi visa, I thought. I was now sure about one thing: I couldn't expect any support from the ambassador and the embassy.

The latter conclusion was soon proven true: Ambassador Kharchev changed his mind about assisting me, and all other options fell through as well, so I never made it to Saudi Arabia. I had to cover Operation Desert Storm from Abu Dhabi. I tried my best and, it seemed, didn't do too badly in the end. At *Izvestia*, I was praised for doing a good job, and I had to pretend that the commendation was deserved, even though I knew full well that relying on sources in the United Arab Emirates — the local press, international agencies, and TV channels — without any first-hand reporting was far from ideal. But there was nothing I could do about it; that unfortunate situation stemmed from the wrong choice I made at Abu Dhabi International Airport. But that was not the only, nor even the primary, consequence of that erroneous decision. There was more to come.

Waking up the next morning in the bright, warm light, I saw clear blue sky in the window, went for a swim in the outdoor pool at the hotel, and ate a delicious breakfast. Life went on, and around me was a rich, engaging and fascinating country. What else does a traveller and journalist need to be happy? To hell with all the Kharchevs and all intelligence services of the world, I thought.

But on January 13, 1991, the stars stood in the fatal configuration – for the USSR, the world, and me. That Sunday, British Foreign Secretary Sir Douglas Hurd was giving a press conference. He had come to Abu Dhabi to discuss the fate of occupied Kuwait. I got myself accredited for that press conference in advance, just in case, although I wasn't pinning great hopes on it, as I didn't expect many newsworthy pronouncements to come from that briefing. The military action was about to begin, but the politicians and diplomats kept their mouths shut. However, it became known that the British were going to organise the evacuation of their expatriates' dependents from the Emirates, which in itself confirmed the imminence of hostilities. It seemed worthwhile to try to find out more.

In the morning, I regretted having obtained my accreditation. My head felt as though it were stuffed with sawdust — I hadn't slept a wink all night. What did I care about 'Desert Storm' when a storm of my own was raging within me?

All through the night, I sat in my hotel room watching television, mostly CNN, which was broadcasting reports from Vilnius — scenes of civilians being gunned down by KGB commandos as they stood up for their freedom. It was sheer carnage.

I realised that hating the KGB made little sense — it was merely a tool, albeit a ruthless one, in the hands of the Communist Party. It was not the face of "Comrade S." that haunted me, but the hypocritical countenance of Ambassador Kharchev. In my ears still echoed his furious cries about 'attacks on the sacred'. Now, the 'Sacred Empire' he had spoken of was striking back — and I could almost see him gloating.

For me, it was a crisis of conscience. I was still a member of the Communist Party, and Gorbachev had only recently been one of my heroes. Now my whole world was collapsing, and the pain was immense.

Still feeling far from normal, I staggered into Douglas Hurd's press conference. I sat there, half-listening as British journalists pressed the Foreign Secretary with questions about the fate of expatriates' families and the broader military and political outlook. Yet all I could hear was Kharchev's voice, echoing in my head. For me, it had become a symbol of everything I despised that day. It was because of him that my head throbbed; because of him that I saw myself, as if from the outside, standing up and putting a question to the British Foreign Secretary:

'Sir Douglas, do you know what happened last night in Vilnius? Don't you think that it is even more important than the impending Gulf War? What can you say about it?'

I was ready to react with a contemptuous smile if the Foreign Secretary would cowardly sidestep my question, mumbling something about the subject of the press conference being the problem of the Iraqi occupation of Kuwait and not the situation in Lithuania. That is what the reaction of the West, in general, will be, I thought. Lithuania is a faraway country that the Western public knows nothing about. Gorbachev is their favourite; they would never say a bad word about him.

But Sir Douglas Hurd took me by surprise. He hardly wasted a second to formulate a response. And what a response it was! The echo of my voice didn't quite die in the hall when his powerful baritone drowned it: 'We are closely monitoring what is happening in Vilnius. I can say that our future relations with Gorbachev depend on what the outcome of these events is going to be and in what way this crisis will be resolved.'

I was amazed that he did not talk about the relationship with the Soviet Union or Moscow. No, his response was clearly and unequivocally personalised: the relationship with Gorbachev was at stake. So, the British, at least, clearly understood that in the Soviet system nothing significant can happen without the consent, if not the direct orders, of the head of the Party. Knowing the Gorbachev style, I was sure that a written instruction on the use of firearms against civilians did not exist, but the KGB chairman, Vladimir Kryuchkov, certainly was given some clear hint that he could go ahead with extreme measures. Otherwise, he would have never dared to act. It was a Soviet version of Thomas Becket's syndrome. 'Will no one rid me of this turbulent priest?' asked King Henry II in exasperation, and the courtiers rushed to kill the saint.

But the king later repented: came to Canterbury Cathedral in rags and barefoot, fell at the altar and humbly allowed the monks to whip him.

Not only wasn't Gorbachev whipped, but he never even repented or appropriately apologised. In his defence, he muttered something completely unintelligible, pretending that he knew nothing in advance of what was going to happen in Vilnius. The perpetrators of the crime were not punished either. In the King Henry's case, there was at least the excuse that the killers escaped to Scotland, which was independent in those days, but KGB Chairman Kryuchkov and his special forces were near at hand.

Back at the hotel, I went to the business centre to look at the news reports and was totally astonished to see that Reuters, AP and other international agencies had put Douglas Hurd's response to my question at the top of their news summaries. It turned out to be the West's first official reaction to the events in Vilnius. And I, unwittingly, became the co-author of a sensation.

But there was a price to pay for that moment of glory. A fellow citizen of mine, probably a junior diplomat from the Soviet embassy, attended that press conference and rushed to inform the ambassador, who cherished the opportunity for sweet revenge, of getting back at me for the idiotic situation he himself had created. He was determined to punish me for his own stupidity, for confusing me with some KGB big shot or a super-agent. Victor Lebedev later told me (and other sources confirmed it) that the next morning, the ambassador convened a meeting of senior diplomats. The only item on the agenda was: *'What to do about Ostalski's provocation?'* The ambassador was inclined to send an urgent encrypted radiogram detailing my alleged treachery — a report that would be read by every member of the Politburo. However, before taking such a drastic step, he wanted to gather some support. In truth, most of the time, embassy staff tend to agree with whatever the ambassador proposes; disagreement can be detrimental to one's career. But occasionally, there are exceptions — and one of them occurred that day at the Soviet embassy in Abu Dhabi.

When it was the KGB resident's turn to speak, 'Comrade S.' duly denounced my so-called 'provocation', but then cautiously suggested that it might be wise to think matters through more carefully before taking any drastic action. 'Maybe we shouldn't rush things,' he said. 'Ostalski is Yakovlev's man, and it's said there's growing tension between the latter and certain other members of the Politburo. Do we really want to stick our necks out and get involved in political quarrels at that level? Should we risk taking sides? Perhaps it would be wiser to wait until the situation becomes clearer. In my view, we should proceed with caution.'

I cannot vouch for the exact accuracy of this account, but something along those lines was certainly said. And Victor Lebedev, who was present at the meeting as secretary of the local Communist Party committee, supported 'Comrade S.' in recommending restraint.

Perhaps he realised that by sending that telegram, he might make a personal enemy of Yakovlev, as well as of Petrovsky, and even fall out with the KGB resident. Maybe he remembered what had happened to him in Moscow, when his career had suffered a serious setback after he crossed influential figures from different factions. So this time, he chose not to take the risk, to postpone his moment of revenge.

'Do you think we should be careful and hold back for now?' he said. And suddenly, it turned out that everyone present agreed.

Had Kharchev gone ahead and sent such a telegram, I would certainly have been fired — *Perestroika* or not. I would have been forced to leave my beloved *Izvestia*. And no Yakovlev could have saved me, especially since I wasn't even sure he remembered who I was, despite the small bits of work I occasionally did for his people in the Central Committee apparatus.

It turned out that 'Comrade S.' repaid his small debt to me with significant interest added to the capital. But I didn't want to have anything more to do with any Soviet officials. As I correctly envisaged, I received no help whatsoever from Kharchev and the embassy. Although I never acquired the coveted Saudi visa and, in the end, had to do my best to cover the Gulf War from Abu Dhabi, I managed to enjoy my stay in the UAE. Apart from my correspondent's work, my life in the Emirates was quite comfortable, even with the modest *Izvestia*'s travel allowance.

'Comrade S.' and his subordinates didn't bother me. Only at the last moment, a couple of days before my return to Moscow, did he reappear, inviting me for a farewell lunch at a Lebanese restaurant. I did not dare to refuse him. I was a bit wary of any dubious suggestions, offers or requests he might come up with, as now it was I who was in his debt. But he surprised me again: his offer had nothing to do with intelligence matters at all. He asked me if I would be interested in leaving *Izvestia* to join a new newspaper with generally democratic leanings. He hinted that if I agreed, I could be appointed its editor-in-chief, which would be a huge promotion. The newspaper was to receive the support of a politician whose career seemed to be on the rise. I got the impression that the politician in question was either a good personal friend of 'Comrade S.' or even a close relative. I answered honestly that I would think about it, but I doubted I would agree.

We reminisced about the idiotic incident which happened on my first day in Abu Dhabi, and 'Comrade S.' chuckled good-naturedly, without trying to claim any credit for his role in my salvation. And I didn't bring up the subject of Kharchev's raging about the so-called 'vile attacks on the Communist Party' and the KGB's supposed 'obligation to stop them'. I didn't discuss any of this with the resident, nor was I prepared to confess to him how those antics had affected me, as they were firmly linked in my mind with the shameful events in Vilnius and what I perceived at the time as Gorbachev's betrayal of the democratic reform.

If Kharchev's hysterical shrieks didn't reverberate constantly in my head, perhaps I wouldn't have rushed things the way I did. But as it happened, the moment I was back in Moscow, I went straight to the secretary of the *Izvestia* Communist Party bureau and asked for my membership to be terminated at once. I might have taken more time to mull things over and even discussed my next move with my friends in the Central Committee apparatus. They, I am sure, would have tried to persuade me not to hurry, arguing that if all the progressives and liberals, and everybody capable of lateral thinking, would leave the Communist Party, only reactionaries and mediocrity would remain there. And the struggle for democratic reform will be lost. But I no longer wanted to hear any of this.

My father-in-law urged me to think twice about leaving the party; he was being rational, but his advice was based solely on his own past experience, which was no longer necessarily relevant.

At that time, *Izvestia*'s party organiser (secretary) was Igor Abakumov — an outstanding journalist who specialised in agriculture and rural affairs. He was, at heart, a liberal and a democrat, and he also had an excellent sense of humour — an essential human quality.

Igor didn't take his party duties too seriously; nonetheless, he always tried to dissuade colleagues who wanted to cancel their membership. He used arguments similar to those of my friends among the Central Committee's liberals, who claimed that the best way to push for reform was from within the Party.

But I came well-prepared. When a citizen applied to join the Party, they had to submit an official application confirming that they had thoroughly studied the Communist Party Programme and Charter, agreed with the former, and vowed to fully adhere to the latter. Mimicking that formula, I wrote in my official statement:

'I have concluded that the idea of communism is a harmful utopia. I disagree with the Communist Programme, and I testify that I am no longer able to follow the stipulations of the Party Charter. In this situation, my continued membership in the Party would be unforgivable hypocrisy.'

'Let's see what Abakumov will say to that,' I thought.

Igor was clearly impressed and couldn't immediately think of a counterargument. Standing up, he took my statement and membership card and dropped them into a drawer, where, it seemed, he kept other similar documents. Then he shook my hand solemnly and wished me good luck and success in my new life.

My family was a bit nervous, but initially, nothing seemed to have changed in my life. As before, I went to work every morning. I still attended editorial meetings, wrote articles and interviewed newsmakers. In the first few days after the event, I felt curious glances from my colleagues in *Izvestia*'s Foreign Desk, and I heard them whispering behind my back. As far as I was aware, I was a rare bird; nobody else among them was prepared to follow my example. After all, this was the most privileged group of journalists in the newspaper, many of whom came from the families of the Soviet 'aristocracy', prominent Party apparatchiks or KGB bosses. At the same time, my action must have endeared me further to the people who at that moment mattered for me most – the liberals, our own homegrown 'dissidents' who were calling shots in some other departments, covering internal politics and economy, etc. Some of them, I heard, may have left the Party already, and many more were contemplating such a move.

Still, for a moment, I did wonder whether I had acted recklessly, hardly able to believe what I had done. After all, throughout my adult life, expulsion from the Communist Party had been regarded as a severe punishment for any offender. It almost always led to dismissal from one's position of privilege. In any case, the person concerned would certainly be denied those much-coveted foreign assignments — the very reason most people joined the Foreign Desk in the first place.

And here was I, someone who had *expelled himself* from the Party of his own accord. Yet times had changed. My supervisors and the personnel department didn't know how to treat me — as a leper, or as if nothing had happened. They waited for guidance from above, but none ever came.

If I were to live my life again, I would never have joined the Communist Party. Yes, it would have meant giving up foreign travel, at least during the first half of my life. But perhaps the writer within me would have been born much earlier — and that, I now realise, would have been more than enough compensation.

But in the first and probably the final version of my life, I had no idea what lay ahead. In early 1991, almost all of us believed that the Soviet Union still had a lot of life left in it. Moreover, the atmosphere thickened, and the political tension was visibly growing. Foreign Minister Eduard Shevardnadze, the man directly and justly associated with the attempts to open the Soviet Union to the world, resigned, warning of the danger of a coup d'état. And he did it with a huge bang, in the most dramatic fashion, while given the floor to speak at a major public gathering, the so-called Congress of People's Deputies. It was an unprecedented scandal, nothing like that had ever happened before. The architect of *Glasnost*, Alexander Yakovlev, formally retaining his position in the leadership, was actually isolated and no longer participated in political decision-making. Later, he told me that Gorbachev even refused to answer his phone calls; his assistants were instructed not to connect them. Gorbachev forgot to block one line of communication, the High-Frequency channel in the president's car. Yakovlev managed to get through to the president through it. The only words he had time to utter were: 'Mikhail Sergeyevich, they are plotting a coup against you'. Gorbachev just swore under his breath and hung up.

KGB chairman Vladimir Kryuchkov, increasingly perceived as one of the true rulers of the country, publicly declared all persons cooperating with Radio Liberty to be traitors and foreign spies. Thus, I officially made it into the KGB blacklist, and more was to come.

A few times in those days, I was buttonholed in the corridors of *Izvestia* by colleagues that I didn't know too well, who, having looked around carefully and making sure that nobody could overhear us, would say in half-whisper: 'Andrei, tread carefully! Whatever you do, don't mess with Liberty, or you will be sorry!'

I did not know whether they were doing somebody's bidding or sincerely wished to warn me of the danger.

Chapter Two

Clear and Present Danger

In mid-August 1991, I was going on vacation. Together with my wife, I planned to spend two weeks at a health spa called *Sanatoriy Druzhba* in the *Klyazma* region, not far from Moscow. The name of that establishment requires some explanation. The word '*sanatoriy*' in Russian has nothing to do with sanatorium, it means something completely different. It was a Soviet invention, a type of convalescent establishment where workers could recuperate and receive medical attention after suffering from serious illnesses. However, over time, the concept of *sanatoriy* had degraded along with everything else in the Soviet empire, becoming just an all-inclusive hotel and spa for the privileged, with some health-enhancing procedures offered as a bonus. *Druzhba*, meanwhile, translates as 'friendship', but there was a hint at some deeper meaning in this word, as this particular establishment served as the place of vacations for foreign communists who were given asylum in the USSR. Typically, though, you could buy a stint there if you had the right connections, even if you had nothing whatsoever to do with foreign Communist parties. That day, I was getting ready to lock up my cubicle in *Izvestia* and get on the way to *Klyazma*, when the telephone on my desk rang.

'Mr Ostalski,' said an unfamiliar voice on the phone. 'My name is ...' (the name meant nothing to me). 'We recently met in Munich, in the Radio Liberty office.'

Much as I tried, I couldn't remember meeting the gentleman.

'I am awfully sorry,' I said, 'but unfortunately, I will not be able to help you today. I am going on vacation, a car is waiting outside, and I literally don't have an extra minute to spare.'

'Oh, no,' the caller said, 'this time it is not about contributing to our radio programmes. We would like you to note the following information you may need. It will not take much of your time.'

Out of sheer politeness, I gave in with a sigh. I took a piece of paper on which some entries had already been made. I turned it over: the leaf's reverse side was free.

'I am ready,' I said.

And the man from Munich started dictating names and corresponding phone numbers. I knew some of these people: they were stringers and commentators, in varying degrees associated with Radio Liberty. But some of the other names on that list were new to me. All in all, there were about ten. The piece of paper proved to be not big enough, so I ended up writing the last two or three names on the page of my desk calendar.

'What kind of a roster is this?' I asked.

'Oh, this is just in case. Just a precaution.'

'Precaution? In case of what?', I asked.

'Oh, if something unexpected and unpleasant happens, you can call these numbers and maybe someone will be able to help,' replied the man from Liberty.

'And what is it that may or may not happen? What are you referring to?', I was becoming somewhat alarmed.

'Oh, no particular reason to worry, it is nothing much. Just a preventive measure. As they say, it is better to be safe than sorry. A safety net, if you like.'

'I don't understand,' I said.

What bloody nonsense, I thought to myself.

Later on, I would remember that conversation, asking myself time and again: How could I not have understood? How was it possible that I didn't get the message? Only a few days earlier, I had told a visiting British journalist that the idea of a coup d'état was in the air; some feared it, while others, the reactionaries, looked forward to it. And many in both camps considered it inevitable. It was a clear and present danger. Yet only one day later, I was in denial about it.

It was another case of doublethink: on the one hand, as an analyst, I spoke of a suffocating, ominous atmosphere, rife with the threat of a political earthquake and catastrophe, while on the other, in everyday life, I couldn't fully bring myself to believe in the possibility of a real coup d'état. It was something that occurred in other countries and affected other people. What does our daily life with its ordinary, petty concerns and chores have to do with it? Feverish packing for vacations and efforts to organise the family trip to *Klyazma* were the genuine reality.

I probably have to say a few words here about Radio Liberty and my association with it. For any Soviet citizen, it was a forbidden fruit. You could go to jail just for listening to it. At the university, we were taught that it was an ideological tool of the West designed to undermine the USSR, and, in a way, it was true. It was indeed an essential instrument of information warfare created by the USA to weaken the Communist regime. It had found the most sensitive, the sorest spot in the Soviet system – the total deficit of truthful news – and was hitting at it hard. The Party and the KGB tightly controlled the flow of information within the country, going to great lengths to keep the population ignorant of uncomfortable facts about the actual state of the Soviet economy and the extent of its lagging behind its ideological adversaries. The Soviet masses were not supposed to be aware of the living standards and freedoms enjoyed by their Western peers. Simply by reporting facts as they were, Radio Liberty, along with the BBC Russian Service and other NATO broadcasters, was indeed chipping away at the Communist edifice. It also provided a platform for dissident voices within the USSR and its foreign critics. The Soviet government was spending enormous amounts of money (more than on all Soviet radio and TV broadcasting together) on jamming those transmissions. Still, it was never 100 per cent efficient: those with enough patience and determination could always find a gap in the wall of howling noise.

There was no way I could have been involved in Radio Liberty programmes before Gorbachev's *Perestroika*. If I had tried, I would have lost my job and probably been exiled to remote provinces or even imprisoned very quickly. However, in 1986, the Soviets stopped jamming BBC and Voice of America broadcasts in Russian. Despite this, Radio Liberty, considered the most dangerous of them all, was still being jammed until the end of 1988, even though the station increasingly resembled other independent media organisations rather than merely a propaganda tool of the Cold War. The time came when Radio Liberty, based in Munich, began openly employing stringers and contributors within the USSR. Still, the KGB viewed them as foreign agents and appeared determined to make their lives difficult. There were reports that these stringers were subjected to intimidation and pressure. If there was any tightening of ideological control, they were likely to be among the first to suffer a new wave of repression.

That was the time when, while working at *Izvestia*'s foreign desk, I was also approached by Radio Liberty. The station was looking for Soviet journalists who would dare to go on air and comment on international current affairs. I hesitated before accepting that offer for the first time: it was a risky decision, one of those I could live to regret in a big way. But at the same time, it was a liberating experience, another step away from suffocating orthodoxy and a big, adrenaline-boosting adventure. Indeed, the first crime is the hardest; the following ones come easily.

In the late 1980s, my infrequent appearances on Western radio waves beamed into Russia began to garner notice from friends and enemies alike. It was then that I started to get warnings, either from genuine well-wishers or by some 'interested persons' who tried to discourage me from giving interviews to the voices from behind the Iron Curtain. But it only whetted my appetite for political mischief.

Then one day, a mysterious alien envelope arrived at *Izvestia*'s address. It had an unusual plastic 'window' which I had never seen before. And through it, a strange green slip of paper with my name on it shone. It was a BBC contract for an interview I had previously given to the corporation, promising me 29 pounds sterling on condition that I sign it. That came as a shock as I didn't realise that one could be paid for giving interviews (Radio Moscow and Soviet TV never paid, at least in my case). Also, the offered payment was not in roubles but in coveted hard currency, the use of which by Soviet citizens remained semi-legal. Throughout the history of the Soviet Union, it was a serious crime punishable by many years of hard labour, but under Gorbachev, that changed as well. It was still not fully legalised, still frowned upon, but tolerated by the authorities.

Twenty-nine pounds was equivalent to nearly forty-five dollars. A meagre sum by today's standards, but then ... Oh, those were the days of the empty shelves in Moscow food stores, while every ten dollars allowed for a fabulous trip to the hard-currency *Sadko* grocery where many sought-after and hard to get delicious things for the whole family (like ham, cheese or Belgian chocolate) could be bought. One such contract with the BBC promised not one, but four luxurious trips, with five dollars left over for change. Or, even better, one super trip resulting in a massive feast with friends and relatives invited to share in the gastronomical joy!

Initially, I was unsure how to handle such a contract. I hesitated, wondering whether it was better to forfeit my fee or ask the Brits not to pay for my contributions. Why boo the geese - the ones that inhabited a vast and forbidding KGB building in *Lubyanka* (officially called *Dzerzhinsky Square*)? But then I thought, what the hell, if I don't take the money, nobody will believe it anyway. And I was already in trouble, as all correspondence with NATO countries was subject to obligatory censorship (called perlustration), and those 'geese' surely made a copy of the green slip and put it into my file – for them, it was proof that I was 'selling the motherland for cash'.

If I were doomed anyway, I may as well enjoy the forbidden fruits of *Sadko* while I am still alive and free, I thought.

The BBC Moscow Office offered to 'monetise' my contract. Then, British and American correspondents began arriving in Moscow to cover the fascinating changes, often seeking my help as a commentator, expert, or advisor. They were paying me for my services, very modestly by Western standards, of which I, however, had at that time no idea. In this way, I managed to save the incredible sum of 160 dollars for our first private trip to Western Europe. Interestingly, Radio Liberty had never discussed any payments for my commentaries. And, as odd as that sounds today, it never occurred to me to enquire about the payments either. I wasn't sure when, why, and how much Liberty paid its contributors, if at all. My contributions to BBC programmes were in English, broadcast by the World Service or Radio 4. And those were considered less evil; working for them was deemed less of a crime than cooperating with the archenemy – Radio Liberty. And I felt I was taking that risk mostly to spite old timers and dogmatists. And, maybe, to prove something to myself. Yes, those were indeed extraordinary times.

On that day in August, I nonchalantly left the list of emergency contacts provided by a man from Liberty on my desk. I didn't even put it into the safe that I had in my cubicle. In a hurry (I hate to be late), I also forgot to hide away a banned book, *KGB: The Inside Story*, written by the most famous KGB defector, Oleg Gordievsky (in collaboration with the British expert Andrew Christopher). On top of everything else, an American diplomat who had lent me that incriminating tome had an annoying habit of marking his books: 'From the personal library of so-and-so, the US Embassy'. So, there was enough 'hard evidence' left on my desk for everybody to see, clearly 'proving' my 'spying' or, at least, 'anti-Soviet activity'. However, the secret police would have had more than enough damning material on me even without searching my cubicle, and some of it would have come to the KGB *Lubyanka* headquarters straight from the same Munich that I was reckless enough to visit shortly before that fateful August.

Initially, I was not planning to go there at all. This idea emerged at the very last moment, just before I went on my first-ever private trip to Western Europe. It was a dream come true: I couldn't believe it was happening to me in reality. Before that, I had only been to the Arab East, Africa, Czechoslovakia, and Hungary, either sent there on assignments or – on one unique and happy occasion – allowed to buy 20 days of vacation on the shores of Lake Balaton in Hungary. That happened mainly thanks to the special respect in which the Union of Soviet Journalists held *Izvestia* newspaper, and that organisation, in its turn, was allowed by the Party to exchange visits with the 'Socialist brothers' – their Hungarian counterparts. The private visit to the West felt like an unbelievable, magical sensation —a life-changing breakthrough.

At long last, I would see the fabled West with my own eyes, going there as a private tourist and not on any official, hurried business. I was free to go and do whatever I liked with my wife being my only 'chaperon' instead of omnipresent party officials or KGB snoops.

My first eye-opening impression of Europe was that the borders between Western countries were, in fact, gone. Or, to be more precise, there was no border control. At the time, very few people had ever heard the word 'Schengen'. That famous agreement, however, had already been signed; however, nearly four years had to pass before it was fully implemented. Nevertheless, at many borders, there were no passport checks, or they happened only sporadically.

I still remember the shock I felt when I saw an empty 'glass' cubicle at the Franco-Belgian border immigration control.

We stayed with my wife's brother in Paris. Afterwards, he kindly took us in his car to see the picturesque French countryside. We mainly travelled along *'les routes nationales'*, the toll-free local, narrow roads, which, in contrast to expensive but fast and boring highways, went through cosy little towns and villages, through scenic woods and green fields. Our pockets were not deep to put it mildly – all in all, we had the already mentioned great sum of one hundred and sixty dollars between us, earned through semi-legal moonlighting for foreign media. It was, of course, an act of foolhardy arrogance if not total recklessness to go on a big European tour with such 'riches'. We had hoped that all the accommodation would be provided free of charge and that we wouldn't have to pay for transportation either – thanks to the generosity of relatives, friends, and colleagues. We were prepared to spend the absolute minimum on food. And it turned out that most of the time we were treated to lovely home meals, but as far as the restaurants, even the modest ones, were concerned, they practically did not exist for us. Food markets and fairs did help too; in the French tradition, you could taste the contents of each stall. Until this day, I remember the charming town of Arles, where we strolled along an infinitely long row of olive stands. I ended up consuming so much of the green, salty fruit in its many excellent varieties that I couldn't have lunch. We also visited Monaco, and once again I was feverishly turning my head, looking for border signs, not wanting to miss the exciting moment when we would cross into that fabled principality. In the end, we did miss it, as there was no control whatsoever. It felt weird after my experience of going through Soviet border check-points with unsmiling, stern-looking *'pogranicniki'* – the KGB officers in full military uniform – who studied your face with utmost suspicion. Those were truly nerve-wracking moments, followed by the unforgettable feeling of triumph when we were finally allowed through. Did I pull it off in the end? Was I somehow miraculously permitted to pass through the once-impenetrable Iron Curtain? What an extraordinary feat. In truth, there was neither triumph nor feat in crossing these now-invisible borders of Europe; it was simply a mundane, everyday occurrence for millions of people — and, for a brief moment, I found myself among them.

I duly played roulette in the famous Casino de Monte Carlo and lost the minimum stake of five treasured dollars. What did we do it for? Well, for the thrill of it, of course. I felt compelled to try something which didn't exist in my country, another forbidden fruit. I put my meagre stake on black, and in total fascination watched the wheel spin and the little ball run, not quite believing that it was happening to me and not to some character in a Western movie, as watching foreign films was the only way to catch a glimpse of capitalist reality available to me for many decades of my life. However, although there were no border checks, we were required to show our passports when entering the casino, and copies were taken. That was a law, but I, tormented by the usual Soviet paranoia, couldn't help fearing that the report of us doing something illicit would somehow reach the Soviet authorities. That kind of paranoia, though, would prove well justified at another leg of our great European tour, but not then, not in Monaco, where I had absolutely nothing to worry about, except losing five dollars – a considerable sum for us at the time.

From Monaco, we returned to Paris, and from there, my brother-in-law kindly drove us to Brussels. We were a bit nervous before crossing into Belgium – we only had a transit visa for that country and were only vaguely aware of what we were entitled to. But once again, there was no one to check our passports.

Having spent a couple of days in Brussels, we took the train to Cologne. Yet again, no one was interested in examining our German tourist visas. But this time, I thought I noticed a visible change in the landscape when the train crossed into Germany. Surely, the contrast was not as stark as the one I experienced when returning to the Soviet Union from socialist Hungary in 1988. Then every second pylon along the railway line suddenly looked askew and rickety. In Belgium, everything was clean and tidy, but Deutschland was just fabulous – the exactness and precision itself, a lovingly scrubbed, spotless, and yet charming reality. Houses, impeccable front gardens, alluring alleyways, and low hedges looked almost like a scene from a movie. All of these were perfect, as if they had been plastered and painted in soft colours just a day before. Oh, it was Germany all right!

But again, nobody cared to check our documents, and I felt slightly disappointed: why had I bothered to exploit my friendship with the German press attaché at the Moscow embassy to obtain the coveted German visas?

Just before I left for my European tour, I mentioned to a Radio Liberty contact that I wouldn't be available for interviews while I was away from the Soviet Union. Unexpectedly, I got an invitation to visit Liberty's Munich headquarters, even to spend a few days as its guest. I hesitated, as it was a scary proposition. But what do I stand to lose? I asked myself. I'm sure I'm already on the KGB's bad list. So, I said yes, thank you, I will be delighted, but got goose bumps at the exact moment, nevertheless. It was a weird sensation, both frightening and delightful, an adrenaline rush. Just fancy, I was telling myself, I will be able to see 'the Lair of the Arch-Enemy' with my own eyes! Radio Liberty, Munich: the combination of these words was supposed to instil terror in any Soviet heart.

In Moscow, I was given the telephone number of Savik Shuster, the renowned editor of *The Country and the World* program on Radio Liberty. I learned a great deal from Savik and the live discussions he facilitated. This experience ultimately helped me later, when I joined the BBC World Service in the 1990s, working first as a producer and then as the editor of the BBC Russian Service. But at that time, in 1991, I had not yet met Savik face-to-face. I called him from a payphone in Paris. I still remember how I stood in the locker room of the *Musée d'Orsay*, my head still spinning after seeing the originals of those beloved Impressionists — Manet, Monet, and my favourite, Renoir. How many magnificent Renoirs were on the top floor! And it wasn't a dream — you could gaze upon those incredible originals from the closest imaginable distance, almost close enough to touch them. You could savour, unhurriedly, every brushstroke of genius, breathing in the very air he had captured for eternity with his brush. And now, after all this incredible experience, I suddenly remembered the possibility of a trip to '*The Lair of the Beast*'. But I was still dillydallying, asking myself whether it was really necessary to go there. Haven't I had enough mind-blowing and eyes-opening experiences for one tour? Too many discoveries had been made. Starting, maybe, with delightful but straightforward things like fresh baguettes – I could never imagine that such an elementary object as bread can bring such satisfaction. And then, croissants, damn them! In dubbed French films shown in Moscow, they were called *rogaliki* – the name of a Soviet bakery product that resembled a croissant in shape. But it was a rather crude affair, not magical, so it did not melt in your mouth as pleasantly as its French counterpart. And a simple espresso in an ordinary *Bar-Tabac* was quite unlike what I had been taking for coffee my whole life (although, I must admit the Hungarian coffees on Balaton were not all that bad). And then came a fantastic find that just walking along *Les Grands Boulevards* could make a man happy. It was much, much later, after maybe twenty-odd visits to Paris, that they seemed suddenly boring and monotonous. But at that very first, treasured moment of losing the Soviet cultural 'virginity', I was clearly in love with Paris, and nothing could be more beautiful in the whole world. And then came the blue waters of the *Côte d'Azur* and the *Promenade des Anglais* in Nice, as well as the already mentioned Monaco. Every day of the trip, I would pinch myself and say, 'Yes, I've been there; yes, I've personally played roulette in Monte Carlo!' We even danced on the world-famous bridge in Avignon and, together with my wife, sang a song of the 15th century, that every French school child knows: '*Sur le pont d'Avignon on y danse, on y danse, Sur le pont d'Avignon on y danse tous en rond* (all dance in a circle on the bridge of Avignon). We failed to form a circle, but we certainly enjoyed kicking, jolting, and roaring. It turned out, though, that the medieval French used to dance *under* the bridge, not *on* it, as the word *sous* (under) sounds so insidiously alike the word *sur* (on). But what did it matter! There is not enough space here to fully express what I felt when I first encountered this bright, smiling, colourful, well-fed world — a world that seemed like another planet to someone arriving from a country of cheerless drabness. My stays in Lebanon and Kuwait should have prepared me for the abundance of food and goods available in shops. But that experience was a pale imitation of the consumer paradise I discovered in Western Europe. Much more importantly, there was something in the atmosphere that mattered far more than shops and food. The general mood in this newly discovered world was astonishingly different from what I was used to — sunny, wonderfully relaxed, and free from the heavy, ever-present gloom of Soviet life. There was no need to constantly glance over one's shoulder or fall silent in fear of the intimidating, omnipresent power of the state. Of course, I couldn't immediately become like the inhabitants of this magical world. But at least I could look, admire, and try to capture the image in my memory, aware that it might be the only chance I would ever have — my first and possibly last glimpse of the West. And by the way, where is this world now? Where has the magic gone?

Thirty-four years ago, there I was, standing in the basement of the *Musée d'Orsay* by a payphone, hesitating, unsure whether to dial the number in Munich. I recalled that a few weeks earlier, I had given another interview to Radio Liberty. It was not a pre-recording; it was going live, something almost unimaginable at that time in Soviet radio and television journalism. The presenter was putting questions in turn to an expert in the Munich studio, then to a correspondent in Washington, and finally to me on the phone. The subject of the transmission was yet another escalation of the Middle East crisis. All went well until the discussion turned personal.

'Mr Ostalski,' said the presenter, 'you have already described the official position of the Soviet Foreign Ministry, but what about the personal viewpoint of Mr Gorbachev? Is anything known about possible differences between him and other members of the Politburo? Are there any nuances there?'

'There is a reason to believe,' I said, 'that Gorbachev...'

'Andrei, Andrei, we can't hear you! There is something wrong with the line,' the presenter sounded worried.

'But I can hear you well,' I replied.

'Oh, it seems you are back now! Continue, please. You said that Gorbachev...'

'Yes,' I said. 'The fact that Gorbachev's position is determined by...'

'Andrei, we have lost you again!'

The same thing happened a few more times. I was perfectly audible as long as I did not pronounce the name of Gorbachev. Every time I did, though, mention him, my voice would miraculously disappear from the airwaves. I did not realise that such technical methods existed: allowing somebody on the outside to suppress just one source on the telephone line.

The presenter, though, was not prepared to give up easily.

'Messrs from the KGB,' he said into the microphone, and thousands, tens, or perhaps even hundreds of thousands of listeners were likely startled by this form of address they had scarcely expected ever to hear. 'Please, allow us to conclude this programme. It's not a recording — it's going out live! Our audience is desperate to learn what is going on in the mind of the Soviet leader. We ask you, very politely but firmly: sirs, for God's sake, let Mr Ostalski finish!' And, incredibly, I was allowed to complete my phrase. I imagined the eavesdropping KGB officer panicking and contacting his superior, a general, maybe, asking him what to do in such a situation. And the general is probably saying: 'Well, we do not need any scandals at this point. To hell with him, this Ostalski, let him say what he wants. You write it down, every treacherous word he utters. We will hold him to it when the time comes.'

And now, standing at the French payphone in that great museum, I couldn't decide whether actually to call Munich. Everything around me was calm, beautiful, and so reassuringly peaceful. Yet I knew that after a visit to the "Beast's Lair", everything might change; my happy mood could vanish in an instant. It might even prove to be a point of no return for me. Still, I despised my own cowardice and, cutting short my fearful thoughts — forbidding myself to linger on them any longer — I turned the dial on the telephone (remember, in those days telephones didn't have buttons yet).

Savik said, 'Yes, Andrei, we are very much looking forward to welcoming you here. We will put you into a good bed and breakfast. We will cover the cost of your stay, but you will need to purchase your own air or train tickets. Still, it will be worth your while as we will ensure you receive all the fees due to you for the programmes you took part in.'

'Fees? What fees? Really? You owe me money?' I was stunned. Didn't expect there would be payments involved. Shall I accept it or what? I thought frantically. Shall I give my enemies yet another trump card to use against me? On the other hand, seven woes, one answer, as the Russian proverb goes (The English equivalent being: one may as well be hanged for a sheep as for a lamb).

'But of course,' Savik said on the phone, 'we will ask our cashier to open his office specially for you if you come at the weekend.'

On the way out of the museum, I casually mentioned to my wife that Liberty would probably pay me for the broadcasting work I had done for them. She hadn't been keen on my going away to Munich, thinking we would be better off just staying in Bonn for a couple of days, but now her attitude seemed to have changed.

'Really? How much?' she wanted to know.

'I have no idea. Well, maybe a few hundred. Dollars or marks, not sure. It should be enough to cover the cost of travel to Munich and back. And still we will have something left for shopping in Bonn.'

Wife brightened considerably, as our measly funds were nearly exhausted. Still, I wasn't sure whether I should be happy with this turn of events.

In Bonn, a friendly *Izvestia* correspondent provided us with a bed, while his kind wife offered to be our guide around the city. We felt so welcome that, on the spur of the moment, I decided to confide in him, despite the apparent risks of sharing a potentially damaging secret with a stranger. I asked the colleague to get me a cheaper train ticket to Munich. He didn't ask any questions, but it was clear he guessed who I intended to visit.

It turned out that every foreign journalist accredited in Bonn was entitled to one free one-way train ticket to any city in Germany each year. *Izvestia*'s Bonn correspondent practically never used this privilege, as the newspaper provided him with a nice car, and he loved cruising crazy German motorways at crazy speeds. So he gave me a Bonn-Munich ticket as a present and persuaded another colleague to give up his entitlement, which ultimately allowed me to get a return ticket for free. Never before have I experienced such comfortable travel. The train seemed to be flying, so smooth was its movement — no sickening shaking and bouncing that I was used to in Mother Russia. The cosy seat felt as if it was gently embracing my body. And, outside huge glass windows, the immaculate German landscapes, picturesque rivers and hills, and perfectly tended fields and groves were sweeping past. I couldn't take my eyes off the perfectly painted houses of little toy-like towns and stations, sparkling under the gentle sun.

In Munich, I stayed in a very modest (but, like everything else in Germany, immaculate) bed-and-breakfast with a shared bathroom and toilet on the same floor. It did not matter: I was not yet spoilt by the luxury of the five-star hotels, and was, in fact, no stranger to the common latrine. What was important was that I had the chance to see Munich, one of the breathtakingly beautiful European cities. I travelled around it by tram, absorbing the architecture, the streets, and elegantly dressed people. I decided to find the notorious "Hitler's Beer Hall", where the Fuhrer, that psychopath, obsessed with hatred of Jews, started his career that proved fatal for millions of people, including the Germans. An elderly woman showed me the way but tried to talk me out of visiting it.

'What do you need it for? In Munich, there are many other attractions. And that one is best left alone,' she said.

But I persisted and made it to the beer hall, the *Hofbräuhaus*. That establishment seemed large, spacious, dull, and not exceptionally comfortable. I drank a massive mug of nice beer, but then beer is nice wherever you are in Germany. Yet I felt nothing remarkable: no sense of awe, no brush with history — only boredom. Later, I learned that the present building had been constructed to replace the original, which had long since been demolished; it was merely a replica of Hitler's favourite haunt, which perhaps explained the absence of any palpable tension in its atmosphere. Still, freaks from all over the world come here to pay their hateful pilgrimage, although I did not see any of them in the hall. Incidentally, it turns out that Lenin once visited the old, authentic beer hall too. But so what? And, by the by, I never felt anything special in Lenin's mausoleum, either — just a bit of cold curiosity. So my advice is: don't go to the Hofbräuhaus, as there's nothing there to see or feel. And ignore the Mausoleum for that matter, too. At least, I'd be delighted if you will, for I am ashamed of my country for hosting a cadaver, or rather, the bits and pieces, shreds and scraps, the decomposed leftovers of bones and rotten skin – nearly nothing is now left of that body. What a barbarism – to exhibit such a sack of organic slop as a proud symbol – of what?

But back to Munich in 1991. The world-famous *Marienplatz* square in central Munich struck me as a real urban beauty, a truly gorgeous place where you feel the breath of history in the air. Its architecture is extremely eclectic because the city was heavily bombed during the war and had to be largely rebuilt. That is why the New Town Hall looks much older than the Old Town Hall. Alongside them, you will see modern commercial buildings from another era that blend perfectly into their historic surroundings, nonetheless. From the variance of styles arises a vivid sense of the natural movement of life.

The headquarters of Radio Liberty disappointed me, though. It was not very grand. Something understated, a bright but simple, unassuming two-storey building, vaguely reminding me of an old school where I once studied in Moscow. But my jaw nearly dropped in amazement when I saw how heavily guarded the entrance to the 'Satan's Lair' was. Every suitcase had to pass through a highly sensitive scanning device, then through a metal detector and an explosives detector — such strict security was new to me. After all, terrorist attacks were still rare in those days. What struck me most was that you had to stand in a confined space between two massive doors equipped with powerful, ultra-strong locks that made it impossible to break through or escape. At the same time, your luggage, clothes and body were thoroughly inspected.

My Munich excursion put me in a rather lyrical mood, but now I suddenly found myself in a completely different, very harsh world: the territory of the Cold War and high risk. It was no joke; the inhabitants of this world were expecting sabotage attacks at any moment. As I learned later, these measures were tightened after the Romanian agents planted a bomb in the building, causing an explosion which injured six people.

I was given something close to a red-carpet reception and taken to meet the top American bosses. I had the impression that I was presented as a showcase, a precedent, being possibly the first ever high-profile Soviet journalist and an employee of an important official newspaper of the USSR to be openly associated with Liberty as a freelance commentator. And yes, the one belonging to *Izvestia*'s privileged Foreign Desk. Seeing this, I for a second had a moment of irrational self-doubt: could it be that I was indeed a traitor, as some of my Moscow colleagues implied? But of which cause? A dead and clearly false ideology, ditched by the world? Or maybe I betrayed Konstantin Mikhailovich Kharchev? Recalling that name helped me to dispel any remaining qualms. And the Cold War was already coming to an end.

In just a few hours that I spent at Radio Liberty, as well as at the dinner, arranged in my honour at one of the nearby restaurants, I learned an astonishing thing. It turned out (I could not believe my ears!) that there were two main emigre factions at Radio Liberty, engaged in constant, albeit discreet, confrontation. The first one was the alliance of Slavophiles and anti-Semites, whose heroes were Alexander Solzhenitsyn and the inventor of the term Russophobia, academician Igor Shafarevich, a brilliant mathematician and fanatical Jew-hater. The second faction united westernizers (their enemies called them 'Zionists', although not all of them were Jews), and their main moral compass was Andrei Sakharov. The US authorities did not fully understand the essence of the disagreement, and they may have thought it necessary to keep the Russian nationalists on board as well. They somehow tried to maintain peace within the team. But the civil war was unremitting and sometimes led to serious clashes. It even reached the point of sabotage, where tapes with pre-recorded broadcast material would 'disappear' a few minutes before transmission.

'And also, you should be aware that our organisation is swarming with KGB agents,' a somewhat intoxicated Liberty journalist whispered in my ear at the end of the dinner.

Only a few hours before that conversation took place, I would never have believed that, dismissing it as a manifestation of typical émigré paranoia. But in the interregnum, something happened that made me take my accidental interlocutor's warning more seriously.

I paid a visit to the Liberty cashier, who kindly agreed to operate outside his working hours for my sake. He happened to be a middle-aged German, with a neat little beard, who spoke excellent English. But I was immediately struck by how woeful he looked, attributing his bad mood to the fact that I had spoilt his weekend. Still, he was polite, efficient and to the point, quickly finding my name in the list. And then all of a sudden, he blushed and started swearing. At the time, I still didn't know the German word 'Scheisse' but correctly guessed the meaning from his tone.

'What's the problem?' I asked.

'The usual. It happened again,' he said.

'How do you mean? What happened again? You don't have the right amount at hand, or the payment hasn't been correctly signed off or what?'

'No, everything is in order,' the German replied. 'It's just that the carbon copy of your payment slip is gone, nicked.'

'How is that possible?!' I was at a loss.

'I guess it's the KGB... Do you know that abbreviation? I think their agents have a habit of stealing the copies of the receipts.'

I almost uttered the silliest question, 'Why?', but cut myself short at the last moment. It was a no-brainer. If it was indeed the KGB at work here, another incriminating financial document would be very soon added to my file in the bowels of the Lubyanka. So, I asked myself, what should I do now? Run? No, it would be meaningless because I was already branded 'an enemy of the people' anyway, and I may as well take the money. And by the way, for how much did I sell my motherland? What? I could not believe my ears.

I was, it transpired, owed more than two thousand marks. Today, it wouldn't be considered too significant a sum for a freelancer to earn, as it only amounted to less than a thousand dollars and had been accrued over a couple of years. But at that time, it seemed to me a mind-boggling fortune. How many trips to the *Sadko* food shop could it mean? I lost count.

After the shocking conversation with the cashier, I was prepared to believe the tale about the KGB men in the ranks of the anti-Soviet Radio Liberty. I have also heard about the scandalous story of Oleg Tumanov, a simple sailor, who escaped from a Soviet ship in Egypt. Once in Munich, he got a job at Radio Liberty as a newsreader. He hardly had the qualifications or experience, even for that modest role, as he had neither attended university nor worked in any media. But somehow Tumanov managed to impress the American bosses so much that he had a phenomenal career, eventually rising to head the Russian section of Liberty. And then one day, he just vanished, surfacing quite soon in Moscow. He then appeared at the press centre of the Soviet Ministry of Foreign Affairs, where he angrily denounced his former colleagues and superiors as vile 'slanderers' of the Soviet paradise.

It was the high office that he held that was so disconcerting. The logical conclusion would be that he must have had many other agents under his wing. In general, my mood after that visit wasn't particularly blissful. Together with my wife, we did a rather lousy job of trying to spend the Liberty's windfall. We were in a great haste, as there was only a day and a half left for us in Germany. We were wary of bringing any hard currency back to the USSR, as the legality of doing so was still unclear. And we definitely had to declare every pfennig at the border. So, we bought a lot of odd and unnecessary things. I can't even remember anything except one suit, which looked much posher and more expensive than it really was, and a superfluous video recorder.

Another surreal detail of that trip, a very telling one, is etched in my memory. When we arrived at the Moscow *Belorussky* Railway Station, it was practically impossible to get hold of an official taxi; you had to queue for an hour or so. But there were plenty of moonlighters offering their services with no wait at all. The one who managed to get our attention led us to his vehicle parked nearby. Astonishingly, it was a large *Ikarus* coach usually accommodating more than 40 passengers. And the two of us had it all for ourselves, plus we tugged along a few boxes hurriedly packed in a slapdash way – all the 'trophies' acquired during our last hours in Bonn. For 10 dollars, the driver was ready to take us anywhere. The huge coach barely managed to squeeze through the narrow passage leading to the entrance of our modest apartment block in *Novye Cheryomushki*.

Soon, our apartment was thoroughly burgled, and no material trace of our trip and Liberty's money remained. I tried to take it on the chin: can't say that I was totally indifferent to that incident, it was truly unpleasant because it felt like a violation of personal space, nearly a rape. It was also definitely disagreeable that the burglars deprived us of certain things, including basic amenities. However, I learned to regard material losses philosophically, as most of it is just tinsel and vanity. It is not worth grieving over them because life is too short for that.

That was the background to the strange warning call I received from Radio Liberty before going on vacation in August 1991. A few days later, early in the morning of August 19, I found myself in the biochemical laboratory of the sanatoriy having a routine blood test. A nurse had just stuck the needle into my vein when a radio above her head spoke in a bold announcer's voice, solemnly informing the populace about the introduction of a state of emergency in the USSR. It was clear that the feared coup d'état had come true. So many saw it coming, but nobody seemed able to do anything to avert it. I mentioned earlier that Eduard Shevardnadze, the liberal foreign minister, went so far as to publicly and scandalously resign, hoping that this unprecedented move would prompt Gorbachev to realise the threat posed by the hard-liners he had surrounded himself with.

The Politburo member Alexander Yakovlev also tried to alert the Soviet leader to the danger. Still, his warnings were met with scorn and dismissed as the ramblings of a political loser. Gorbachev chose not to believe not only those who, until his recent bromance with nationalist reactionaries, had been closest to him, but also the foreign leaders. George Bush Sr. personally tried — in vain — to warn him (the CIA and NSA were already picking up ominous signals). Even Radio Liberty knew what was coming and wanted to alert me to the real and present danger, but I ignored their warning — what an idiot! I even managed to leave the precious safety net list behind.

As soon as I heard the radio announcement, I knew that Gorbachev was arrested and isolated, probably even killed, with all the power passing into the hands of the junta, headed by the most sinister figure of the time, the KGB chairman Vladimir Kryuchkov, the very one who had publicly declared individuals like me traitors and spies.

Blood seemed to have literally frozen in my veins. The nurse began to squeeze and knead my arm, saying: 'I don't understand what happened, it does not flow ... Probably, I will have to jab again'.

But I immediately lost all interest in medical matters. Muttering some vague apology, I got rid of the needle and ran to see my wife in the room.

What I physically felt that moment is incomparable with anything I had experienced in my life, not even the stress caused by bullets whizzing over my head and shells flying around me in Lebanon and Iraq. Or any other frightening situations that had ever befallen me. It was a strange mixture of despair, fear and hatred. I did not doubt that the relevant KGB departments had already received the lists of suspects to be seized, and I was equally sure that my name was on it, albeit perhaps not at the top. Probably, somewhere closer to the bottom.

I was certain that the *Izvestia* office was already being searched, and that my cubicle would soon be combed too. Perhaps the KGB officers were already there, examining with wry smiles the banned book on my desk and then, with more keen interest, the suspicious list of names and numbers scribbled on a strange slip of paper. I rushed to the payphone, trying to call every *Izvestia* number I could remember. None of them answered. And then the telephone at the Sanatoriy broke down, and the line went dead. There was no communication link left with Moscow. (Mobile phones did not exist yet).

Should I try to escape? I was asking myself. One option would be to swim across the Bug or some other river on the border. Or try to smuggle myself on board a foreign ship in the Crimea. Or get to Turkey through the Caucasus mountains. I will not bore the reader with all the insane, senseless plans that went through my head. I knew deep in my heart that it was all pure fantasy, but I just had to occupy my brain with something. I considered suicide, too, and it was the only realistic option in the circumstances. But it wasn't easy to overcome the self-preservation instinct, and I didn't fancy the prospect of suffering severe pain.

Together with a small group of like-minded liberals, we went to the entrance of the nearby Klyazma holiday retreat of the Communist Party Central Committee. We chanted anti-communist slogans, and hysterical voices insulted us back. 'You are all dead, you kikes!' someone shouted from behind the wall. That was a surprise. Why bring up the issue of ethnicity? I looked around and noticed that in our small group, hardly anyone had a distinct Jewish appearance. I had to remind myself that for a specific category of people in my country, the word 'Jew' defined a liberal Westernizer, a human being to whom personal freedom was fundamental. The one who 'reads too many books' and 'too literally' takes the Christian (aka Jewish) view of the world. In the end, I felt ashamed: it was a stupid, completely senseless action taken out of total desperation. Most likely, we were spatting over the fence not with any serious Party apparatchiks but some miserable flunkies and menials serving the Party toffs.

Back in the room, I began to twist the radio knob feverishly, and suddenly got an incredible surprise: I stumbled on a familiar name and voice. The BBC ran an interview with a counsellor of the Soviet Embassy in London who strongly condemned the action of the putschists, calling it an illegal coup d'état. His name was Alexander Ivanov-Galitsyn, and his words were a ray of light in the darkness, a message, a signal: hold on! All is not lost!

Sasha Ivanov-Galitsin, nicknamed '*Knyaz*' (meaning 'The Prince'), was a very good friend of mine, the person with whom I always felt a close affinity, sharing the same values and views, as well as a very similar sense of humour and a shared feeling of the absurdity of this world. We had known each other for a long time, having become close friends while working in North Yemen in the early 1980s. The fact that he appeared in the news at such a critical juncture seemed to me a happy omen. I took heart, as they say, life went on, and there was hope.

The next day, our son Dima was supposed to go to Holland on a school exchange. The wife had been sent to Moscow to accompany him to the railway station. We agreed to encourage Dima to seek political asylum in the Netherlands. We reasoned this way: as the son of a 'traitor', he will have no chance of a normal life in Russia. In the unlikely event that we could escape abroad ourselves, we could be reunited with him there.

I didn't doubt that the putsch would succeed. After all, it had the full might of the Soviet state machine on its side: the army, the KGB, the police, and the still-powerful Communist Party, with its extensive network covering the whole country. The population was passive and despised Gorbachev. They blamed their continuing impoverishment not on the decrepit and decaying economic system, but on their grandiloquent president. The stratum of intelligentsia ready to fight for freedom was extremely thin. Brave men who were prepared to put their lives at risk for its sake were even less numerous. But there was, of course, at least one maverick — a powerful and fearless man prepared to lead the resistance — and his name was Boris Yeltsin. The masses liked his image as an honest and straightforward, quintessentially Russian 'mouzhik', even if they didn't understand what he stood for. The fact that he hated Gorbachev (and the feeling was mutual) also contributed to Yeltsin's popularity. So I could pin some hopes on him. But I was sure that the KGB would immediately move to neutralise Yeltsin. He somehow managed to reach the seat of the Russian Federation's parliament, nicknamed the White House, which was to become a focal point and symbol of resistance.

Only a few months later, the reason for the incredible, impossible and illogical defeat of the putsch would become known. It was the pathological cowardice of its leaders. These people were the product of the Party's genetic selection, pathetic figures of the stagnation era. Not a single one of them proved capable of taking responsibility for determined action.

The commander of the KGB elite Alpha special force, Victor Karpukhin, refused to move against the protesters without a written order. But none of the Emergency Committee members dared to sign it. General Alexander Lebed was ready to use his tanks against the defenders of the White House, who, as a result of a ridiculous misunderstanding, took him for their supporter. But Lebed, a military man through and through, also needed a formal order to act. Had the putschists found the will to issue it, all resistance would have been crushed in less than two hours. But they didn't, only half-heartedly trying to talk Karpukhin into acting without any written authorisation. He, quite logically, declined: Why on earth should he take responsibility for the inevitable bloodshed and a terrible, illegal turn in the country's history?

Upon arrival in The Hague, our son Dima gave a short interview to the prominent Dutch newspaper *De Volkskrant*. The next day, his face was on the front page with the headline: 'My parents told me to stay in the Netherlands for good'.

But in the event, he didn't have to. Three days later, the strange coup-d'état dissipated, the putschists surrendered and were put behind bars. However, a different coup occurred (and succeeded) at *Izvestia*. The journalists banished Nikolai Efimov, the editor, who had supported the putsch, and unanimously voted to replace him with Igor Golembiovsky, the informal leader of our anti-communist faction. My fate also took an abrupt turn. Contrary to all expectations, I suddenly became a rather big shot, a member of *Izvestia*'s editorial board and its Foreign Editor. And to think that only recently I was ruefully preparing to leave my beloved newspaper! By cancelling my party membership, getting associated with Radio Liberty, and by committing some other 'mortal sins', I put myself in the line of fire. I knew that black clouds were gathering over my head, and it was becoming clear that I would have to go soon. I had already negotiated and secured a job offer at The Associated Press's Moscow office. I was to join it in the autumn. Golembiovsky himself was being pushed out of *Izvestia* by the powers that be. He had made many enemies in high places, and I had unwittingly contributed to his problems.

Chapter Three

Yevgeniy Primakov, My Nemesis, My Enemy

Several times on that day, under different pretexts, I had been coming to see Igor Golembiovsky, who, in the absence of the editor-in-chief, was running the show. I had been waiting apprehensively for a reaction from the powers that be to my scathingly critical piece that was being published in the evening issue of the newspaper. And finally, it happened: a light-yellow telephone with the USSR state emblem on it rang on the chief's desk. It was ATS-2, a secret government communications device, connected to the Kremlin's automatic telephone exchange. Nicknamed '*vertushka*' ('turner'), it had been an important symbol of Soviet power since Stalin's time. Then it didn't have a dialling disc; instead, you had to rotate a handle to get connected to the exchange, hence *vertushka*. The exchange had been automated a long time ago, but the name stuck. When I was appointed *Izvestia*'s Foreign Editor, I also became entitled to ATS-2, inheriting it from my predecessor. In contrast, Golembiovsky, after becoming the Editor-in-Chief, would even get ATS-1 – a higher calibre government telephone line, generally reserved for ministers and above.

But on that memorable day in late 1990, none of us had any idea of what lay ahead. The political reforms were slowing down and staggering. Gorbachev was wavering, trying to salvage his *Perestroika* while keeping the loyalty of the orthodox party apparatchiks, who, worried by the prospect of losing their privileges, were exerting relentless pressure on him.

Having picked up the receiver of his *vertushka*, Golembiovsky visibly stiffened, his muscles hardening on his face. According to the formal rules, I had to leave the room to avoid overhearing confidential negotiations, as any exchange on the ATS government line was officially deemed secret material. But Igor gestured with his hand: stay. 'Good afternoon, Yevgeniy Maksimovich,' he said into the receiver guardedly. I froze: I guessed who the caller was, since there was only one person of political importance with that combination of first name and patronymic. It was bound to be Evgeniy Primakov, a member of the Soviet Union's Presidential Council and one of the country's most powerful figures. And I had every reason to suspect that his call directly concerned me and my piece. It looked like I got much more than I bargained for: a short article, just a few paragraphs in fact, that I had written in a hurry, had had a much more potent effect than could have been expected. The great man wanted my head, demanding that I should be fired from *Izvestia* with immediate effect.

Talented and well-educated, Primakov was a revealing, if unusual, case of a highly successful apparatchik. He prospered under Khrushchev and even more so under Brezhnev, but joined the highest echelons of power thanks to Gorbachev's attempts to restructure the workings of the Soviet behemoth. Paradoxically, it was in the new democratic Russia of Boris Yeltsin that he reached the pinnacle of his career, serving as head of the foreign intelligence service, then as foreign minister, and finally, albeit briefly, as Russia's prime minister. This paradox itself highlights the ambiguity of Gorbachev's and Yeltsin's attempts at democratic reform and possibly even explains their ultimate failure. In their efforts to change the Russian society, they had to rely on people like Primakov, who was quintessentially Soviet.

Still, he was not your typical apparatchik. To begin with, Primakov was a Jew (or at least half-Jewish). His ID (the so-called 'internal passport'), though, didn't reveal this fact, and that made his advancement in the Soviet hierarchy possible.

There was a notorious '*pyatyi punkt*' ('entry five') in the Soviet personal identity documents. It was misleadingly called 'nationality', but in reality, it indicated ethnic origin and was widely used by authorities for furtive discrimination. If Primakov had a word 'Jew' stamped in his internal passport, all the avenues of Soviet political career would have been closed to him. Not quite a 'yellow star' but something not dissimilar in concept if not as deadly in practice.

The Soviet system (at least since 1949) was profoundly, though not overtly, racist and anti-Semitic, camouflaged under the veneer of utterly hypocritical slogans of 'communist internationalism'.

People like Primakov, who were fortunate to have a Russian-sounding surname and could claim the privileged ethnicity of one of their parents (in his case, nobody knew who his real father was), were considered lucky. Still, they not only had to go to great lengths to conceal their 'dirty secret' but to show extraordinary dedication and fervour in serving the orthodox ideology if they wanted to do well in the Soviet hierarchy. The fact that he didn't look typically Jewish in appearance also helped, although his detractors from early on in his life suspected that 'something was not right' with his ethnic background. So, he had to double down on proving both his loyalty and usefulness to the system.

And he did. Graduating from the prestigious Institute of Oriental studies, he made a quick career in propaganda apparatus (surely, we shouldn't call it journalism), rising in the early 60s to a staff position in the most important Communist party's newspaper 'Pravda' and becoming its Cairo correspondent. It was there that he met and befriended Saddam Hussein, who was exiled to Egypt at the time, and this bond later played a momentous role in Primakov's life and career. And, strangely, in my life, too. One can say that it was the Saddam connection that brought us into that clash with potentially catastrophic consequences – at least for me.

But how did I manage to enrage a member of the Soviet Presidential Council?

All this happened on the eve of the start of Operation Desert Storm, and consequently, a few weeks before I left for my fateful trip to Abu Dhabi, as described in the first chapter of this book. The coalition led by the United States was determined to achieve the liberation of Kuwait, which was occupied and annexed by Iraq, by military force, if need be. Iraq, in its turn, persisted and bluffed, hoping that its 'Soviet friends' and China would be able to stop the military operation. In a similar situation at the height of the Cold War, it would have been quite a realistic hope. But Saddam Hussein did not realise that the times had changed. Many in the Soviet government, secret services, and Foreign Ministry did not understand that either. Or, rather, didn't want to accept the change. They hoped the Gulf conflict could again drive a wedge between Moscow and Washington, thereby burying the hated *Perestroika* and *Glasnost* and turning the clock back. Already, the impending putsch was in the air. Promoted by Gorbachev himself, its future leaders were gaining power by the day, emboldened by what they saw as widespread support for their reactionary intentions. For them, the prospect of a major confrontation with America over the Gulf crisis was a godsend. Hence, there was a direct link between the fate of my country and what was going on in Iraq.

Having returned a few days earlier from one of his shuttle voyages to Baghdad, Primakov insisted in an interview that there was still a realistic chance to avoid military action – a clear case of wishful thinking. But what angered me even more was his insistence that hundreds of Soviet citizens stuck in Iraq were free to come back home at any time. I knew it was a lie: there was a pile of desperate letters on my desk from these same Soviet advisers, who were prevented from leaving under various pretexts; in some cases, their passports were seized clearly to keep them in the country, perhaps, to use them as 'human shields' in the event of the war. Apparently, such situations were quite common. I quickly wrote a little piece – a page and a half, no more – describing the situation as I saw it and accusing Primakov of lying through his teeth. I didn't have much hope of getting it published; it was too daring, even for the *Glasnost* era, and could have got *Izvestia* in serious trouble. Besides, it was too late as the paper was about to be finalised, and all the deadlines for submitting new material had passed. Still, I showed the piece I wrote to Igor Golembiovsky anyway. He read it in silence and then, to my astonishment, picked up the intercom receiver and called the printing press manager. He asked him to replace the editorial on the front page (there was such a genre at the time) with my exposé.

As soon as a copy of the latest issue reached the Kremlin, the lightning struck.

So I did give Primakov grounds for disliking me. In my turn, I had reasons to detest him. His 'friendship' and personal relations of trust with Saddam Hussein exasperated me. How can one be friends with a monster and a pathological sadist? Primakov seemed to take great pride in this close relationship, which began in the 1960s, and allegedly utilised it in the interests of the USSR and then Russia. But I can't cite a single case in which anything tangible was achieved through this 'friendship'. I saw him at close quarters in Baghdad, when he was on a secret mission shuttling between Syria and Iraq, trying in vain to reconcile the two fascist (National Socialist) Ba'athist regimes. And now once again, he was engaged in some murky game with the dictator, trying to find a vague compromise with him. What compromise, I thought, it is a straightforward case when international law should prevail, period! A sovereign UN member state had been subjected to banditry and now had to be freed with its sovereignty fully restored without any conditions or concessions. I thought it was obvious. I couldn't believe that Primakov really expected that Gorbachev would agree to play the dubious role of a 'mediator' between the insolent aggressor and the coalition set up to help his victim. I hoped that Gorbachev, despite his flirtations with the reaction, wouldn't want to jeopardise his relations with the West for the sake of some muddled geopolitical fantasies.

It occurred to me that Primakov might have badly underestimated Saddam's perfidy and the danger hanging over the Soviet advisors. He didn't realise that the dictator was perfectly capable of using them as 'human shields'. In fact, he wouldn't have minded if a few Soviet citizens were killed or injured by American fire. The vaunted special relationship with the Soviet Union and personally with Comrade Primakov wouldn't have counted for much.

In the new era of Putin, Primakov again tried to use his connections with Saddam, this time to prevent the US invasion. In 2003, he came to Baghdad, suggesting that the Iraqi strongman would have to resign to avoid a new war, but again his intervention came to nothing. In theory, that proposal was the right one: the problem of Iraq and its quarrel with the West boiled down to one person. However, it was whispered at the time that Primakov's suggestion was somewhat disingenuous, as Saddam, stepping aside for a while and putting a puppet at the helm, could remain the éminence grise and pull the strings from behind the scenes. Anyway, it did not work: Saddam's pride and vanity wouldn't allow that; he couldn't bear the thought of anyone else, even if it were just a figurehead, taking his place at the top. And, generally, the Eastern tyrannies operate in such a way that anyone who ascends to the throne would never voluntarily vacate it.

To be fair to Primakov, I later learned that in 1990 he had raised the issue of Soviet advisers in confidential conversations with the Iraqis. And allegedly, he was assured that they would be free to go. Some of them might have been indeed allowed to leave, but not all, and if none of our fellow countrymen were hurt by the American bombing, it wasn't thanks to Saddam's 'kindness'. The Americans just tried very hard to avoid hitting the areas with a large concentration of Soviet advisers.

This story demonstrated what was unacceptable to me in Primakov's creed: his belief in secret diplomacy conducted beyond the scrutiny of public opinion. This often ends badly, especially if you're dealing with treacherous dictators.

In my mind, a clear logical chain had lined up, connecting the Soviet patrons of the Iraqi dictator, who readily forgave him his little misdemeanours, like the slaughter of the Kurds, Shiites and even Moscow's favourite Communists, to Yevgeniy Primakov and his ilk. Even today, they are still looking for excuses to support similar monstrous regimes and secretly engaging in murky games with them for the sake of some spurious geopolitical aims ('make Russia great again!') and the entrenched anti-Americanism inherited from Stalinists. It seems to be ingrained in the bones of the Russian political elite. I remembered the murder of my colleague Sasha Bolmatov and shameful attempts of our 'deep state' to cover it up, exonerating the Iraqi secret police of that atrocious crime. All of that was for me a symptom of the same malaise, afflicting both the state and the society as a whole in my country, which still hasn't recovered from it today. I call it 'Saddam Hussein's syndrome', but may as well assign it the name of Yevgeniy Primakov, who became for me a symbol of that disease. And this, even though at the university, we were friends with his bright, talented, and charming son, Sasha. I was shocked and devastated when he died suddenly of a heart attack in the early 1980s.

Now, looking back at Russia's recent history, the figure of Primakov appears more ambiguous. Especially, if you compare him with those who came to take his place.

A lot of blood, destruction and horrific civil wars usually accompany massive tectonic ruptures like the ones that happened in our country. The fact that this fate has been somehow avoided is a miracle, owing to Gorbachev and Yeltsin, as well as to some representatives of the old Soviet elite, such as Primakov. In August 1991, when the putschists tried to restore the Stalinist regime, he bravely came out in strong opposition to the coup and supported Gorbachev and Yeltsin, and the latter never forgot it. When the Foreign Intelligence Service was embroiled in a crisis and refused to accept outsiders as its leaders, Yeltsin chose Primakov as a compromise. When he needed a reserved Minister of Foreign Affairs with the reputation of an experienced statesman to replace a flamboyant and unpopular among the elite Andrei Kozyrev, he again turned to Primakov. And when the rebellious Duma triggered a near-fatal government crisis after the 1998 financial crash, Primakov proved to be perhaps the only politician acceptable to both Yeltsin and the parliament as prime minister. He was needed in this capacity for only a few months until the situation calmed down. And he had discharged this role honourably.

One day in the mid-1990s, I sat in the office of Aleksandr Yakovlev, the man who, as the architect of *Glasnost*, played a significant role in history and in my life as well. Suddenly, the telephone on his desk rang. Yakovlev spoke to someone in good humour, calling his interlocutor 'Zhenya' (a diminutive form of Yevgeniy). They apparently discussed a family reunion. It turned out that Primakov was at the other end of the line. I was stunned. If the main Russian liberal is friends with someone, it means ...

No, I give up. God only knows what that means.

Primakov was a person who, in his capacity as the prime minister, famously (or notoriously) turned back his plane over the Atlantic, rudely cancelling by this act his official visit to the USA in protest against the American bombing of Yugoslavia. Arguably, it was he who turned not only that aeroplane but Russia itself around. Many believe he was Putin's mentor in foreign policy, almost the initiator of the anti-Western lurch now associated with the Russian president. His role in this unfortunate turn cannot be denied.

But nothing is ever black and white. I recall a lengthy interview that the liberal TV presenter Yevgeny Kiselyov conducted with Primakov in the early 2000s, in which the latter discussed the differences between Russia and the US and the West, advocating for Russia to assert its viewpoint and defend its interests forcefully. But he stressed that under no circumstances should Russia completely sever ties with the West; it should never choose the path of isolation. 'It would be a great folly,' said Primakov.

For all his apparent support of the Kremlin's policies, one could clearly read between the lines his concern that Moscow might be going too far. He openly criticised the zealous Russian propagandists for stirring up militaristic fervour. 'War is the last thing Russia needs,' he said.

His worldview, of course, was in many ways a relic of the Soviet era; yet, he was undoubtedly a pragmatist—a man who disliked extremes and reckless foreign adventures. I do not doubt that if he had been in Putin's place, Russia's relations with the West would have been at best lukewarm but not openly hostile. He would never have started wars in Georgia or Ukraine, nor would he have so brazenly violated international law and treaties by annexing Crimea. And I cannot for a moment imagine him authorising murders on foreign soil (or within Russia itself) — certainly no poisonings of so-called 'traitors' under Primakov's leadership.

I hate to admit it, but the world might well have been a safer place with my old adversary in the Kremlin instead of Mr Putin.

But I could not possibly feel so charitable towards Comrade Primakov at that fateful moment at the end of 1990, when he was doing his utmost to destroy my life and journalistic career.

I was standing in Igor Golembiovsky's office with a thousand butterflies flying in my stomach and thinking, 'Is that it? Am I finished?' But even if my *Izvestia* career was terminated, I was telling myself, it wasn't the end of the world. Life would go on. These were new times; there was no Stalin, nor Brezhnev, and

Primakov would not be able to send me to jail or exile. There would probably even be a chance to find another job.

As upsetting as Primakov's threats were, they were far less devastating than some other news I had received a little earlier. That other, shattering message came in a different phone call. It did not appear to pose any immediate danger to my personal safety, yet it left me rooted to the chair, as though pierced to the core. That news changed my life, setting me on the path that would ultimately lead to a perilous confrontation with Primakov himself. There was an invisible, straight line connecting those two events — those two phone calls.

The day was bright and sunny, and I was in an excellent mood. Everything was going swimmingly; I had just published a piece that everybody seemed to like, and was quite happy with another one I was finishing writing. Then the phone rang on my desk, and I picked it up, still smiling. And then the sun went down in my world.

A representative of Aeroflot called to tell me that Alexander (Sasha) Bolmatov, a man who replaced me in 1986 as the TASS correspondent in Iraq, died in a car crash in Baghdad. The sinister chain immediately lined up in my head: I had to leave Baghdad urgently after I was seriously hurt in a car accident, which I had reason to believe was not an accident at all. To allow me to return to Moscow for urgent treatment, I was temporarily replaced by a very friendly, cheerful and kind guy – Alyosha Vlasov, who soon also was caught in a car crash with much graver consequences; he was actually maimed for life. And finally, Sasha Bolmatov came to Baghdad to take my place – and now he was dead.

Always calm, balanced, benevolent – one of those wonderful human beings, about whom they say: 'He wouldn't hurt a fly'. This turn of a phrase means, of course, that such a person does not offend people: neighbours, colleagues, acquaintances and even strangers. He never speaks ill of anyone, neither to their face nor behind their back. He is not prone to intrigue and malice.

Even finding himself at the end of somebody else's nasty joke, he would not get angry but only smile good-naturedly and maybe shake his head. TASS shift editors liked him a lot as Sasha was always conscientious and reliable in his work.

An appointment as the Iraqi correspondent was considered one of the most lucrative in TASS, at least in its Middle Eastern department. A portion of the small salary was paid in dollars, and then you also received an extra 20 per cent for working in a country at war. (We called it *'grobovye'* – 'the coffin money'). The climate of Iraq is very harsh, with monstrous summer heat and 'khamsins', nasty winds blowing from the desert that bring sand, which clogs your eyes and crams your mouth. And there was a war with Iran going on, and not to forget all the nastiness of a cruel dictatorship. Sasha was still keen to go, hoping to save some money before retirement, but, having heard rumours about my troubles, he wavered. He decided to seek my advice.

My advice – to accept the posting – was totally, fatally wrong. That is why I was so shocked by the news of his death, for I felt a sharp pang of guilt. But when we spoke in the autumn of 1986, I sincerely believed that, if certain elementary precautions were taken, Sasha could happily work there for three years or more without any significant trouble and stack a bit of dosh for the family. I told him: by all means, take the offer, but don't do the stupid things I did, and you'll be fine. Try to avoid trips to the front, as they can be dangerous. Refrain from contact with any anti-Saddam opposition as well as intelligence services, be they Iraqi or Western ones. Minimise your exposure to the activities of 'neighbours' (the jargon term for Soviet spy organisations, both the KGB and the GRU). Avoid them altogether, if humanly possible, while trying not to antagonise them. Play the fool, if need be. Under no circumstances have any dealings with the Palestinians; they are the source of trouble, and keep your distance from the American journalists, especially female ones, as that's what nearly destroyed me. (The final part of this phrase I didn't say out loud; Sasha didn't need to know about the exact nature of my personal predicaments).

I proudly told him about the new premises of the TASS bureau in Baghdad, which I had found after a long and arduous search. It was a spanking new, clean house, and even though it was only half the size of the previous place, it was much more comfortable. It was conveniently located in the best area of Baghdad, the blessed *Al-Jadriya*, almost on the banks of the Tigris River, in a quiet, secluded alley with no through traffic. And on top of everything else, the villa was surrounded by a wonderful date grove, a real oasis. I managed to install reliable telex and telephone connections, with two teletypes operating around the clock, printing news from the local news agency INA in both Arabic and English. Thanks to its proximity to the presidential palace, there were almost no interruptions to the electricity and water supply. To top it all, the Soviet embassy and the Iraqi Ministry of Information were just a 10-minute drive away. You really don't need to travel anywhere else, I said, and you can always rely on the services of our loyal driver, Juma'a, a jovial Shiite from the Baghdad slums. This extraordinary man was not very literate, but, having been gifted with exceptional linguistic abilities, managed, with practice, to become nearly fluent in spoken Russian.

Actually, I told Sasha, TASS only needs statements of the Iraqi military command, which have to be very quickly translated into Russian and sent by telex to Moscow as they appear on the INA teletype, plus all kinds of other official announcements concerning the ongoing war with Iran, plus reviews of the local press. The rest is optional, which means it is not necessary; they will easily do without anything else in Moscow. Please don't repeat my mistake of trying to play a real journalist; it is dangerous, and no one in the world will appreciate it anyway. I also advised Sasha to be more careful around Subhi Haddad, the Reuters correspondent. I couldn't believe I was saying this, though, for Subhi was a very good friend of mine, to whom I owed nearly all my knowledge of modern Iraq and its internal convoluted politics, and to whom I might have unwittingly done some serious harm. For more than three years, I had been an involuntary yet constant witness and spectator to his unfolding tragedy, and, unfortunately, to some extent, a participant as well.

Part Two

THE ANGRY GODS OF BAGHDAD

Chapter Four

On The Eve of the Armageddon

The culmination of that drama for me came one night in the spring of 1985. It was about 1.00 AM when the telephone in my house rang. It was Subhi, and I knew from the start that something absolutely extraordinary must have happened. Previously, he called me that late only in case of exceptional events, for example, when an Iranian ballistic missile struck Baghdad for the first time. Accidentally, it was a Soviet weapon, called 'RF-17' and nicknamed 'Scud' in the West. Moscow's dear friend Qaddafi has resold it to Tehran without permission. He was mildly reprimanded for doing that afterwards, but the flow of Soviet weaponry to Libya continued unabated.

Subhi didn't give me any details, just said: Please come right away. And I didn't ask for an explanation, as it was obvious that he wouldn't have woken me up in the middle of the night for some trivial reason. I just leapt into my car and drove off.

The great city of Baghdad at night looked dead; there were no people in the streets and almost no cars either, only strange shadows were looking at me from behind the corners. It wasn't a long journey. When I arrived, Subhi looked gloomy, intense, and strange. He was dressed as if for some official occasion. Without saying a word except 'hello', he led me into the garden. That didn't surprise me, as it was where we usually went if we had to discuss something serious and sensitive, hoping to avoid the microphones of the Iraqi eavesdroppers. But this time, something was not right, so I immediately pricked up my ears.

Subhi looked impressive in his white suit. His greying hair and moustache were well-groomed and elegantly trimmed. He reminded me of a movie star — perhaps a touch of Clark Gable from *Gone with the Wind*. But it wasn't an accident that he made me think of actors and Hollywood as he posed in the middle of the garden in a dramatic, *unnatural* posture. It was so much not like the humorous Subhi I knew, the man capable of irony and self-deprecation, who would wince at false pathos and smugness. So, what did this charade mean? And then I guessed: this obvious unnaturalness concealed a warning that he hoped I would be able to decode.

Subhi began reciting – as if reading from a prompt – things that were incredible and impossible, and my jaw must have dropped in shock. He told me that one of his cousins who served in Saddam's palace had just brought him extraordinary news: Iraqi intelligence received "absolutely reliable information" that at dawn the Israelis would strike at the Iraqi nuclear reactor 'Tammuz' (known also as 'Osiraq'). It was sold to Saddam Hussein by France in the mid-70s, and the French technicians also helped to install it. The reactor was later destroyed by the Israelis, who got worried by the prospect of anti-Semitic Iraq developing a military nuclear capability.

'But they already bombed it in 1981, didn't they?' I asked, surprised.

Subhi hesitated for a second, but then quickly came up with an explanation:

'It has been partially restored since the previous raid. The Israelis figured this out and decided to finish the job with another strike. Apparently, the plan is to use a tactical nuclear weapon this time.'

I was lost for words.

Subhi made a long pause, looking as if absent-mindedly at something in the bushes, where, probably, the camera was installed, and this weird glance served as an extra warning – in case I wasn't receptive enough to have guessed already what was going on.

And then came the coup de grâce:

'Saddam has decided to respond blow for blow. He, too, has something up his sleeve – the so-called 'atom bomb of the poor'.

Then came another pause, followed by the conclusion:

'Tomorrow, a new and most terrible war will start in the Middle East,' Subhi said and fell silent.

I stood there, dumbfounded, unable to utter a word in front of him, and thought hard: what should I do now?

Oh, I did understand what he was trying to intimate: we were being watched. He was making it clear that he had no choice; he had to play the role assigned to him by the secret 'script-writers', hoping that I was intelligent enough to see through it. They were probably filming us too and would later analyse face expressions, every word we uttered, and every gesture we made. There was a strange void in the expression on his face: no hint, no tips, no regret. Unlike his usual self, he was as cold as ice: he couldn't show any emotion. But surely, he was sending me a signal: be very careful and think hard about how you react, what you are going to say, and what you are going to do.

By that time, I had long known that the *Mukhabarat*, the dreaded Iraqi equivalent of the KGB, had recruited Subhi. It was not just a counterintelligence service but a brutal secret police. Their job was to torture and murder Saddam's real and imagined opponents. They were also closely watching us, foreigners, and trying their hand at the favourite KGB sport of the so-called 'active measures' (disinformation and manipulation), too.

Subhi was no ordinary rank and file informer, no, he was a very special case, somebody with whom the local 'Himmler', the great and terrible Barzan al-Tikriti himself, regularly had meeting sessions with compulsory tea-drinking. How did I know this? Subhi himself told me this in great detail. He said that every time he sipped tea in that office, sitting opposite the most frightening man in the land, he would think: Is there thallium in this cup? That poison was the *Mukhabarat*'s weapon of choice for quietly dispatching the undesirables. Subhi was sure: sooner or later, his thallium time would come.

After arriving in Iraq in May 1983, I was immediately introduced to Subhi at the Ministry of Information, where all the foreign journalists accredited in Baghdad regularly gathered. Actually, almost all of them were Iraqis; they were mostly stringers, that is, freelancers. The only foreign correspondents working permanently in Baghdad were three Soviet journalists representing the *Novosti* agency, TASS and Soviet radio, plus reporters from the East German agency ADN and the Yugoslav TANYUG. There was yet another radio journalist from the former Yugoslavia accredited in Iraq, but she deserves a separate chapter in this book. Despite being an Iraqi, Subhi was, by all accounts, the informal doyen of the foreign journalists in Baghdad. He was not some paltry stringer but the full-fledged chief of the Reuters bureau, arguably the most prestigious position among foreign correspondents.

For the time being, it was the only Western agency represented in Iraq at such a high level, and his reports made up the bulk of all the world's information flow from this country. And Iraq was quite important, mainly because of its ongoing war of attrition with Iran. Other major world media periodically sent special correspondents to Iraq, and almost immediately, nearly all of them visited the Reuters bureau. Its head was almost a worldwide celebrity, and this status certainly helped him to stay afloat and, perhaps even survive in this utterly ruthless state, a miraculously enduring kernel caught inside the giant mill that was grinding lives and human destinies by the hundreds of thousands.

Subhi's authority stemmed not only from his official position. Above all, he stood out for his remarkable erudition, his vast knowledge of Iraq's history, Arabic literature, and tradition, and his deep understanding of the country's realities — not to mention his flawless, beautifully spoken English. He was the foremost local expert, always ready to help, and journalists from all over the world flocked to the Reuters office seeking his assistance.

Was he also being used by Iraqi intelligence at the same time? Oh, undoubtedly, he was — but he was by no means their willing or submissive tool. He despised Saddam's regime more than anything else in his life and was engaged in his own perilous game. A telling example of this was the way he quietly, persistently opened my eyes to the macabre and sickening reality of one of the most brutal and despicable dictatorships in history — turning my world upside down in the process.

As a journalist, I also had a great deal to learn from Subhi. He was a true master of the news agency style: concise and restrained, yet somehow vivid and expressive. His reporting was consistently accurate and written in impeccable English. With rare exceptions, he never missed an important story — even those the local press ignored. His work was of the highest calibre, certainly not Iraqi propaganda, and his editors in London were thoroughly satisfied. Yet the task before him was almost impossible: he had to meet the demanding standards of his British superiors, remain faithful to Reuters' golden principles, and at the same time avoid provoking the wrath of the Ba'athist authorities — never crossing that fatal red line. It was like walking a tightrope every single day without a safety net.

Over time, I came to see the toll it took on him — how he had to manoeuvre, dissemble, conceal, feign ignorance, and play one powerful figure against another. Such a game could only end badly, and eventually, it did. But the denouement came later — after my departure (or rather, my near flight) from Iraq.

For the first couple of months, he was wary of me. He looked away. Something was wrong; I could see it clearly. I decided to wait until we could talk privately. That moment came when we went together on a frontline trip, organised by the Iraqi Information Ministry. We shared a few laughs and jokes. Suddenly, when no one else was around, he began talking about Moscow, about Russia, asking many questions and listening raptly to my answers. All kinds of mundane details interested him, as well as exhibitions, concerts, what people talked about, and who the most popular writers and singers of the day were, etc. He admitted that he had been to Moscow several times. But it was a long time ago – in another life, he said. And I thought I felt a tinge of remorse or even bitterness in his words.

Soon, I noticed that Subhi started using all sorts of pretexts to try to be alone with me as often as possible. And then he invited me to a dinner at a restaurant on the banks of the Tigris River, where excellent *mazgouf* was on the menu (a local fish, fried on charcoal, which looked and tasted much like carp, but not so bony and generally tastier).

And finally, during another exhausting front-line trip, having been under Iranian shelling, sweaty, drained and dog-tired, we once again found ourselves together, while waiting for a coach to take us back to a hotel in Basra. We were sitting on some old tyres, at a distance from the rest of the group, voraciously gulping water. Subhi was talking about the USSR and then suddenly said in a low voice:

'I am a former communist; there was a time when I was even a candidate member of the Central Committee.'

I was shocked: I never expected to hear anything like this. I quickly glanced around: could anyone overhear such a terrible, dangerous confession?

The Iraqi intelligentsia had been deeply infected with communist ideas. Teachers, doctors, and engineers were often either members of the Party or at least sympathetic to Marxism, which they believed offered a way out — a glimmer of hope amid the hopeless, harsh, and cruel reality in which they lived. Naively, they equated it with the dream of a fairer, more just, and more humane society.

The main rival of the Communists in Iraq was the Ba'ath Party ('Revival') — a national-socialist, or, to put it bluntly, a classical fascist movement. Hitler and Mussolini were among its idols, while Saddam Hussein hero-worshipped Stalin. At his request, the Soviet authorities even organised a secret pilgrimage for him to visit places associated with Stalin in the USSR. It was, in its way, a touching friendship between a dying, senile pseudo-socialist state and a young, power-hungry Ba'athist predator brimming with malice.

Inevitably, the nationalists destroyed their rivals — with characteristic, unrestrained brutality. Communists were shot, hanged, beaten to death, crushed by bulldozers, or buried alive. Sometimes, Saddam himself took part in such atrocities. Unlike Stalin, he was not merely infinitely cruel; he seemed to derive a physical pleasure from inflicting pain — a true sadist, in the strictly medical sense of the term.

The repression, of course, extended far beyond the Communists. The Shiites and Kurds were kept under control through sheer terror. Any sign of dissent — even the slightest lack of deference to Ba'athist authority — was punished by death or prolonged torture. A person could be executed merely for accidentally placing a shoe on a newspaper bearing the leader's portrait.

Regular purges also took place within the Ba'ath Party itself. Following the example of his idol, Saddam eliminated his own 'Old Bolsheviks' — those who, directly or indirectly, through family ties or other connections, were linked to 'wrong' factions within the Party.

Somehow, a short film of a major Ba'ath Party conference was smuggled out of Iraq and shown to the world. In it, Saddam, seated at the presidium, calmly denounces one party member after another. Each is seized by secret policemen and dragged from the hall to be executed. The remaining delegates applaud wildly, their eyes glazed with terror. *What if my turn comes next?*

The USSR was, in fact, complicit in those crimes. Moscow forced Iraqi Communists out of the underground so that they would enter into a 'progressive anti-imperialist coalition' with the Ba'athists, who played along with this farce and created the so-called Popular Front in which the Communists were incorporated. When the Communist Party cells came into the open, the Ba'athists began to destroy them systematically.

What was the reaction of the Soviet Union, that 'beacon of communist solidarity', to the massacre? You would think the Soviets would have to do their utmost to defend their coreligionists. That they would tell Saddam: stop immediately, or do not count on our military and other assistance any more. No, nothing of the kind happened. But surely, a strong and loud protest was launched? No, not even that.

Veniamin Likhachev, the erstwhile Soviet ambassador in Baghdad, was authorised to say something not too harsh in private, to express, off the record, some mild dissatisfaction with the killings and arrests. For this sin, he was immediately declared persona non grata and sheepishly went home. The Soviet government decided to swallow its pride and avoid any angry posturing, accepting the destruction of 'the brotherly Party' it had nurtured for many decades and letting the ogre do whatever he liked with it. The political, economic and, most importantly, military cooperation with Baghdad continued on the same scale, as if nothing happened. Ambassador Likhachev was 'exiled' for

11 years to an African department of the foreign ministry, possibly as a sign of contrition – appointing the man who had drawn such ire from 'the great leader of Iraq' to any high-profile position could have been seen as a sign of defiance, risking more trouble in the relationship with Baghdad.

What was the reason for this humiliating stance? Why did the Soviet government so easily sacrifice its favourite Middle Eastern communist party, bowing to a foreign tyrant? It was done for the sake of the so-called 'common struggle against world imperialism', i.e. the United States and the West. Moscow gerontocrats saw in the Ba'athist Iraq an important ally in this 'existential struggle'. Its feral anti-American and anti-Israeli, anti-Semitic rhetoric was music to their ears. Their ideologies were related. The realisation of this fact marked the beginning of my own moral crisis. It was a bitter, painful catharsis from which I came out a changed person.

...We were sitting on those stupid, dirty tyres, Subhi and I, quite close to the front line in south-eastern Iraq. Subhi, it seemed, could no longer hold back; he had to unburden himself completely. Half-whispering, he confided the most extraordinary things to me. He warned that he was obliged to report regularly to the *Mukhabarat*, detailing his conversations with foreigners — including me. I should therefore be extremely cautious about what I said in his presence, he explained.

If I decided that I could trust him, though, he would be willing to let me see and agree upon what he wrote in those reports, ensuring that nothing in them could harm me. On the other hand, he would fully understand if, after this conversation, I chose to break off all contact with him. The only thing he asked — pleaded, in fact — was that I tell no one his terrible secret, for by revealing it he had, as he said, placed his life entirely in my hands.

I sat speechless for quite some time, then mumbled something incoherent. Only then did I realise why the Soviet embassy had warned me against getting too close to Subhi: they knew that he had been 'burned'. (As I later discovered, it was Subhi himself who had passed that warning to them through other Communists — unwilling to betray his beloved Soviet comrades directly.)

On our way back to Basra, we sat side by side on the coach, but I kept my eyes fixed on the window, not knowing how to speak to him after what I had learned. I couldn't make sense of it all. Was it possible that this was, in fact, a game of poker being played by the *Mukhabarat* — an attempt to get closer to me through Subhi? Such a possibility, I thought, could not be ruled out. Yet I found it hard to believe that Subhi would consent to such a devilish scheme. In any case, I had nothing to hide from the *Mukhabarat* — not at that time, at least. But perhaps they didn't know that, suspecting instead that I was a KGB operative or something of the sort.

'I have yet to explain something to you; it is essential,' Subhi said.

Under some pretext, we lingered outside the hotel where our group was staying. There and then, speaking in a strained, unnatural voice and avoiding my eyes, Subhi hurriedly told me how he had been recruited.

The Ba'athists had a problem with education. Their power base — and indeed their ranks — mainly consisted of the semi-literate small shopkeepers, market traders, and peasants. After they had shot, hanged, imprisoned, or exiled about half of the Communist Party members and their known sympathisers, they suddenly realised they lacked the engineers, doctors, teachers, and accountants needed to keep the country running. Their Bolshevik predecessors had faced a similar problem after the 1917 Revolution, but in Iraq, the issue was far more acute, owing to the nation's generally low levels of literacy and basic skills.

In the early 1970s, a solution of sorts was found. An order came down from on high to try to 'turn' those who had survived the purge. Among them, they discovered Subhi — half-dead in the dungeons — and offered him a position serving the Ba'athist regime. He refused. 'I was hoping to die quickly, but I failed,' Subhi told me.

The Ba'athist *Gestapo* had its psychologists. Someone had realised that when dealing with a finely tuned, sensitive individual, brute force and the usual methods of torture were not always the most effective way to get results. Subhi was, of course, tortured first — beaten until he lost consciousness, but that was merely a kind of initiation, a prelude. The trouble with such fragile intellectuals, they found, was that they fainted too easily, and once revived, did not necessarily 'see the light' or grasp the wisdom of the Ba'ath Party.

So, there were other, more subtle techniques — and one of them was reserved especially for people like Subhi, those bound by deep attachment to their loved ones.

Subhi's beautiful wife was brought into the room where the interrogation was taking place and chained to a radiator. The Ba'athist interrogator, speaking without much emotion, remarked that because of Subhi's foolish stubbornness, 'a good woman may have to suffer.' He explained that a platoon of soldiers, who had been without women for many months, was waiting in the next room. They could be allowed to do whatever they pleased with Subhi's wife, in front of her husband.

'But you can stop it at any time,' the interrogator told him. 'All you need to do is raise your hand.' That would signify Subhi's willingness to renounce his membership of the Communist Party, to sign a statement declaring that the current Communist leaders were all KGB stooges, and to pledge in writing that he would cooperate with the Iraqi security services for the rest of his life.

Subhi did not wait for the doors to swing open — especially as his beloved wife had already begun screaming in terror. He raised his hand immediately. He surrendered. And he quickly signed everything they placed before him.

'Tell me, Andrei, what would you have done in my place?' Subhi asked.

'Of course, I would have signed everything too,' I replied at once, without hesitation.

The last thing I wanted was for him to think, even for a moment, that I might be some arrogant, heartless bastard who could listen to such a story and still maintain an air of moral superiority.

It took me a couple of weeks to muster the courage to see Subhi again at the Reuters bureau. I smiled at him, but the idea of being alone with him didn't appeal to me for a while. Looking back now, I suppose that that smile did send a wrong signal to him, nevertheless. He decided that I had been given permission, either by the Soviet embassy, the KGB, or possibly even the

Central Committee of the Communist Party in Moscow, to resume contact with him. The long wait was over, he probably thought; his loyalty had been appreciated. A deadly but exciting game had been authorised.

That's what I understand now, but at the time, the possibility of such an interpretation of my actions didn't occur to me. And Subhi couldn't for a moment imagine that a TASS correspondent, even as young and inexperienced as I was then, would be so naïve and heedless as to engage in such a game without a go-ahead from a high authority. If only he knew that I had refrained from informing the embassy, or anybody else, for that matter, about the conversation we had in Basra. If only I knew what consequences my reckless action would bring.

According to the formal rules, I was required to report my contacts with foreigners and even write transcripts of any meaningful conversations I had with them. Special attention had to be paid to potentially suspicious suggestions, which were referred to as 'recruitment approaches.' But what should be considered a meaningful conversation, let alone a suspicious approach? Criteria were blurred. In Stalin's time, it is said, a Soviet citizen abroad had to rush to the embassy to report any fleeting foreign contact, doing so in writing and in every detail. Anyone who did not literally follow that rule was automatically suspected of spying. But after Stalin's death and the Twentieth Communist Party Congress, which denounced his terror, rules were gradually relaxed or at least pursued less vigorously.

At some point, after I arrived in Iraq, those rules, it seemed, were given a new life, albeit in somewhat lighter form. Now every Soviet citizen working for the state organisations abroad was required to fill out a special card for every contact with a foreigner. I vaguely remember that you had to register the date, the place, the contact's name and nationality, and write a very brief, one-sentence summary of the conversation. What has been etched in my memory is that there was an entry on the card indicating who had initiated the encounter. What a silly question. We regularly ran into each other with my peasant landlord in the blind alley where we both lived. 'Shlyonok?' ('What is your colour?') he would ask, a funny equivalent of 'How are you?' in the Iraqi dialect. Of course, I have to tell him that I am fine and ask about his colour in return. And then politeness demands that we exchange some other pleasantries and mundane family news. On whose initiative was that contact established? Or in regular briefings at the Iraqi Ministry of Information, you willy-nilly had to engage in rather senseless chit-chat with many colleagues. Who should be named as the initiator? Cards were stored in a small room at the embassy, under the control of the so-called 'security officer' nicknamed *'Stepanych'*.

He was a gentle giant, an always cheerful KGB man, who loved his drink and good food and did not take himself too seriously, lived well himself and allowed others to live, the complete opposite of his counterpart in Yemen, who tried – and not unsuccessfully – to recreate the atmosphere of Stalin's purges in the Soviet colony there.

'If I'm really to fill in a card on every contact I have, there will be no space left here soon,' I told *Stepanych*. 'And I will not have time for anything else! I have dozens of those wretched contacts every day!'

Stepanych winked, outlining his vision: that the instruction shouldn't be taken too literally, some creativity is called for, and only substantial and interesting contacts should be registered on those cards. And, of course, I had to be careful and vigilant at all times, paying close attention to suspicious cases and immediately reporting anything that suggested espionage or provocation that could compromise my safety or integrity in any way. I eagerly agreed. Of course, if I ever get any basis for a suspicion like that, I will come rushing to see *Stepanych* right away, filling in the card!

After that conversation, I banished all thought of those useless cards from my head. Periodically, *Stepanych* would buttonhole me in the embassy corridor and whine: 'Listen, there has been nothing from you for quite some time. Be a good boy, do a couple, or we will both get into trouble.'

I had to agree with *Stepanych*; he was right. I would sheepishly go and do as asked. Only to forget about the whole business until the next reminder. Of course, I had to do a card on Subhi, too. And soon I was invited for an unofficial chat with another member of the KGB station in Baghdad. He was polite but to the point: I should stay away from the Reuters correspondent for my own sake; it is a perilous liaison that could do me enormous harm. He said he couldn't go into details, though. Well, I didn't need him to, as I knew a lot myself, but I wasn't going to discuss it with the KGB.

'But I can't avoid him altogether, can I? And I can't be seen as being rude to him,' I said. 'He is the doyen of our journalistic corps, and we regularly meet at the Information Ministry.'

'That's okay,' said the wise spy, 'as long as you don't get too close to him. Try to avoid confidential tête-à-têtes, and you will be fine.'

I couldn't argue against that. I nodded, promising to follow that prudent advice. I was sincere in that undertaking, but would soon start breaking that promise. A few days later, my Yugoslav friend Zoran took me for a fleeting visit to Reuters' bureau on our way to his place (we were having lunch there). He said he urgently needed a consultation with Subhi on a piece he was writing. Zoran said it would last no longer than five minutes, but we ended up spending more than an hour there. And so, step by step, one thing leading to another, I began to get closer to Subhi again. He was too interesting a companion to ignore, an incredibly precious source of knowledge for me as well as a brilliant journo from whom I could (and did!) learn a lot professionally. In fact, I soon realised that he was irreplaceable. Without his help, I wouldn't have had the slightest chance to fully understand what was going on in modern Iraq and at the front, or to absorb the nuances of Iraqi culture and traditions. Without him, all other avenues would have remained closed to me as practically all other Iraqis I knew or could hope to meet were reluctant to talk to me frankly about anything of importance, for communicating freely with a foreigner was tantamount to a crime punishable by a lengthy prison sentence. After one of our front trips, Subhi told me he was terribly upset by the reckless behaviour of a visiting American colleague who tried to interview a sentry at a military depot. The sentry, out of sheer politeness, probably tried to answer something in English. 'An idiot, now the *Mukhabarat* will put him through hell, and after that he will be either shot or sent to the frontline to be killed,' he said. And added: 'Will you maybe talk to our American friends and explain to them how things are set up here and how their lazy curiosity can cost innocent people their lives?'

I promised to do that and did, but the problem with those Western correspondents who came for a short visit, maximum for a week or two, was that they knew nothing about the country and didn't have time to learn. And then, in their place, others came. The Iraqis had a deliberate policy of not letting the same journos in a second time; they wanted only the ignorant and ill-prepared, so they would have to rely solely on the information the official guides fed them. There were a few exceptions - for example, a famous roving correspondent for Newsweek, Elaine Sciolino (who later joined The New York Times and became a star there), was personally invited to Iraq and treated as a celebrity. There were rumours that Saddam himself was going to receive her, but then he changed his mind at the last moment. Later, I thought that it was an example of his strong animal instinct, which often served him well, except in moments when it was overpowered by his enormous pathological ego and pride (which, in the end, was his undoing).

Nevertheless, Sciolino was allowed to interview many other bigwigs, including Saddam's deputy in the Revolutionary Command Council and the chief ideologist of Ba'ath's Arab national socialism, Izzat Ibrahim, a red-haired, skinny fanatic, who thirty or so years later astonished all the orientalists by reinventing himself as one of the leading military commanders of the terrorist Islamic State. To Tariq Aziz, Saddam's glib foreign minister, she had talked, if I am not mistaken, several times. Why the Ba'athists chose to trust her so much, I have no idea; she must have invented some clever trick. She was able to get the Iraqi visa promptly and without any problems. And came several times. We had been to the front together and chatted a lot. Once, we came under severe Iranian shelling, hiding under some hangar together, almost in an embrace. Nearby, two meters from us, a mine fell, but did not explode. An Iraqi officer said, '*Maku natija*,' which meant 'no result,' and made a mark in his notebook. I must tell you that such incidents and experiences forge a bond like no other. That's how we became friends: she began visiting us at home, and she loved our little daughter. Once I drove her around Baghdad in my car – an episode which may have played a role in my personal troubles. Oh, how heartily we both laughed, imagining what the *Mukhabarat* would think about us showing up together. Well, the time came when Iraqi spooks certainly remembered that episode and started thinking hard about its meaning.

Elaine deceived the Ba'athists. She published a long feature piece in the New York Times Magazine, in which she revealed the brutal and terrifying truth about Saddam's regime and the leader himself. That article went off like a bomb; Sciolino was declared an enemy of the Iraqi state and its people. A big investigation was launched. Who helped her, who supplied 'the saboteur' with information? There couldn't be any doubt that my name was on that list. Especially, as Iraqi authorities had other grievances against me, in fact, a whole pile of them. I annoyed them with awkward questions, feeling fed up with the information ministry officials lying through their teeth during those frontline trips. They were exploiting the ignorance and naivety of visiting Western journalists, who often knew little about the military situation and didn't understand the war's basic geography. After many trips to the front, and with Subhi's help, I could reasonably orient myself and quite often saw through those lies. Once, we were visiting the northern sector where, allegedly, Iraqis had achieved a small victory by reclaiming the Kardamand mountain, considered a strategically important height. Not surprisingly, Western correspondents wanted to see that mountain with their own eyes. The guide waved toward a nearby hill. Subhi prudently remained silent, but I couldn't stand such an outrageous falsehood and chipped in:

'Sorry, but this is not Kardamand! There it is, that highest peak in the distance. Why don't you take us closer to it? From here, it is impossible to determine with certainty who controls it.'

I suspected that, since the military situation was fluid, the Iranians managed to regain control of Kardamand while we were being driven to the frontline from Baghdad. But the Information Ministry was loath to admit it, as it would mean losing face.

The guides quickly changed the subject and took us back into our coach. Several similar episodes occurred, which angered the *Mukhabarat*. Once, we were taken to Basra again, this time to monitor the alleged violations by Iran of the agreement, recently brokered by the UN, that prohibited the shelling of cities. Typically, both sides accused each other of breaching that deal.

On our first day in Basra, nothing happened, but on the second, as we sat down to dinner in the hotel's restaurant, the distant cannonade became clearly heard. Our excited ministry guides started shouting: 'Do you hear that? Iranians are shelling Basra!'

All journalists, Iraqis and a few visiting foreigners, leapt from their seats and rushed to the teletype room – they wanted to report the news as quickly as possible. I was the only one from the whole group who remained at the table, quietly continuing to eat. Within a few minutes, one of the guides came back on my behalf.

'What is the matter with you, Mr Ostalski?' he said, 'Are you not concerned with falling behind your colleagues? You may be late with important news!'

'I'm sorry,' I said, 'I didn't quite get it – what news do you mean?'

'Come on, Mr Ostalski, can't you hear the sound of the artillery shelling?'

'Oh, yes, I can certainly hear some cannonade going on. But how can I be sure who is shelling whom from this distance?'

The furious guide stormed out of the restaurant, and I returned to my shish. I nearly finished the meal when the same ministry official came back.

'The governor of Basra would like to talk to you on the phone,' he pronounced solemnly.

Of course, I had to abandon my coffee and go into the hotel's hall where the receptionist was waving at me like mad.

'I can tell you officially,' said the governor on the phone, 'that exactly twenty-five minutes ago, Iranian artillery started shelling the living quarters of Basra. We don't have the full picture yet, but it is already clear that there are heavy casualties among the civilians. This is an outrageous violation of the accord reached recently with the help of the United Nations.'

I thanked the governor and promised to transmit his statement to Moscow immediately. And I did, because in this way I didn't have to lie or fantasise. My urgent telegram mentioned the distant sounds of artillery fire and then quoted the governor word-for-word in inverted commas. Moscow could then add a short report to this dispatch, citing the Iranian counter-accusations.

I learned this method from Subhi (who wasn't with us at that time for some reason). He would always describe exactly what he could see or hear without jumping to his own conclusions, and then add the official interpretation, always precisely attributing it. The Iranian take on the events could always be appended to the story in London.

Actually, at some point, I suddenly realised how lucky I was to work for TASS, rather than Novosti, newspapers, or radio. Why? Unlike my less fortunate colleagues, I did not have to engage in lies, except in rare cases. Most of the time, I had to work like a normal journalist, honestly reporting the truth to Moscow – things that I saw, heard, and read in the local newspapers, always accurately quoting the source. Did it make me a real journalist, as this profession is seen in free countries? Hardly. But my *modus operandi* was not that different from Subhi's, and it helped me retain some measure of self-respect and hone my skills, learning as much as I could from Reuters. The main difference between me and any normal Western correspondent was that my audience was very narrow. Ninety per cent or even more of what I reported was not intended for the general public, but rather for the select group of government and party bureaucrats who had access to the semi-secret TASS bulletins and newsletters. The rest of the population was not supposed to be subjected to the free flow of information. As with everything else in the Soviet Union, the news was also rationed, and access to it was determined by an individual's place in the state hierarchy. The Politburo members and ministers were receiving the so-called 'White TASS' bulletins – complete, uncensored, concise, and urgent news from around the world without any propagandistic spin. No attempt to slant the news reports was required in other 'For Official Use Only' daily bulletins called 'A' (most important international news) or regional newsletters. There was, however, a bulletin called 'AD' which had a more restricted distribution and to which the 'anti-Soviet' reports were confined. These reports reproduced foreign 'hostile publications' or official statements that were critical of Soviet policy and the actual situation in the country. I worked for a stint as the TASS copytaster (a senior sub-editor who reviews and selects material for publication) and as such had to produce my own unofficial bulletin during the night shifts, which in the mornings would land on the desks of important Central Committee apparatchiks and big shots of the KGB and military intelligence. My official guidance stated that there shouldn't be any ideological caveats; everything resonating around the world should be included in that bulletin, whether deemed 'anti-Soviet' or not. But then I was advised off the record that there was just one exception: personal attacks against comrade Brezhnev had to be buried. I heard rumours that the KGB, too, was ordered to ignore, even in its top-secret reports, any personal slurs that could upset the General Secretary. That was censorship of the highest order: the Soviet leadership was censoring itself!

My report from Basra on the alleged breach of an important international agreement probably qualified for a couple of lines in the 'White TASS' bulletin for the government and Politburo, but certainly not for a special one that would wake up the ruling gerontocrats.

The artillery barrage continued through the night, and in the morning, we were taken to see the destruction it caused in the city. My conclusion was that both sides likely violated the agreement and shelled each other's cities, but it was impossible to determine who initiated the conflict. Tehran claimed that it was forced to respond to the Iraqi provocation; Baghdad insisted on the opposite version of the events. There was no way to verify what really happened independently. From the dirty looks the ministry officials were giving me, I deduced that I didn't win myself any favours, to put it mildly.

After returning to the hotel that day, I found that the glass in my room's window was broken and a shell splinter was embedded in the wall above my bed. I suspected fabrication, although I couldn't entirely rule out an unpleasant coincidence either. In any case, the view of the rough-edged hole in the wall was highly unpleasant. Subhi grew pale and shook his head reproachfully when I later told him about it. Probably he wanted to say: next time that shell could get into your room while you are inside, if you continue poking them. And he was absolutely right, of course, it was useless, as unmasking the crude propaganda concoction didn't achieve anything.

Subhi taught me many things, including how to behave at the front and what to look for to avoid being accidentally caught by a sniper bullet or a mortar attack. But more importantly, he enlightened me about the real power anatomy of the country — information that could never be found in any open sources — and nobody else would ever dare to discuss such things with a foreigner. From him I learned about the Ba'ath Party's structure, and about the underground Shi'ite organisation Dawa, which regularly organised bombings and other acts of sabotage, but whose existence was never acknowledged in the media – not a single word! Even mentioning its name was tantamount to a crime. A visiting Japanese journalist once asked officials from the Information Ministry about Dawa's actions. He never got any answer; the officials pretended they didn't know what he was talking about. Subhi just shook his head and then whispered in my ear: 'Our dear Japanese guest will never get a visa again'.

Only at the end of my stint in Iraq did I finally grasp what Subhi thought about me and our relationship. I wasn't entirely sure about the accuracy of this analysis, but I think I was close to the truth.

For several years, he waited for the Russians to come to their senses, to recognise at last what a terrible mistake they had made by giving Saddam the green light to annihilate the Iraqi Communist Party. Or, at least, they will appreciate his, Subhi's, personal loyalty and give him a chance to be helpful to the Cause again. Not for nothing was he rubbing shoulders with some Ba'athist bigwigs and was close to Saddam's eldest son Uday, and therefore could be a source of important information which would, of course, help the dear Russians to realise at last what kind of a monster they have fallen in with.

He was desperate to regain some self-respect, and becoming useful to Moscow would have helped him achieve that. Yes, on the surface, it looked as if he were working for the *Mukhabarat*, but surely the Russians would see through it, recognising it as nothing more than a sham, a deliberate game. That humiliated and debased by Ba'athists, Subhi, of course, hated their party with its fascist ideology and Saddam personally, as well as the whole clique around him. It was an intense and ferocious hatred, made so much more hurtful because he had to hide it deep inside, forcing himself to smile at his tormentors daily.

For many years, I tried to understand how he felt, to put myself in his shoes. Of course, my situation was considerably different. I was lucky enough not to experience such a brutal, mind-excruciating treatment from my country's rulers and hence didn't feel the unbearable emotion of the same strength as he did. It would be preposterous even to attempt a comparison. Yet we also had something in common. At some point, I also had to admit to myself (after a long period of denial) how much I disliked the system and the ideology I had to serve. How repulsive I found its untethered, utter hypocrisy. And how much I despised myself for continuing to serve it. There was, though, a fundamental difference between my fate and his: I could hope to change mine while he didn't stand a chance. Not one in a million.

So he clutched at an illusory straw. All these years, he was waiting for some super-agent from Moscow, some Soviet James Bond, to come to his rescue. That brilliant spy would come, establish contact, engage in a sophisticated game against the *Mukhabarat* and Ba'ath, helping Subhi to wreak his vengeance on fascist monsters. And – who knows! – maybe even promise a great prize for this successful and important work. This prize, of course, will be a refuge in his beloved Russia. For Subhi himself, his wife and his children. Flight to the Mecca of all the progressives, of all the people of goodwill, to the most magnificent city in the world – Moscow. Let it be just a dream, an illusion of light at the end of the tunnel. Even a tentative promise, a vague hope, a distant possibility was better than nothing. That would mean some other theoretically possible outcome in his life apart from a dose of thallium-poisoned tea or death from unbearable torture in the notorious Abu Ghraib prison.

But that Russian Bond was not coming. The Russians he met shied away from him, as if he were a ghost. And in a sense, he was. Hadn't he himself warned them to stay away?

And still, he hoped that one day the Soviet friends would decide not to leave him to his fate, despite all the warnings. Would take the risk.

I was young and clearly inexperienced. Didn't look like a super-agent, not in the least. This youngster behaved strangely, didn't offer to sign any secret agreements, and didn't hint at any possible tasks or assignments. I never invited him to a restaurant, although, in theory, I had to reciprocate, since Subhi did take me for nice meals from time to time (Reuters paid, while TASS's hospitality fund was so meagre that it wouldn't have been enough for a single lunch). However, I did invite him home a few times for modest dinners, but never alone – always in the company of others – so as not to put him in a compromising position. However, neither Subhi nor his curators from the *Mukhabarat* could for a moment imagine that I maintained a regular contact with him without encouragement or at least permission from the relevant Soviet authorities. That, on the contrary, I had to go to great lengths to conceal how closely we communicated. I was officially advised to stay away from him. To be polite, smile, engage in small talk, and exchange trivial phrases. Ask: 'Shlyonok?', 'What is your colour?'. And that should be strictly all.

I don't think there was ever a moment of conscious decision on my part to ignore the wise advice of the embassy. It was an incremental process. First, I allowed myself to talk to him on our trips to the frontline, say, for fifteen minutes or so, with others present. Then, gradually, the length of our interlocutions increased. More and more often, we would talk without anybody else overhearing us. Sometimes, we would go somewhere in his Volvo together, taking turns at the wheel. And so on. Practically every day, foreign correspondents were coming to the Reuters bureau, which had become something like an unofficial press club in Baghdad. I couldn't ignore those gatherings. That was my main excuse for not keeping away from Subhi.

And then, when I realised that our relationship had bloomed into a close friendship and a dangerous liaison, it was too late. I didn't want to end it, while hoping that I could still do so if push came to shove.

It was an absolutely one-sided exchange. I was getting knowledge and information from him, some of it really sensitive, while I had no secrets to share. I knew very little about the Soviet embassy and the secret services' operations. There were rumours

I heard and bits and pieces I accumulated willy-nilly, but Subhi never, not even once, tried to get anything of the sort from me. He was extremely delicate in that respect. It seemed that the only thing he really wanted in return was the opportunity to chat about Russia, its history, culture, and so on. That is why I didn't feel any acute danger emanating from our friendship.

And then came that late-night phone call and a surreal conversation in the Reuters' back garden. I had ample warning that something like that might happen one day, but I was still completely shocked when it actually occurred. Clearly, it was some deadly provocation, no doubt, authorised at least by that Iraqi 'Himmler', Barzan al-Tikriti, if not by Saddam Hussein himself. But to what end?

Why summon me in the middle of the night in this fashion, trying to impress on me that a new terrible war was likely to break out the next day? The war that could potentially engulf the entire Middle East and possibly the world? I tried to calm down and break the problem down into components. I had to presume that the story was a pure fiction from start to finish, total bunkum. A pure provocation. But what could be the practical purpose of it? The deception, if passed to Moscow and, say, published in an urgent 'White TASS' bulletin, would have only survived until the next morning. Surely, Saddam's sadism didn't stretch so far as to seek pleasure from denying the Soviet gerontocrats their sleep.

No, the target of this weird operation was not in Moscow; it was here, in Baghdad. It may have been me, Subhi, or someone else.

I stood there, looking at my friend with astonishment and thinking hard. Some other explanations of the thriller at hand sprang to my mind, however unlikely they might have been. For example, what if the Israeli intelligence services were playing their disinformation games and managed to bring Saddam to panic? He got seriously scared and – oh, how touching that would have been! – counted on my help. And then the most horrifying possibility of all: what if, against all odds, the improbable story was, after all, just true? What was the probability of that? Very, very unlikely, yet there was still a remote chance, maybe one in a hundred, but still more than zero. I could not entirely rule out the possibility that the Israeli strike would happen, and Armageddon would begin the next day. How could I sit on this information and do nothing about it? That would have been too much of a responsibility for me to shoulder. So, the question was: what should my next move be? I was at a loss, and Subhi was clearly not in a position to help me, as he was acting under duress, with every word and gesture being monitored. But he had every reason to hope that I understood the peculiarities of the situation and would act accordingly.

After considering all the options, I made a decision. Whatever this mystery is about, I should react to it in a 'natural way'. Strictly natural. What is every Soviet citizen working abroad supposed to do in the event of an emergency? Surely, he must run to his country's embassy. And that was precisely what I was going to do too.

I played dumb, asking Subhi a couple of meaningless questions and went home. There, my wife woke up and looked at me with fear in her eyes. I just put a finger to my lips: silence, don't say a word! I didn't have time to explain anything, always conscious of what the *Mukhabarat*'s microphones in our home would pick up.

I rang the embassy and asked the guard who answered the phone if I could speak to a diplomat on the night shift. All Soviet embassies had a general rule: a diplomat had to be on duty at all times in case of emergencies. Usually, they would hide away in one of the offices and have a nap. Should anything extraordinary happen, the duty guard had to wake them up.

Diplomats had to do it in turns, regardless of rank or affiliation. Only the ambassador himself, his deputy, the counsellors and the so-called 'residents' (the chiefs of the KGB and GRU stations) were exempt. Who would become my contact person in this emergency was purely a matter of chance. In the worst-case scenario, I could have encountered pure hostility from a malicious compatriot who might try to turn the whole affair into a scandal, portraying my role as gross misconduct. But I was relatively lucky: the diplomat on duty that night, whom I should call Michail Ivanovich, was not a spiteful person and was not involved in my disagreements with the ambassador in any way. On the other hand, his actual position at the embassy was a complicating factor, as he served as a deputy to the chief of the Baghdad KGB station.

In theory, I should not have had any way of knowing what his real job was. However, everyone at the embassy was aware of everything and spoke in whispers. Of course, nobody ever uttered the words 'KGB' or 'GRU'; no, everybody used the names and patronymics of the relevant bosses for gossiping. 'Who is this tall young guy who arrived yesterday?' a nosy wife of a technician would ask in a half-whisper. 'He is Vasiliy Borisovich's man,' her husband will answer in a hushed tone. The spies were not very well disguised. They kept together and looked and behaved in their own peculiar way. It didn't require special powers of observation to realise who was who. It was a serious flop and a clear sign of the Soviet system's growing lethargy.

In response to my rambling tale, Michail Ivanovich said a terrifying thing:

'Do you know what you just did to me? You have blown my cover.'

It sounded scary, as if I were guilty of treason. It felt as if I betrayed him to the Iraqis.

'What does your cover have to do with it?' I exclaimed. 'As far as I am concerned, you are just another Soviet diplomat on the night duty shift, that's all. I am not even supposed to know who you really are, and anybody else could have been in your place. Why don't you proceed the way any 'clean' diplomat would?'

Michail Ivanovich only shook his head and sighed, as if to make it clear that I was talking nonsense.

'It is a fact, my cover has been blown, and from now on I won't be able to conduct any high-risk operations until the end of my assignment in Iraq,' he said.

He sounded desolate, but I suspected that deep inside, he was pleased. Just imagine, in the fascist Iraq where seven or eight security services were after you, following your every move, an operative suddenly gets himself a dispensation allowing him to refrain from doing any dicey jobs, clandestine meetings, etc., confining his duties to paper pushing inside the station. What bliss! At least I would have definitely rejoiced in his place.

But I was alarmed. Recently, TASS foreign correspondents were summoned to a training session in Moscow. One day, a KGB counterintelligence officer came to speak to us. He tried hard to instil in us the fear of the alleged machinations of hostile intelligence agencies. He warned: exposing Soviet agents working undercover abroad constitutes a criminal offence and is punishable by imprisonment of up to six years of hard labour. So, have I unwittingly committed a crime? But what was I supposed to do in the circumstances? I had no idea who the duty diplomat at the embassy would be that night. Officially, for me, he was just an employee of the Ministry of Foreign Affairs of the USSR, period!

On the other hand, it was true that I had been warned (though not officially) to stay away from Subhi, and that could theoretically be used against me. Why on earth did I allow myself to be drawn into this mess by meekly doing Subhi's bidding and turning up at his office at such an ungodly hour? That would be a legitimate question to put to me. Defying the advice would probably not qualify as a criminal offence. Still, it could be construed as a serious enough misdemeanour that might cut short my foreign assignment and even end to my journalistic career.

On the way home, I reflected that, in the hellish situation I found myself in, I managed to choose the correct course of action. Yes, it may easily have dire repercussions, and I will have to face the music. In the worst-case scenario, I may indeed be sent back to the USSR, but that is undoubtedly not the worst thing that may happen to a human being in my precarious position. Yes, I may also face a ban on foreign assignments, but, with a bit of luck, it will be for only a limited period, say, three or four years. And then I might hope to be forgiven, possibly, with some help from my well-connected father-in-law. But even if I lose the privilege of foreign travel forever, it was still possible to live in Russia, provided this life was not spent in a hard-labour camp, of course. With such selfish thoughts, almost pleased with myself, I was driving through Baghdad at dawn. And only at the third *filka* (as the Arabs call roundabouts), it suddenly dawned on me what Mikhail Ivanovich might have meant. Let's suppose he does not want to wake the ambassador; the rumour had it that there was no love lost between him and His Excellency, who, if woken up like that, could get seriously angry.

Meanwhile, the chief of the KGB station was away, so Mikhail Ivanovich reckoned he would have to expound this convoluted story to the Moscow centre using his own personal code. He probably also believed that there was one chance in a hundred that the Iraqi warning was a genuine one and a big war would start early in the morning. If it really happened, while he, as the acting chief KGB spy in Iraq, would have decided not to pre-warn Moscow about it, it would not only ruin his career but might turn him into everybody's fool. His name may even be included in intelligence school textbooks – as a spy who made one of the biggest mistakes of all time.

Another hypothesis occurred to me: what if the Mukhabarat was actually going after Michail Ivanovich? But, on the other hand, what would they hope to achieve? Breaking his code? Yes, but I heard the spies were using a one-time code for such occasions. OK, it could confirm his affiliation with the KGB, but so what? This was a fierce dictatorship and not one of those mellow Western democracies with limited resources for surveillance; here, every foreign diplomat and journalist was presumed to be a spy anyway, watched on all sides around the clock, with every word and every fart duly noticed and registered. There was no limit on funds or on the number of people available for this task. No, I still couldn't see the point of the weird affair I had got myself entangled in.

Then the morning came, and no Israeli strike occurred, and Armageddon did not ensue. Two days later, I saw Subhi. He said hello and smiled at me as if nothing had happened on that fateful night at all. As if I dreamt the whole thing. Life went on as before. But what surprised me most was that the Soviet embassy and the KGB seemed to have forgotten the entire episode, too. No reprimands, no investigations, no questions asked. Nothing! Not to mention the untimely return to Moscow for which I had already braced myself. What could be the answer to this enigma? Could it be that in the end, Mikhail Ivanovich decided to take the risk and buried the story after all? And then another crazy idea occurred to me: what if the whole affair from start to finish was a little joint operation of the KGB and the *Mukhabarat*? Why not, considering that there was clearly a love affair blooming between the two? Another senior position was created at the embassy for a counsellor, filled by a KGB general who had to serve as an advisor to the *Mukhabarat* and act as the liaison between the two organisations. To further this brotherly collaboration, Vladimir Kryuchkov, Andropov's confidante and future KGB chairman, secretly came to Baghdad on a special flight. He negotiated something with the Iraqi spies and, as rumour had it, signed an agreement on wide-scale cooperation. So, could it be a joint effort to check me out? Maybe they wanted to see what I would do with the sensational information provided? What if, after my rendezvous with Subhi, I went not to the Soviet Embassy but to the Baghdad Sheraton, where, by chance, one of my American journalist friends was staying at the time? A lady with whom I seemed to have developed a suspiciously close relationship. Or maybe I would go home and get a dusty transmitter from under my bed to send a message to my British, American, or Israeli masters. Well, in any case, I did the right thing by going to see a duty diplomat at the Soviet embassy right away. As far as Subhi was concerned, I didn't worry about him too much. I suppose he took good care of me, giving me an invisible warning. He, I believed, shielded me from the *Mukhabarat* as much as he humanly could, and without that protection, I could have got myself into bigger trouble.

I could see that the whole set-up was becoming more astonishing if not bizarre. My closest Iraqi friend was courting disaster to keep me safe. My unforgettable driver Juma'a – a destitute, defenceless and nevertheless always cheerful Shiite (and Shiites were second-class citizens in Saddam's apartheid state), took horrendous risks too to warn me. He used to drive me to the Rafidain Bank, located in the very centre of Baghdad, where there was no parking space anywhere nearby. The only solution was for the driver to go in circles around the bank while I attended to TASS business. Once, when he was taking me there, he suddenly asked an absolutely crazy question:

'Tell me, Andrei, what do you think about our president, Saddam Hussein?'

Coming from Juma'a's mouth, that question sounded so blatantly unnatural, so bizarre, so impossible that any idiot would have pricked up his ears. He still had to ensure that I was warned and understood what was going on, and went further. He pulled a miniature tape recorder out of the left pocket of his trousers and, slowly and clumsily (as he had to hold onto the car steering wheel at the same time), moved it into his right pocket. And then glanced at me: did I see it? I nodded and winked at him: Don't worry, everything is all right, and started shooting the bull. Everyone knows Saddam as an outstanding figure, even his enemies respect him, and we, the Soviets, are not the enemies of Iraq; on the contrary, we are its friends, don't you, dear Juma'a, know about the Soviet-Iraqi friendship and so on. That was more or less what I said for the benefit of the *Mukhabarat*.

But I still couldn't quite bring myself to say that I personally loved or at least respected Saddam, though I probably should have made an effort and lied. What stopped me was the thought of our four-year-old daughter Vasechka (officially Vaselina) and her constant exposure to harmful Ba'athist propaganda. The nature of my work made me keep the local TV constantly on, and the little girl could not help but watch it. Saddam Hussein was always present on the screen, either making some historic pronouncements or chairing the government's and the Ba'ath ruling bodies' meetings, and – more and more often – feigning his affection for children who always presented him with gorgeous flowers. As a result of this brainwashing, Vasechka started repeatedly expressing her admiration for this clearly charming and kind 'uncle' with the wonderfully funny moustache. And the worst thing of all was that we couldn't object to it in any way. We just had to smile, pretend we didn't understand who or what she was talking about, and try to change the subject. I had an absolutely burning desire to tell my daughter: no, my little darling, this is a real baddy, a cruel, detestable and damned man, perhaps the most terrible villain that you will ever see in your life. Oh, how desperately I longed to say those words, but couldn't. Firstly, there were definitely listening devices installed in my home; our conversations were surely eavesdropped upon and recorded. And secondly, it would have been impossible to prevent Vasechka from repeating my utterances in the wrong company.

Juma'a was clearly ordered to provoke me into revealing my true feelings about 'the great leader'. A pretty stupid idea, come to think of it, but who said that an average *Mukhabarat* operative was necessarily clever? Somebody had to tick the box to add another report to my file, double-checking Subhi's accounts, testifying to my loyalty and innocence.

Of course, I couldn't tell the truth in response to Juma'a's mad question, but nor did I go far enough in expressing a positive attitude towards the dictator. I was hoping that my spin would be deemed upbeat enough.

That was not the only episode of that kind. Once, late at night, I heard a slight knocking on my door. My landlord, the owner of the villa that I had found for TASS premises, that simple, illiterate peasant, sent his son to tell me (in a whisper) that people from the *Mukhabarat* came and interrogated his father about me. I took him out of the house into the garden, as he insisted on delivering the full list of questions put to the old man.

'My father says you need to know the details, just in case', he whispered.

During the three and a half years that I spent in Iraq, several strangers went to considerable risks to warn me of the dangers. Some of them just put their fingers on their lips at the right moment, or just shook their heads and winked, or used some other gesture to alert me. Those people did it not only out of the hatred they felt for Saddam's infinitely cruel 'Gestapo', although it was, of course, an important motive, I am sure. But I think, first and foremost, it was dictated by a sense of self-respect and human decency, which turned out to be stronger than fear. Amazingly, such qualities can survive in humans (at least in some of them) in the most challenging conditions, under the heaviest of yokes. And a self-deprecating thought would come to my mind: was I really worthy of such empathy, a care of these ill-fated people, whose life was an absolute and total hell compared to my relatively comfortable and easy existence? I had no answers to those questions.

And then I let Subhi down.

Chapter Five

A Death Sentence in a Letter

Till the day I die, I will not be able to forget the moment when I first picked up and began reading Rita Nephew's 'open letter', realising in a few moments that it was not just an ordinary epistle and not only a denunciation, but, quite possibly, a death sentence. What a sensation it was. What would be an appropriate metaphor to describe it? Making my hair stand on end? No, not strong enough. Maybe more like being hit in the sternum with all the air whooshing out of my lungs.

This letter was brought from Baghdad to Moscow by a colleague who, at my request, had been checking my mailbox while I was away on holiday.

It totally spoilt my vacation. My wife Sveta and I were enjoying the temperate climate of the European part of Russia. After the scorching heat and all the horrors of the war-ravaged Iraq, travelling in the colourless and shabby but calm and cool Russian heartland felt like bliss. Even the political system seemed humane and gentle in comparison. On TV, instead of a moustachioed heavy-set man with the eyes of a murderer and heaps of corpses in the reports from the front, there were the recurrent pictures of a shameless, impotent old man and joyful news about harvesting. What a blessedness! We went on a cruise on the Volga River, and it didn't matter much that the food on the boat was worse than mediocre. The portions were too small, often leaving us feeling a bit hungry. The food shops on the Volga banks were also nearly empty, and grocery supplies were rationed. Still, we enjoyed ourselves and the picturesque little towns we were passing by. The cliffs, the green hills, and the forests were pure magic. Walking around the old wooden houses of Kostroma made us feel as if we were in some fairy-tale movie, and the city of Kuibyshev looked delightful, although its name didn't fit it. The Bolsheviks had renamed it after one of their own. We couldn't guess that in just a few years, it would regain its old, beautiful name of Samara.

We returned to Moscow in a great mood. And then it was suddenly shattered by this threatening letter. I felt a strong urge to do something about this serious, possibly existential threat —to run, to hide away, to escape —but where to?

That Rita Nephew I saw only once in my life. I presumed that she was one of those Western journalists allowed a flying one-off visit to Iraq so that they could be fed with the information ministry's propaganda. I felt sorry for them, identifying with their common frustration and their desire to gain at least some understanding of what was really going on inside the country and at the war front. I was willing to help by sharing some background information off the record, and the word about a sympathetic TASS correspondent spread. So, I wasn't particularly surprised to learn that yet another American journalist was seeking to meet me and pick my brains. The manner of this contact was unusual, though, and the name of the media organisation she claimed to represent should have put me on my guard. But I was still a babe in the woods.

A certain Third World diplomat, whom I had met only fleetingly, brought her to my place one evening without any advance notice or phone call. He said that Ms Nephew was a very good friend of his and had come to Baghdad on a journalistic assignment. He asked if I would mind talking to her and sharing my thoughts on the current war situation and local politics.

The diplomat astonished me by inviting us, along with Rita Nephew, to an exclusive restaurant that was entirely out of bounds for me and my friends or colleagues because it was ridiculously expensive. My monthly salary wouldn't have been enough to pay for one dinner for the three of us there.

I'd heard all sorts of stories about that place, but I never thought I'd actually get the chance to eat there, so of course, I was curious. Only the Ba'athist big-wigs of a very high calibre and the richest wartime profiteers (that is, relatives or close friends of the same party bosses) could frequent this place. Well, perhaps, the heads of foreign corporations or high-level government guests were sometimes entertained there, too.

The diplomat muttered under his breath that the accounting period was coming to an end and that his hospitality funds remained underspent. It did occur to me that it sounded a bit phoney, as if he was trying hard to explain away his indulgence. It probably should have given me pause, reminding me of the wisdom of the old Russian adage: 'It's only in a mousetrap that the free cheese is available'. Should have but didn't.

That night, Rita Nephew was drinking quite a lot. The diplomat also tried to make me drink an exorbitant amount of some crazily dear whiskey. At some point, I started resisting his attempts, not out of caution and wisdom but simply because I hate to surpass my modest alcohol limit, as I immediately get unpleasant sensations if I do. (A happy property, some say, your body itself automatically switches on a 'stop' signal). But in the end, he did probably manage to pour enough into me to weaken my critical thinking.

I remember that Nephew was particularly interested in my relationship with Elaine Sciolino. How much time did we spend together? Where had we been, and so on. I'm afraid I let myself talk too much. I recalled driving Elaine around in my car. My main, my fatal mistake was to brag about my role in helping her to write her dramatic exposé of the Ba'athist regime.

In reality, my contribution was not particularly significant. Still, I preferred to think otherwise; I wanted to wear it as my badge of honour, which I couldn't do in the presence of the Iraqis or the Soviets, for that matter, while an American journalist seemed the right company to let my hair down and show off a bit. In the state of intoxication, I probably wasn't very coherent and now remember that conversation only vaguely.

It is true, though, that I did offer some insights to Elaine. I shared things I saw or heard myself, but mostly those I had learnt from Subhi. How much did I see myself? Well, evident traces of the Iraqi use of chemical weapons against Iranian troops at the front. Intolerable, stomach-churning scenes of Iranian children taken prisoners of war. They were kept on their knees for hours on end, and those identified as grown-ups (older than 16 years old) were separated from the rest, most likely to be shot.

Or perhaps I told her — though I can't be certain after all these years — about the legendary General Rashid, the most popular Iraqi commander, whom Saddam, of course, later had killed. Rashid had once cheerfully, and in gruesome detail, described to me how his men had captured an Iraqi Communist near the front line and spent some time torturing him — gouging out his eyes and then slowly cutting him to pieces, taking great pleasure in the process.

I also knew from my own sources that the *Mukhabarat* had gone to great lengths to discover whether any Jews were among the Soviet experts working on projects being carried out with Soviet assistance. Those suspected of possessing 'such a terrible human flaw' often found themselves facing all manner of unpleasant incidents.

Another episode comes to mind from the corridors of the Ministry of Information. A middle-ranking official, whom I barely knew, stopped me and whispered that Saddam had broken off negotiations with Kurdish leaders because he could not resist making a racist pun. In Arabic, the plural forms of 'Kurds' and 'monkeys' sound very similar. Saddam could have secured the favourable neutrality of the Kurdish *Peshmerga* militia in the war with Iran in exchange for minor concessions, such as greater autonomy for Kurds. Instead, he chose to mock and insult the Kurdish negotiators. When one of them dared to show his indignation, he was killed.

Why my chance informant — apparently of mixed Kurdish descent — risked his life by sharing such a dangerous secret with a stranger, I can only guess. Perhaps he was sick to death of the regime's brutality and wanted the Soviet government to learn the truth about their so-called ally in the 'anti-imperialist struggle'. He likely remembered the Soviet Union's long history of flirtation with the Iraqi Kurds. But the Soviet government did not want to hear anything about the plight of their former allies.

When I went to see the Soviet ambassador to pass on this story, he was clearly displeased by my initiative. He told me, in no uncertain terms, that he was not the least bit interested. Evidently, he had learnt from the fate of his predecessor, who had destroyed his own career by trying to intercede on behalf of the Iraqi Communists.

At the time, I could not have imagined the terrifying turn Saddam's policy on the 'Kurdish question' would soon take. It was probably then that the regime decided that genocide was a better strategy than negotiations. The next logical step was the large-scale use of chemical weapons against the Kurdish civilian population. In the small town of Halabja alone, around five thousand people — including hundreds of children — died the most excruciating deaths imaginable.

Other stories — about the mass torture of political prisoners in Abu Ghraib, or the virulent anti-Semitism permeating the Ba'ath Party and its members' admiration for Hitler — I learned from Subhi. I cannot recall how many of these I shared with Miss Sciolino.

She also met Subhi privately, without my presence. I do not know how open he was with her, but I thought I recognised one of his typically sarcastic metaphors, which Elaine attributed to a 'taxi driver':

'This is a car. But if Saddam says it's a bicycle, then it's a bicycle. And he can kill me for telling you that.'

I do not know for sure where she heard the words uttered by an anonymous Iraqi white-collar worker, who complained about the incessant humiliation and fear: 'We're reduced to the level of animals here. We sleep, eat, work, but can't think. We are inefficient, because we're all afraid of the person above and the person underneath.'

I have heard something very similar from Subhi many times, as well as the joke quoted by Elaine in her article. Question: 'What's the population of Iraq?'. Answer: '28 million. 14 million Iraqis and 14 million portraits of Saddam.'

The cult of the dictator's personality knew no bounds, sometimes going beyond all realms of lunacy. Saddam looked at you from everywhere: not only in every official's cabinet, but in every school class, from covers of students' notebooks, from the walls in every public institution, in hotels, restaurants, shops, kindergartens, and finally on the façades of houses – it was hard to find a single street in Baghdad and other major cities, from where at least one picture of his wouldn't be visible. Or two. Or three. And of course, from early morning to late at night, radio and television kept chanting the slogan: 'Birrukh, biddam, libeyyak ya Saddam!' – an offer to sacrifice the soul and blood for the beloved leader.

Here is another typical poetic glorification quoted by Elayne in her essay: 'Saddam is the perfume of Iraq, its dates, its estuary of the two rivers, its coast and waters, its sword, its shield, the eagle whose grandeur dazzles the heavens. Since there was an Iraq, you were its awaited and promised one.'

The super-expensive restaurant disappointed me: an ordinary *mazgouf* in a cheap family establishment on the waterfront would be so much more delicious than all its costly delights. The only thing that fascinated me was the glass floor in the hall; it served as the roof of a giant aquarium, where fish swam. You could, if you wanted to, show the waiter which of them you were sentencing to death in honour of your dinner. I suspected, though, that it was a gimmick: you wouldn't have a way to check whether it was the fish you had chosen that was brought to your table. Of course, over the years, I have often seen something similar in different countries: the option to select live fish through a transparent wall. But the trick here was that the aquarium was under your feet, and the floor was made of glass. I did not expect to find such sophisticated amusements in wartime Baghdad.

In general, life in the Iraqi capital had a feel of schizophrenic duality. On the one hand, the endless, ruinous, murderous war was visibly strangling the economy. Tens of thousands of coffins were quietly transported from the front line to every corner of the country, with *Mukhabarat* making sure that families kept their grief private and buried dead soldiers secretly, so as not to spoil the mood of the government and the public. When Saddam attacked Iran in September 1980, he promised a quick and easy victory, but the fighting turned into a war of attrition and dragged on and on with no end in sight. The Iraqi youth were sent to the front; there was no one to work in the factories and at the construction sites. The powers that be had to replace them with cheap labour from Egypt. These guest workers were treated like animals. I myself witnessed disgusting scenes: the representatives of the authorities considered it good form to show their contempt for these unfortunate, downtrodden wretches, dressed in dirty blue gallabiyahs. They worked hard while being paid peanuts and constantly mistreated and humiliated, while it was them who kept the Iraqi economy afloat. It was a clear demonstration of the utter hypocrisy of the official slogans of the Arab Brotherhood and pan-Arab nationalism of the Ba'ath party.

All the hardships of the war coexisted with the ostentatious luxury of bars, restaurants, and nightclubs. Close to ninety-nine per cent of the population could never afford such indulgences; they were the exclusive domain of the elite, including important foreign guests, Ba'athist bigwigs, and well-connected nouveaux riches. First-class hotels, such as the Meridien and Sheraton, were oases of calm and comfort; they served as a haven for diplomats, spies, and journalists alike. During the day, it was easy to get a good cup of coffee, tea, or even a relatively inexpensive lunch there. On the top floor of another hotel – Babylon, which was owned by Saddam's son Uday – I tried a drink under the mysterious name of 'cappuccino' for the first time in my life.

The hotels competed to present Western-style shows, featuring foreign, scantily clad dancers and singers. Those performances were not for me; they were totally beyond my grade and budget. Only once did I have the chance to glimpse the lavish lifestyle of the privileged few. What an impossible contrast: after travelling back from the front line and witnessing death, destitution, and the dereliction of a war-torn nation struggling simply to survive, I suddenly found myself attending a 'Night of Hawaiian Cuisine'.

An official delegation of Soviet journalists was being entertained at one of the exclusive nightclubs. To my surprise, I was also invited; the idea was that I would act as an interpreter for the guests. I noted the names of the exotic dishes offered to us, but the records are gone. I recall only some kind of seafood and puddings made from coconut milk, as well as edible lotus roots with other mysterious ingredients added. I didn't find any of it particularly tasty, but surely those dishes had to be awfully expensive. We were seated right next to the podium, where a cabaret show was staged. One of the most stunning, half-dressed black girls, with incredibly long legs, suddenly reached out to the elderly leader of the Soviet delegation and playfully placed a hat on his balding head. He didn't know what to do or how to react; he sat there with a confused half-smile on his face, looking at the Iraqi hosts in the hope that they would save him from this predicament, but they were laughing happily. The mischievous dancer felt encouraged and went further, grabbing the poor fellow's tie, trying to pull him to the podium. He fought back in horror, snorting and panting, and she finally let him go when he started to squeak. He was probably terrified by the idea that this 'adventure' would somehow get reported to Moscow.

In comparison with such amusements, what happened to me in that ritzy restaurant where the diplomat took me with Rita Nephew was an epitome of moderation. We only ate and drank, although our host did not fail to mutter casually, glancing at the menu prices, that we could just as well have had dinner with black caviar in a posh establishment somewhere in Manhattan.

Ms Nephew asked her questions in a friendly way and did not object when I, turning to whisper, called Saddam's regime 'fascist'. She did not seem to mind it at all, and therefore her open letter, in which she later denounced me in severe terms, came as a shock.

The letter in which she expressed her concern about my 'anti-Iraqi views' and my poisonous influence on American journalists, and especially on Elaine Sciolino, was addressed to me. More importantly, copies of this missive were also forwarded to others. It was an impressive catalogue. It featured high-ranking American officials and editors. It wasn't particularly pleasant to see all those addressees in that list, but I wouldn't have lost much sleep over them. It was the first line in it that was a real killer, both figuratively and literally. A copy was sent to the Iraqi embassy in Washington, personally to His Excellency Ambassador Nazar Hamdoun. I heard that Hamdoun was a very influential figure with a direct line to Saddam. It was a major blow, to put it mildly; I was clearly in jeopardy. The Ba'athist government of Iraq and most probably Saddam Hussein himself were informed in no uncertain terms that they had a dedicated enemy in Baghdad, and his name was Andrei Ostalski.

Nearly forty years have passed since it was written, but today, I re-read it, and it still gives me shivers.

"Dear Andrei: after much reflection since my return from Baghdad, I have decided to speak up on the conversations I had with you... I do not need to point out that as a correspondent for TASS, you have an inordinate amount of influence on world public opinion about Iraq, and consequently the Iraq-Iran war and its outcome... Personally, I was very disturbed by much of what you told me about Iraq because I not only found it misleading and most disparaging but incorrect. If what you say

about your extensive input into Elaine Sciolino's New York Times Magazine piece is true and that you were actually quoted in a 'well disguised' manner, then this is not a matter to be taken lightly. In my opinion, that article was misleading and has been extremely damaging to Iraq because it was one of the first major articles written about the country after diplomatic relations with the U.S. were restored. It served to set the tone for much of our coverage of the war by influencing U.S. editorial opinion".

The letter went on about the potential damage Elaine and I had allegedly done to the prospect of ending 'the bloodiest war that the world has seen in 40 years'. It was an absurd contention. But even more ridiculous was a rhetorical question that Rita Nephew had put in that letter of hers as a sort of rebuff to my assertion of the repressive character of the Iraqi state and its unreserved brutality.

"If, in fact, Iraq is such a stringent police state, how do you explain the fact that you have been allowed such liberty of action and have been given complete access to the foreign press and diplomatic community, the most sensitive of sectors to a country fighting a war?" she wrote.

Oh, really? I wanted to shout. So, does Miss Nephew seriously think that I should be grateful to Saddam and the *Mukhabarat* for allowing me to communicate with fellow foreigners? As far as I was aware, neither Stalin nor Hitler forbade foreign journalists from speaking to each other. Did it make those dictators paragons of democracy and freedom then? And, by the way, exactly what kind of 'liberty' was I 'allowed' by the Iraqi authorities? Occasionally, putting awkward questions to the information ministry officials about their endless lies? Oh, yes, it had been sort of tolerated (not really), at least I was not killed (yet), nor even jailed or tortured as any Iraqi would undoubtedly be for daring to ask for the truth.

The biggest absurdity of all was surely Nephew's assertion that even the outcome of the Iran-Iraq war itself depended on me, and it could end badly because of my irresponsible behaviour. I should have been flattered!

She didn't mention an insignificant fact that it was Saddam who started the war with Iran in the first place, hoping to achieve a quick and easy victory over its old enemy, weakened by the

Islamic revolution. The plan was to annex the oil-rich province of Khuzestan, where a significant number of ethnic Arabs lived, possibly even constituting the majority there. However, it didn't work out that way, as the Iranians offered rigorous resistance.

Among other things that I gleaned from that sinister letter was the answer to the mystery of why Elaine Sciolino had been acquiring Iraqi visas so easily and given such free access to the Ba'athist bigwigs, and even allowed to travel a bit without the *Mukhabarat* minders (though of course she was constantly followed and often eavesdropped upon). The Iraqi authorities made a typical mistake of misunderstanding what makes free societies tick. They projected their own norms onto America, believing that a correspondent from an important media organisation, with recommendations from the State Department and support from the American embassy, would toe the line and write a complimentary article celebrating the resumption of diplomatic ties between the two countries. They knew that the State Department and the White House would most probably welcome a positive spin in such a piece, too, as Washington decided at that time to support Iraq against Iran. The Reagan administration was seriously worried by Tehran's attempts to expand its influence in the region and sponsor anti-American upheavals there. As an adage goes, an enemy of my enemy is my friend.

But what Saddam and his underlings failed to understand was that the American authorities didn't control what journalists wrote.

Elaine's piece did indeed go against the grain and quite possibly upset the American officials somewhat. Before this, only fragments of anecdotal evidence of the reality of the Ba'athist regime occasionally appeared in the American press. Here, everything was generalised with such force that Rita Nephew was partly right when she accused Elaine of setting a new, much more critical tone in the American media. If there was a bigger political and philosophical message in Elaine's piece, it was that it is terribly wrong to fight one monster by allying yourself to another. The end never justifies the means; the latter will always negate the former. And, of course, the subsequent events fully justified this view. But at the time, official Washington was annoyed with what Elaine did.

I assumed (wrongly) that Rita Nephew's actions were part of a damage-limitation operation by the CIA or another American government agency. But I also saw her denunciation as an attempt on my life.

Any unbiased reader had to acknowledge, though, that Elaine's feature was a masterpiece of thoughtful and honest journalism. No angry invectives, disparaging insults, nor howls and hot air so common in the Soviet press or in western tabloids. If a picture of an unmitigated nightmare emerged in the reader's mind, it was accomplished by listing the well-corroborated facts and quoting opinions. The article was objective: the author paid tribute to Iraq's pre-war economic successes, although these were achieved thanks to high oil prices. Elaine noted the progress of literacy programs and the development of infrastructure. But at the same time, she accurately and mercilessly demonstrated the regime's hypocrisy and its incredible cruelty, showing what the war meant for the country trapped in the senseless, endless slaughter. The style was simple (but not simplistic), restrained, almost dry, yet somehow still expressive and beautiful, without any distracting semantic games. I found the article's structure and logic to be flawless as well. There were no attempts to exert emotional pressure on the reader or impose a ready opinion, but that made it all the more convincing. I still believe that Elaine's feature is an ideal training material for any journalistic college.

When I look back today, I see that Iraq was surely the nightmarish chapter of my life, but Subhi and Elaine, both in their own ways, unwittingly became my mentors in the profession. I am very much obliged to both of them. Closely following Subhi's work, I saw and admired how he combined maximum precision and thoroughness with brevity in reporting, scrupulously choosing every word to remain impartial and concise in presenting facts in the best traditions of Reuters. Meanwhile, Elaine demonstrated the techniques of the most challenging journalistic genre, the investigative feature, showing how to tackle complex and explosive issues and how to go against the grain, overcoming received wisdom, prejudices, and stereotypes, without succumbing to the temptation of cheap sensationalism.

In a way, America's flirting with Saddam could be seen as a mirror image of the Kremlin's position. Moscow was prepared to close its eyes to the reality of the situation in Iraq in the name of the 'common anti-imperialist struggle'. At the same time, Washington was willing to look the other way because of the danger emanating from Tehran. But there was also a cardinal difference: American journalists working abroad are not subjected to direct pressure from their embassies, and they can't be prevented from telling the story as they see it. In my case, even my timid attempts to report facts objectively – for publication in TASS bulletins of limited circulation ('For Official Use Only'), often provoked an angry reaction. I recall picking up a story from *Alef Ba*, a government-controlled magazine dedicated to the 40th anniversary of the end of World War II, and sending the detailed account to Moscow – no commentary from me, just the quotes. The article was called 'Iraqi-German cooperation 1941-1945'. The author of the article praised 'fruitful contacts' between the nationalist, anti-British and anti-Semitic government of Rashid al-Ghailani and Nazi Germany during the Second World War.

'How dare you mislead Moscow!' the ambassador asked sternly.

'How do you mean – mislead?' I was honestly surprised. 'The only thing I did was to quote the article published in that magazine, that's all. Can you point out any errors in my translation from Arabic?'

'No, but you took it out of context!'

I was amazed: what kind of context was he talking about? Apart from the abovementioned piece, there were only two other items in the Iraqi media coverage of that anniversary, both in the semi-official daily *Al-Jumkhuriya*, and both were interviews. The first – with the Romanian military attaché – could, with some stretch of the imagination, be interpreted as a relatively positive account of the actions of the anti-Hitler coalition. However, the correspondent made a rapid transition to modern times and encouraged the interviewee to talk about the special relationship between the two dictators - Saddam and Nicolae Ceaușescu, which he did with great enthusiasm. A few days later, the same paper ran another interview, this time with a British Holocaust denier, who claimed to have proved beyond a reasonable doubt that the mass genocide of the Jews during the Second World War was but a harmful myth invented and circulated by the Zionists. And the interviewer did not question the truth of those statements for a second. Considering that the Iraqi press was heavily censored and closely controlled by the Ba'athist government at all times, the picture in the media certainly reflected the attitudes of Baghdad to Nazism and war. Yes, my report inevitably led its readers to an inevitable conclusion, but it was a pure fact, hard to argue against.

The ambassador was furious. It turned out that the 'context' I couldn't be privy to was the positive statements allegedly received privately from senior Iraqi officials. My experienced father-in-law called this technique, regularly practised by Soviet ambassadors, 'putting your words into the other's mouth'. That's how it worked: as per usual, the embassy would receive instructions from Moscow to urgently collect something called *otkliki* (feedback) – local reaction to yet another 'brilliant performance' of Brezhnev or, as in this particular case, to some major political event like the widely celebrated 40th anniversary of the victory in World War II. The ambassador then would request an urgent meeting at the highest possible level. There, he would read out loud the text explaining the historical significance of various topics. The interlocutor would be bored to death but would nod politely, overcoming the urge to fall asleep. Perhaps he would mumble something from time to time; some sounds emitted could be interpreted as a sign of agreement, almost of approval of what was being said. Upon returning to the embassy, the ambassador would then send an urgent telegram to Moscow, describing how a prominent Iraqi figure had highly praised Comrade Brezhnev's speech or expressed full solidarity with the Soviet position on various issues. I have heard of one ambassador who honestly responded to all the endless requests for local reactions. If the host country did not pay the slightest attention to another proclamation of the Central Committee of the Communist Party and/or Leonid Brezhnev's speech, that was what he would report to Moscow. So poor fellow was constantly criticised and considered a laggard. For those, *otkliki* gradually became the primary measure of any embassy's success or failure in information and analysis, which, in turn, was considered the priority in any embassy's activities.

All Soviet journalists had to do something similar as well. I was regularly pestered by TASS, demanding quick feedback on the Soviet leadership's pronouncements. Luckily, as long as I offered at least some kind of fudged reaction from the press or fellow journalists, I would be left alone. My superiors were wise enough not to demand too much from me in that regard as long as the 'Baghdad box' could be appropriately ticked. Still, those requests did annoy me and took up too much of my precious time. Once in the embassy's corridor, I ran into a KGB operative who asked me why I looked so grumpy, and I couldn't contain myself and started complaining about the total pointlessness of such chores. He looked at me miserably and said:

'Do you think we don't have to do it? I have been dealing with the same nonsense the whole day.'

I was gobsmacked. I wanted to say: 'What is going on? You should spy, sniff out secrets and reveal the true state of affairs. And if you, like us mere mortals, are spending so much of your time and effort on fabricating flattering feedback to please the gerontocrats of the Politburo, then it is just insane and a true sign of the imminent end of the whole system.'

But aloud I did not say any of it, of course, just shook my head.

Not out of mischief or vanity, I started sharing what I knew about the situation in Iraq with American colleagues (Elaine was not the only one who genuinely sought my insights). Once, out of desperation I wrote a so called 'information letter' for a more secret TASS bulletin called IPK (*'Informacionnye pis'ma korrespondentov'*) about the deeply rooted and officially encouraged anti-Semitism in the Ba'ath party, citing as an example the adverse reaction of the party members to the hard-hitting Soviet film *Idi i Smotri* (*Come and Look*) by Elem Klimov depicting the Nazi atrocities in the occupied Belorussia. The Ba'athists were annoyed by its demonstration in Baghdad, calling it 'Zionist propaganda'. And then I added a few things I learned from Subhi on the same subject, attributing them to anonymous sources. The letter was published in a seriously abridged form, and I received a quiet, off-the-record advice to avoid such themes in the future.

I was frustrated by my inability to present a true picture of what was happening in Iraq to even my limited audience. How could I live with this knowledge, smile and pretend that everything was hunky-dory and long live the Soviet-Iraqi friendship? That was becoming physically unbearable. I could no longer watch the *Danse Macabre* of Saddam and his cringing henchmen without a shudder.

American diplomats and intelligence officers knew only too well that by and large the nightmarish picture drawn by Elaine Sciolino reflected the actual state of affairs. However, for reasons of geopolitical expediency, they did not want the American public opinion to turn sharply against Saddam. But what could they do about it? Not much, but at least they could try to get rid of a suspicious TASS correspondent, who, for some reason, had gained influence over Western journalists. Placing myself in the shoes of an American analyst, I would not doubt that the correspondent was playing a game, most likely guided by one of the Soviet intelligence services. And the goal would seem clear – to provoke a falling out between the United States and Iraq. That view would seem utterly logical. What this hypothetical analyst wouldn't be aware of was that such risky bluffs and complex double-edged games were totally beyond the grasp of senile Soviet leaders living in their sealed ivory towers on cloud nine.

John Maynard Keynes invented an unusual metaphor to describe Soviet socialism: the Bolsheviks, he wrote, 'prefer the mud to the fish', meaning that they knowingly sacrificed economic efficiency for the sake of their rigid ideology and pretentious slogans. Now their frail successors, presiding over the irreversibly degraded pseudo-socialist system, preferred silly flattering fabrications to real diplomatic and intelligence work.

That was certainly a reality, but I was prepared to acknowledge that it would have been a stretch too far for that analyst to imagine that the young Soviet correspondent in Baghdad would engage in a daring and dangerous relationship with American colleagues on his own. In his place, I wouldn't believe it myself. That is why I supposed (wrongly) that Rita

Nephew did what she did to me on behalf of the CIA or some other US intelligence agency. I was sure that the Americans were trying to banish me from Baghdad. Or have me killed. That view seemed confirmed by other strange goings-on. An American lady, called Lisa (if I remember correctly), moved to a house in my neighbourhood and started actively courting our friendship. Once, she invited Sveta and me to a cocktail party, and I suddenly got seriously drunk, having consumed just a single, not particularly strong drink. My wife managed to drag me home before I collapsed. That was the benefit of living close by.

But then Sveta left for Moscow. She always spent July and August there, it being the hottest season when, according to the Iraqi saying, 'the nail melts'. One day, the doorbell rang. It was my new neighbour who came without any notice or warning, arriving at my door dressed in a thin, semi-transparent pink robe, clearly with nothing under it. She was not ugly, but certainly not beautiful. But the robe flattered her figure, and despite myself, I was impressed. I stood on my own threshold, completely stunned and lost for words.

More was to come. My not-so-ugly neighbour almost pushed me aside, entered the house, and found her way into the living room. Having settled into one of the chairs, she told me a sad story about her air conditioner breaking down. I had to admit, though, that the sun was merciless, boiling the air up to 45 degrees Celsius. If what she was saying was true, anybody in that situation would be prepared to defy any conventions to hide from the unbearable heat.

'Will it be okay if I stay at your place for a few minutes until somebody comes and gets my air-conditioner fixed?' she asked.

Of course, I couldn't be so cruel as to refuse.

I don't remember what our conversation was about. I probably mumbled something incoherent, trying to look away and half-expecting her to shuck off her robe at any moment. I didn't know how I would have reacted to such a development without being explicitly rude. The only thing I could think of was to offer her a glass of water while figuring out how to ask her to leave without offending.

But then there was another ring at the door. By a remarkable coincidence, someone else descended on my place again without warning, and that someone was the Soviet military attaché, Colonel Yurchenko. Dressed in his summer uniform, in full regalia. He probably wanted to consult me on a canine issue because we both had the same breed, a cross between a bulldog and a Great Dane. I did not keep him at the door, inviting him into the house right away, managing, though, to whisper in his ear a few words quickly. Something along the lines of, 'Look at her, she has come without invitation, and I have no idea what to do with her.'

Yurchenko stepped into the living room and froze. I introduced the two 'guests' to each other. The neighbour looked us up and down and then leapt out of her chair and hurriedly took her leave. She seemed pretty angry, and I realised that she did not believe in coincidence, deciding that I managed to somehow contrive, in five minutes, the colonel's appearance on the stage. Or, maybe, she thought that I had a military attaché hiding somewhere nearby, calling upon his services any time when I needed to frighten somebody off. In short, Lisa disappeared from my life after that. Yet I came to a worrying conclusion that I had become the object of some American ploy.

Copies of Sciolino's article, meanwhile, started circulating among the diplomatic corps. I saw one in Subhi's hands, too; I didn't know how he had obtained it. Possibly, Elaine herself or somebody else had sent it to him, not by mail, of course, but with some other visitor. At the very same time, one of Newsweek's senior staff members visited Iraq, bringing me a wonderful present from Roman Polanski – his memoirs, brilliantly called *Roman,* and with a witty autograph too: *To Andrei Ostalski from Roman Polanski, one thousand and one miles away from Baghdad.* Possibly, the copy of Sciolino's piece reached Subhi through the same channel. Unfortunately, I lost Polanski's book when my Moscow apartment was burgled, while the damning denunciation by Rita Nephew somehow survived all my travails and vicissitudes and still sits in my little archive, albeit faded and creased.

When we were alone, Subhi pulled the magazine out from the drawer in his desk and, in total silence, showed it to me.

Saddam's face was right on the cover. The main topic of the issue, after all. Subhi held the magazine cautiously with his fingertips, as if it were poison, which in a way it was. He didn't say anything, just asked with a gesture: Have you seen it? I nodded. Then he just shook his head in despair. Did he want to say that I had let him down? Or was he annoyed with Elaine or himself? With an awkward gesture of my own, I tried to convey my opinion that the magazine should be destroyed right away, preferably thoroughly burnt so that nothing but ashes remained. Keeping it in a drawer was dangerous. I could easily believe rumours that an Iraqi could be hanged for the possession of that text.

Having received Rita Nephew's letter in Moscow, I had to decide whether to return to Iraq from my holiday. Common sense said: No, why take chances with your one and only life? But those were the times when naïve self-confidence and adventurism often clouded my judgment.

I went to see my highly experienced father-in-law, who had been through hell and high water of the Soviet Byzantine system, asking for his advice: what should I do? He was clearly taken aback. All he could think of was to advise me to speak privately with Sergei Losev, the TASS director, and confess all my sins. He did not know him well, but heard that he was not a malicious person. That seemed true from my limited experience dealing with him, and I had considered this option but ultimately rejected it. I might as well refuse to return to Baghdad under some plausible pretext or another. I could claim that I was unwell or profess a nervous breakdown, even the shameful weakness of the spirit, saying: I can no longer work in a country at war. I am sick and tired of having to walk by the piles of dead bodies during the visits to the frontline and waking up at night to the sound of air raid sirens and explosions. If I took that course, I would have to be prepared to be deemed a coward, which could damage my reputation. But what did it matter if that was the price to pay for staying alive? The consequences might be unpleasant, but bearable. Of course, it would have damaged my career prospects, but that would have been nothing compared to the terrible consequences that my sincere confession could have had. Malicious or not, as soon as Losev heard about my unauthorised contacts with American journalists and the far-reaching political implications of my reckless behaviour, he would have no choice but to fire me on the spot. And not only that, according to the rules, he would have to inform the Central Committee, the notorious '*zagrankadry*' ('Personnel working abroad') department, which would no doubt investigate the incident with the help of the KGB. And it was clear how the matter would end: I would never have another chance to go abroad, nor would I be able to work in international journalism. I would have to confine myself to translation jobs, which would be the best-case scenario. I expounded these considerations to my father-in-law, and he had to admit that this was a very realistic prospect. And that even he, with all his connections, would not necessarily be able to pull me out of such a pit.

Here I must say a few words about my father-in-law, Valentin Vdovin. I have always respected him deeply. I was amazed that it was possible to reach such a high level in the Soviet hierarchy and remain a decent human being – kind, humorous, and capable of self-irony and empathy – a rare case, an exception that only confirmed the rule. One explanation of that was that he did not have to go through the whole career ladder of the corrupting system, where amoral cynicism was instilled in you in the process. He also managed to avoid the debasing influence of the Komsomol (the Young Communist League) apparatchiks, the milieu in which he found himself in the mid-50s. Not all of them were morally rotten, though. After all, it was the generation of the Twentieth Communist Party Congress that denounced Stalin's crimes and heralded the beginning of a short-lived but uplifting thaw. Among that group, there were many bright and likeable personalities, including Mikhail Gorbachev and Eduard Shevardnadze, with whom my father-in-law had been on friendly terms since his youth. But there was also a much darker stratum in the same bunch, very different people – vicious and illiterate nationalists and anti-Semites. My father-in-law always despised them and tried to avoid having any dealings with them (but not always succeeding). In private, he would sometimes mock them and parody their pompous, bombastic, inane language. I recall his novella about Sergei Pavlov, the first secretary of the Komsomol Central Committee in the 1960s, who later served as the Soviet Ambassador to Mongolia. Feeling frustrated and angry with this posting, which he saw as a demotion, he would regularly get drunk and, for lack of other Jews among the embassy staff, would direct his hatred at the portrait of Karl Marx hanging on his office wall. 'Oi, you, kike, a Yiddish snout!' snarled His Excellency in the presence of other Soviet diplomats.

Valentin received his first ambassadorial appointment when he was only thirty-seven years old, and held that position in several countries throughout his career. He regularly came into conflict with the Soviet bureaucracy, fought against its lunacy on the side of elementary common sense, clashed with ministers, and even occasionally emerged victorious in those battles. Privately, with no strangers listening, he would allow himself seriously scathing criticism not only of individual big shots but also of the inefficiency of the entire system. (Having listened to my father-in-law's invectives for so long, I knew precisely where Gorbachev was coming from when he started his Perestroika reforms).

My mother-in-law Elena went even further in her scornful diatribes against the communist ideology and Soviet power, holding bluntly dissident conversations in the kitchen. There was, of course, an element of convenient hypocrisy in all this, intrinsic to those (myself included) who, understanding the rottenness of the system, nevertheless served it, comforting themselves with the idea that they could do some good, softening its cruelty and moderating its absurdity from the inside. Heroism and self-sacrifice can't be demanded from everyone, and kitchen dissident conversations also served their purpose. They were crucially important for those of us who desperately needed to prove to ourselves that we were still capable of critical thinking, resisting the attempts of the system to turn us into thoughtless cogs in the machine. If a cog begins to think for itself, then sooner or later it will fall out of the rut. The moment will come, and the number of the disaffected party members will reach a critical mass, and then the whole edifice will collapse. And that is precisely what happened. In the end, the USSR was not toppled by a handful of heroic dissidents – tragically unsupported by a public that saw no connection between the absurd government and the empty shops – but by the profound disillusionment of the elites. All the same, the dissidents were extremely important:

somebody had to risk everything, making enormous personal sacrifices to keep the sense of shame alive in us all.

My father-in-law didn't join in anti-Soviet kitchen conversations, but he did not try to stop them either; he was only concerned that none of us should repeat his wife's seditious words outside the apartment or while on the phone.

Agreeing that opening up my heart and soul to the head of TASS was not such a brilliant idea after all, my father-in-law made another suggestion: confiding in the Soviet Ambassador to Iraq, Victor Minin. I was sure that, in this case, too, he was utterly wrong. Anyone who wanted to get rid of me could have done so very easily: all they had to do was forward Rita Nephew's open letter to the Soviet embassy in Baghdad. I had no doubt whatsoever that, upon hearing about my problems, the ambassador would send me back to Mother Russia within 24 hours. And he would greatly enjoy doing so, as there was no love lost between the two of us. And a *'telega'* (literally meaning a 'cart' but standing in the jargon for an incriminating encoded embassy radio cable) will fly to Moscow ahead of me. The consequences of that might be even worse than I could imagine.

I had an understanding with my father-in-law that he wouldn't interfere with my career. With his support, I could easily find work at the Foreign Ministry and perhaps even secure postings in Western countries with a mild climate and a strong currency, rather than in the fire-breathing Iraq. Valentin had influential contacts not only in the Foreign Ministry but also in the Central Committee apparatus. But I was vain, and it seemed to me that I would cease to respect myself, and lose the hard-won esteem of my in-laws too if I turned into a common '*blatnyak*' (a person using family nepotistic ties to forward their career). No, it seemed important to me to do everything on my own. But now, when it came to survival, I was ready to accept help. And my father-in-law obliged, arming me with a photograph of himself standing side by side with his old friend Gorbachev, nearly hugging him. Valentin was the Soviet ambassador to Portugal at the time, and Gorbachev was on a visit to the country, staying as a guest at the ambassadorial villa in Lisbon. Chernenko was still in power, but everybody in the establishment knew that his days were numbered. Gorby was officially number two, and persistent rumours were doing the rounds that he was about to become number one.

I could no longer afford moral maximalism. At the first opportunity, I showed that photograph first to the ambassador, and then to the KGB resident. It was a message: do not touch me, or you can break your teeth. That was, of course, a pure bluff, as my father-in-law would never involve Gorbachev in my problems. When Gorby finally became the General Secretary of the CPSU Central Committee, all sorts of old friends, real and imagined, immediately rushed to pay their respects in the view of possible career advancement. One of Gorby's assistants hinted to Valentin that he should reserve his place in the queue of sycophants and also personally congratulate his long-time comrade. Yes, and incidentally, Mrs Gorbachev wanted to gently remind him of a small favour she had asked of Elena while in Lisbon. But my father-in-law considered it humiliating to fawn on the new boss in this way. He would have been happy, of course, had Gorbachev thought of him on his own, possibly offering some new, interesting job. But he hated the idea of imposing himself to exploit their familiarity. A lovely Portuguese leather handbag bought as a present for the new First Lady was delivered through an assistant. And that was all. If I am not mistaken, my father-in-law never saw Gorbachev again. Shevardnadze, though, did promote him after becoming foreign minister, making Valentin the head of an important department. And he was surely on his way even further up when a serious illness put an end to his career.

Meanwhile, I had several chances to exchange a few words with Gorbachev. Once, in Madrid, I got a rather angry answer to my question at his press conference (I will describe it in more detail in one of the following chapters of this book). And then, long after his retirement, I recorded a lengthy radio interview with him. He never asked me about my father-in-law, probably not realising that there was a connection.

But at that time in Baghdad, I had no idea what was awaiting me. Gloomy premonitions tormented me, although I received an unexpected and vigorous support from the deputy head of the International Department of the Central Committee, Karen Brutents, who visited Baghdad and was present at one of my showdowns with the ambassador. After all, it was Brutents who for many years oversaw the relations with the Iraqi Communist Party, and could not forgive Saddam for its destruction. Apparently, he was disgusted by the embassy's attempts to gloss over Iraqi reality, although this immoral course was fully consistent with the cynical political line that had prevailed in Moscow. Brutents clearly liked my attempts to add a spoonful of tar into a barrel of honey – a traditional Russian saying corresponding to the English expression of a 'small fly in the ointment'. In general, the Central Committee's International Department felt humiliated and considered itself a loser in the political struggle over Iraq's policies. The Ministry of Foreign Affairs and the KGB believed that sacrificing the Communists was an acceptable price to pay for the so-called 'strengthening of the anti-imperialist front'. The malicious anti-American rhetoric of Saddam and the Iraqi press was music to their ears. For it, they were ready to forgive all.

The International Department of the Central Committee might not have liked it, but the problem wasn't confined to Iraq; it was becoming increasingly clear that relations with the Third World's Communists were being relegated to a lower level in the hierarchy of Soviet foreign policy. And generally, the department was losing its weight in the Soviet system. Its chief, Boris Ponomarev, along with his subordinates, was pushed aside, and their opinions were often ignored. But inertia still existed on the periphery of the Soviet system. Ambassador Minin clearly feared Brutents, and after the latter's intervention, he left me alone for a while, although sometimes, at meetings, I caught the ambassador's dirty glance, which did not bode well for me.

It was clear that no father-in-law, despite all his connections, and no Brutents would have saved me had the contents of Nephew's letter become the subject of official investigation. This could not be allowed to happen.

But why did the Americans fail to inform the Soviet authorities about my 'anti-Iraqi activities'? I asked myself. I could think of only one explanation: they did not doubt that the embassy knew about my actions only too well.

It sounded quite logical - but if homo sapiens were always guided only by logic, life on earth would have been more reasonable and safer, although, perhaps, more boring. There have always been and will be 'white crows', odd men out, capable of surprises and defying the received wisdoms. People, thank God, will never be entirely predictable.

I was a totally spoilt brat – not materially, though. I was accustomed to modest living and didn't mind subsisting on a humble monthly salary if there was a roof over our heads, a clean bed, hot water, and no one in the family went hungry, of course. No, the problem was different: I always led a charmed existence, cossetted and cherished in my childhood and youth practically by everybody close to me, in the family, at school, at the university and at work, although from time to time the haters would also appear out of the blue but would always be defeated and disappear from my life. Quite often, I acted as a smart alec, who took it all for granted (for which I am now ashamed).

From time to time, I was visited by doubts. Do I really deserve such sympathy and support? Or am I just unconsciously manipulating people, always making the right impression on them? At least, I can swear that I never knowingly played such a game.

But the love of my family, first of all, my grandfather Porfiriy Feofanovich, who taught me to read, write, think, and love literature, seemed to me to be the source of strength in my life.

Chapter Six

The Power of Doublethink

The grandfather's love was probably a vent for all his unspent emotional energy. For most of his long life, he had to pretend to be somebody he was not, hide his 'wrong social background' - there had been many generations of priests in my family on the paternal side. His education wouldn't have earned him any laurels in the eyes of the Bolsheviks either (he had studied philology at Warsaw University with a specialisation in Latin); he also had to conceal his range of interests, not to mention his political views. After the Bolshevik revolution, he worked as a simple bookkeeper, invariably refusing any offers of promotion, as he couldn't risk being vetted by the Soviet secret police. His deadly, thoroughly guarded secret was that he was closely related to Bishop Arkadiy Ostalski, his cousin, whom the Bolsheviks hated for refusing to bow to their rule. He was declared a 'dangerous enemy' and shot. (After the fall of communism, Bishop Arkadiy was canonised by the Russian Orthodox Church). My grandfather's only aim in life was the salvation of his family, and he was prepared to sacrifice everything for it. Until the mid-fifties, he kept a little suitcase with dried bread and linen ready, in case of arrest. Before the revolution, my grandfather taught Latin until the Soviet authorities deprived him of this opportunity. Only at the end of his life, in relatively more liberal times, did he return to teaching the same subject and continued to do so until he was eighty-five.

My father, Vsevolod, believed that our family had been almost supernaturally fortunate to survive all the vicissitudes of the twentieth century. He cited numerous cases of incredible luck as evidence, such as miraculously surviving World War II despite serving with the special commando forces, which were regularly airdropped behind German lines. Once, their detachment got dispersed, and he had to hide in a rye field, on its very edge. Suddenly, a German tank appeared and stopped at a distance of less than ten metres from my father's hiding place. He was preparing to die, hoping to take as many enemies with him as possible. But when a red-haired young German emerged from inside the tank, my father unexpectedly found it hard to shoot him – he had a nice face and a gentle smile, and looked younger than eighteen, more like a kind and sympathetic school boy than a soldier. He clearly didn't notice my father at first, as he probably just wanted to enjoy a lull in the fighting and the nice weather. And then he suddenly saw the crouching figure of the Soviet army officer in front of him. The smile was still there for a few seconds, but then it slowly faded away. For a few seconds, the two of them were looking into each other's eyes. Then the German turned around and dived inside the tank. My father was angry at himself: why did he miss the chance to shoot at least one German before being killed himself? But then an astonishingly weird thing happened: instead of either crushing my father or shooting him with the machine gun, the tank reversed and quickly drove away.

Another amazing fact was that Vsevolod was never even injured while deep behind the German lines. The commandos had the order to finish off their own comrades if severe wounds incapacitated them, as they had to be on the move all the time and couldn't carry anybody on a stretcher or otherwise. And when a deadly, dangerous injury did happen to Vsevolod, his detachment was already on its way back, close to the Soviet line and a field hospital, so he was safely delivered there. But the shell splinter that had entered his body stopped at the distance of two and a half millimetres from his heart, and doctors believed it was something just short of a miracle that they managed to operate on him and extract that fragment before it moved any further. After the successful surgery and quick treatment, my father was sent to a medical spa for convalescence. There, he met the head of a large air force training school, who became so attached to him that he offered Vsevolod the position of his aide-de-camp. Later, my father even started teaching at that school, while nearly all the rest of his comrades were killed, just four of the entire battalion survived.

After the war, my father graduated as a theatre director, worked briefly at the *Maly Theatre* in Moscow, and then spent most of his life coaching future actors. Quite a few of them later became massive stars in the Russian thespian world. My maternal grandfather was also a prominent theatre director, while my grandmother, his wife, was an actress. It seems it was expected of my brother and me that we should carry on 'sowing the good seeds' with a pen and a voice. I always liked speaking to all kinds of audiences, and I probably had some abilities in that respect. I don't remember how it started, but from year six at school, the teachers were regularly asking me to talk to the class at the end of the lesson if there were a few extra minutes left. I was mostly telling my mates about the books I was reading at the time, but occasionally I could slip into my own fantasy world. The audience, my class, seemed to have developed an addiction to this strange activity.

I never took my father's theory seriously, and he himself did not really insist on it; it was a hypothesis he put forward half in jest. But it was true that the family had survived all the horrors of the twentieth century almost intact. Nobody was killed or maimed during the revolution and the nightmarish civil war in which tens of millions perished. Stalin's purges also somehow passed the family by; in the end, no one got hauled into the Gulag, although all the omens were there, indicating a very high probability of the most tragic outcomes. The Second World War brought many privations; both my father and my uncle fought in the war and were seriously wounded, but again, nobody in the family was killed, which was considered a rarity.

In any case, whether mystical or not, the family definitely owed its survival to the quiet, inconspicuous stoicism of grandfather Porfiriy. If not for his wisdom, excellent self-control and self-denial, none of us would have lived.

He passionately hated the Soviet power, but did not allow his emotions to show through under any circumstances. To survive and save us all, he had to totally cut off all ties to his pre-revolutionary circle of friends and acquaintances. He sealed his lips tight and, swallowing his pride, allowed the new society to bring up both of his sons as true 'young pioneers' (the Soviet equivalent of the scouts, only with a lot of communist brainwashing added; membership was compulsory) and Komsomol members, realising that otherwise they would have been doomed. But it wasn't easy for him to silently observe this happening. Even more painful, I think, was for him to watch how the same fate seemed to befall his beloved grandson. But in my case, he took some countermeasures, giving me a chance to discover his true feelings. After all, Stalin and his terror were gone, and with Khrushchev and his thaw came what Russian quipsters called 'the vegetarian times' (relatively mild repression). In the intervals between reading Walter Scott or Mayne Reid to me or delivering improvised lectures on comparative linguistics, he started, carefully and in little doses, to pour little bits of poison (or rather an antidote to the poison) into my ears. Alas, I was confused and couldn't appreciate his viewpoint at the time. I took his seditious speeches either for a joke, or for the grumbling of an elderly, politically naïve man of the *'Ancien Régime'*. Who refused, for example, to admit the obvious aptness of his younger son's position. My father, Vsevolod, wholeheartedly believed that everything bad in the Soviet reality was brought by Stalin, who had totally distorted the beautiful communist idea. Lenin, meanwhile, was the shining light, and we had to work hard to cleanse his great legacy of Stalin's filth. Grandfather Porfiriy wouldn't comment on such pronouncements, later whispering in my ear: 'Lenin and Stalin were *odnovo polya yagody* (literally meaning: 'berries from the same allotment', the Russian equivalent of 'birds of a feather').

Only a few decades later, I realised that the subversive thoughts my grandad had planted in my mind were not lost; they were preserved, deposited deep in my subconscious, waiting for their time to surface.

As a university student, I wasn't totally immune to some frivolous nonconformist thinking, albeit on quite a modest scale – nothing to be particularly proud of. I rebelled against the ideological rigidity of some of the professors there, especially the tyranny and incredible ignorance of the dean of our journalistic faculty Lev Strzhizhovsky. I collected the pearls from his dull and ill-informed lectures. He didn't bother to prepare appropriately, spoke poorly, mixed up dates and names, misquoted well-known sources, and ignored grammar rules. It was clear he couldn't teach, but, having come from the staff of the Communist Party newspaper Pravda, he didn't require any qualifications to get his position. I made fun of his puffy demeanour and pompous style. As a result, I was declared a 'subversive element' and almost expelled from the university. Luckily for me, the dean also fell out with some influential figures in the Soviet hierarchy (I have no idea what it was all about). More importantly, some of the professors came to my rescue. As soon as the dean made it clear to his subordinates that he was going to get rid of me, his deputy immediately found a way to warn me. The dean, meanwhile, went to see the brilliant Vladimir Segal, my mentor in Arabic, and asked him bluntly to fail me in the upcoming exam, thus facilitating my expulsion. Segal was so furious that he not only immediately informed me of that conversation but also went to see the Rector (University head) about it. I suspect he also ensured that I would receive a higher mark in the exam than I actually deserved. As the foremost Arabic interpreter of the International Department of the CPSU Central Committee, Segal could afford a quarrel with the head of the faculty. A few other prominent professors petitioned the Rector, pleading with him not to allow an injustice to happen. Soon, Strzhizhovsky resigned and went back to Pravda, and I survived. If it were not for this amazing salvation, my life would have taken a different track, and you would not be reading this book.

Once again, I asked myself: why did all those nice people go out of their way, even taking certain risks, to save my neck? Am I so exceptionally talented or charming? I somehow doubted it as I never took myself too seriously. At some point, I inferred that somebody like me found it easy to shine in the USSR because Stalin had killed off the whole host of much more brilliant people, while I was lucky to be alive. I guess I am not entirely devoid of certain abilities and skills, and my grandfather had taught me many things at a very early age. Still, my modest talents would have surely paled in comparison with those who were murdered and their unborn descendants. Stalin's system was specifically honed to find and destroy the best and the brightest, but even before he came to power, the revolution and the civil war had taken their terrible tolls. All in all, Russia is probably the number one case study of negative (and unnatural) selection among humans. As a result of this process, a rare, perfect *kakistocracy* (a system of government run by the least qualified or most unprincipled citizens) was created and perpetuated. At the end of Stalin's rule, only half-literate simpletons totally devoid of human empathy were left to rule the party and the country. In the time of my youth, these perceived leaders of the foremost Marxist state were hardly capable of reading and understanding even one page of *Das Kapital* (with the possible exception of foreign minister Gromyko and the chief ideologue Suslov, but they were both also uncouth and tongue-tied with lower-than-average general erudition). They could only echo the simplistic slogans invented by the Bolsheviks for illiterate workers. Many of the catastrophic problems and deficiencies in modern Russia can be traced back to that peculiar system of government.

It took me a lot of rather painful soul-searching to arrive at this conclusion many years on, while in my youth I was prepared to tolerate the communist orthodoxy (after all, I knew nothing else) even if I despised Brezhnev and other vulgar and poorly educated Politburo members and loved 'anti-Soviet' jokes.

My favourite at that time was about Brezhnev's supposed criticism of the quality of meat products in the USSR. Speaking at a party conference, the General Secretary seemed to have declared that 'the sausages are shit'. (*'sosiski sraniye'* in Russian). That was, the joke went on, a distortion, the result of the severe speech impairment that had befallen the Soviet leader after he suffered a stroke in the mid-70s. What he really was struggling to say was not *'sosiski sraniye'* but *'socialisticheskiye strany'*, i.e. 'socialist countries'. It was hilarious not only because it sounded absolutely authentic (Brezhnev did have a stroke and his speech was indeed impaired), but also because the Soviet sausages, at least those available to the general public rather than the clientele of the Party elite's special food stores, were indeed dreadful. In fact, even those shitty sausages were seen as a luxury by the inhabitants of Russian hinterlands, where any meat products were rarely available in general shops. In the same measure, Moscow's colonies-satellites, aka the 'socialist countries', were also 'in the shit' – because of the stifling control that the Soviet Union exercised over them, choking their economic and cultural development.

Such a joke, if overheard by the wrong person, could mean not only the inevitable expulsion from our privileged MGIMO (International relations) university but, most probably, a few years behind bars. I first heard it from Leonid Florentyev, my pal and the son of a full member of the CPSU Central Committee. I then delighted in repeating it to Nikita Golovanov and Kirill Rozhnov, who were also intelligent and talented young men, both offspring of the Soviet aristocracy. Sergei Kaminsky was another friend from my school days, whom I could trust with my life. I remember that he liked that joke a lot. His father was a very prominent Moscow lawyer. I was sure that neither of them would ever betray me, and of course, none did. But I wouldn't repeat it to anybody else outside that very narrow circle.

Anyway, we were regularly laughing like mad at the expense of the Soviet senile gerontocrats, although the sad results of their rule were hardly a laughing matter.

In the 1990s, after the collapse of the Soviet Union, Russians were free to tell whatever jokes they fancied. Today, in Putin's Russia, people are persecuted as extremists for reposting 'wrong' jokes on social media. We have come full circle.

I remember what a delight it was to read, in my third university year, Orwell's *1984*. I borrowed it from another privileged MGIMO student whom I didn't know all that well, so it was a serious risk, as the book was strictly banned material, being found in possession of it would have been an even more serious criminal offence than telling 'anti-Soviet jokes'. It would have undoubtedly meant many years in jail.

I hesitated but, in the end, decided to take the risk – the temptation was too strong. I couldn't resist it. But I took the book from that student (hidden in a copy of *Pravda*) quite late in the evening. I read through the night like mad and finished it in the morning. I didn't sleep a wink and went to the university very early, patiently waiting there for a chance to get rid of the dangerous volume right away, the whole idea being that even if the student in question were a *stookach* (a snitch) I wouldn't have left the KGB much time to organise my arrest, given the fact that I surely wasn't important enough for such a hasty operation. Nothing ever happened to me because of this episode, so I concluded that my anxiety was groundless and the man was innocent. But it did bother me a bit that he would be so reckless as to lend such 'subversive material' to a stranger. Was he the kind of heedless risk-taker who, after a glass or two, might start boasting in public about the book and its circle of fans? When he asked whether I liked the book, I preferred not to answer.

However, even after reading and admiring Orwell, I still believed in the possibility of a 'socialism with a human face', as well as in the insidiousness of the Americans. It was surely an example of the doublethink so brilliantly described by Orwell in that very book, but the irony of it was lost on me at the time.

In the autumn of 1975, my tutor, Segal, invited me to dinner at his place. Over the food, he suddenly asked me:

'Andrei, have you been following the events in Portugal? Do you realise 'the Reds' nearly took over? What a terribly sad development, what a catastrophe it would have been! Can you imagine: the Communists wanted to nationalise all the land.'

That was really something – hearing such a blasphemy from the man who frequented the Kremlin and was regularly translating for the Central Committee bosses, even for the Politburo members and at times for Brezhnev himself.

I nodded my sincere agreement without trying to reconcile what I had just heard with the other, more orthodox views I still held in my head simultaneously. I considered Segal a genius, one of the absolutely brightest and wittiest men I ever met in my life, and felt immensely flattered to be accepted by him as a junior friend, not to mention the fact that he played such a significant role in delivering me from the clutches of the dean. How on earth could I not agree with him, especially as he showed such an absolute trust in me, the confidence that I wouldn't betray him?

And while the possibility of the communist takeover and Bolshevik-style land-grab in Portugal did bother me, in other respects, I somehow still considered myself a 'Soviet patriot', whatever it really meant. And although doubts were piling up, my real awakening happened only in Iraq. I could not forgive my government for its friendship with the monster. Tell me who your friend is, and I'll tell you who you are. This ancient wisdom applies not only to individuals but also to international relations.

The United States, however, sometimes allied itself with some pretty odious regimes too, supporting them financially and even arming them. It was done for geopolitical reasons – to deter Soviet expansion. But in America, unlike in the USSR, public opinion was strong and didn't take kindly to these tactical alliances. But to begin with, the public needed to know the basic facts about those countries, and that is where the journalists played their crucial role. Elaine Sciolino's hard-hitting article was a typical example of such eye-opening journalism. The Fourth Estate is part and parcel of the democratic society and its system of government, and the American administrations can't ignore it or would do so at their peril.

Besides, the employees of the State Department, the White House and the intelligence services themselves often felt unease about close relationships with cruel and mendacious dictators. As they say, lie down with dogs, and you get up with fleas.

Under pressure from the Fourth Estate, administrations were often forced to lower the level of relations with dubious partners and expose such fellow travellers to public criticism, on occasion even disavowing them.

In the Soviet case, everything was fundamentally different. There was certainly a strong sense of affinity between Moscow and Baghdad. There came a moment when it dawned on me: naïve Iraqi Communists turned out to be superfluous to this happy marriage; there was not much left of Marxism and socialist internationalism in Moscow, just empty slogans and hollow incantations. One-party unopposed rule with the dominance of security services and secret policemen – that was the substance of both regimes and the basis of their true kinship, of mutual understanding and lasting union. And what kind of ideological clattering and blathering was used to justify oppression was of secondary importance; their essence was the same.

When this understanding finally dawned on me, something happened; an internal change occurred. I remember the day when I stood in front of the mirror, shaving, and suddenly saw a new, not wholly familiar person. The full implication of this change, though, did not become clear to me until much later. It took many months. I was fortunate that it was during the same period that the era of *Perestroika* and *Glasnost* began in the USSR, and unexpectedly, I got a chance to leave TASS and join the editorial staff of *Izvestia*. This newspaper was changing too, quickly moving in the same direction as I was.

But in 1985, in Baghdad, I didn't have time to think through what the transformation in my world meant in practice. I had to attend to a much more urgent matter – how to stay alive.

I returned to Iraq, and the very next morning, I rushed to the Ministry of Information and asked for an urgent appointment with Minister Latif Nassif al-Jassim. Usually, one had to wait weeks or even months for such an appointment. Not so in my case; I was given an audience in just a couple of days, although, at the last moment, his deputy took the minister's place. I heard the rumour that he was, in fact, a general of the Iraqi foreign intelligence service. He was undoubtedly a much more polished figure than his boss, who had had hardly any education at all and generally gave the impression of a rather thick and uncouth type. Trying to compensate for the lack of sophistication, he was emanating an overwhelming sense of his own importance, a real Ba'athist, in a word. Besides, the Deputy Minister spoke excellent English, while al-Jassim not only didn't know any foreign languages but even his '*al-fusha*' – the classic, literary Arabic that we were taught at the university – seemed dodgy. And I didn't feel very confident when trying to communicate in the Iraqi dialect.

The general greeted me cordially, smiled, offered me a comfortable chair and a customary cup (or rather, a glass) of sweet tea. After some small talk and exchange of pleasantries, I took the bull by the horns.

'Do you happen to know anything about a so-called open letter addressed to me by an American journalist, with a copy sent to the Iraqi embassy in Washington?' I asked.

My interlocutor was clearly an experienced spy and a great actor. I was astonished by how brilliantly he imitated surprise and bewilderment, how naturally he sounded when asking to repeat the journalist's name, and how convincingly he frowned. It was such a great piece of acting that I was almost ready to believe him and accept that he really knew nothing about any open letters. I had to remind myself that the probability of that being the case was extremely low.

'No, it's the first time I hear anything about this matter,' he assured me.

I handed him the fateful letter, experiencing an extraordinary sensation, as if I were leading myself to the slaughter.

As he read the document with a sceptical frown never leaving his sleek face, I began delivering my well-rehearsed diatribe against American imperialism, its perfidy and dangerous intrigues.

Our enemies were trying to provoke a rift between Iraq and the Soviet Union, I said, vehemently rejecting what I called 'insinuations' and firmly declaring that I had never voiced the slanderous opinions of friendly Iraq that had been attributed to me by 'that woman' — what an insolent, shameless fabrication! I was making all those pronouncements, surprising myself with the ease with which I could lie without flushing, while until that moment I believed myself rather talentless in that respect, a lame-ass, practically. Allowing imagination to carry me away a bit, embellishing a story to make it sound more interesting – that happened to me a lot. But a blatant, self-serving lie? My grandfather Porfiriy Feofanovich took an extremely dim view of liars and managed to instil in me a similar instinctive revulsion, which wasn't easy to overcome. *It seems I can actually fib quite well if it becomes a matter of life and death* – that was the thought that crossed my mind as I demonstrated unexpected talents as a newborn fabulist.

The general kept nodding and making encouraging noises. There was not a shadow of a doubt in his wide-open, seemingly gullible eyes. In the right places, he would scowl, sharing my righteous indignation, and at other times, he would reassure me with a warm smile, radiating friendship and trust.

'Of course, we believe you,' said the general, summing up the conversation. 'Don't worry, just carry on working as normal. Everything will be fine.'

And I sincerely thanked him.

So who duped whom in that surreal little scene? Nobody deceived anybody, and nobody was fooled. Both sides knew only too well that the other side was lying, but pretended to take those bogus mutual assurances at face value. The necessary ceremony was performed.

And what, in the final analysis, was the message I was trying to deliver to the Iraqi authorities? It was possible to sum it up with a straightforward, childish sentence: I will not do it again! That's actually what I promised. The question was: would they believe me? And, even if they would, how could I trust their benign assurances? Saddam might still decree that the crime shouldn't go unpunished, which would be typical of him.

Everybody is occasionally tempted to overrate their importance. But I don't think that the TASS correspondent in Baghdad at that time was seen by the Ba'athists' bigwigs and, in fact, Saddam himself, as too small a fry to be bothered about. Fully-fledged foreign correspondents based in Iraq at that time were few and far between; they could be counted on the fingers of one hand. In terms of its weight, TASS was probably second only to Reuters among them. Still, the latter was represented by Subhi, an Iraqi citizen who was supposedly under the control of the *Mukhabarat*. Out of the three Soviet journalists, I was the only one who regularly went to the front and covered the war. All of that left me rather exposed. It felt as if I was in the spotlight all the time.

Nevertheless, leaving the general's office, I thought I had done well and increased my chances of survival somewhat. I had already opened the door to get out when the general stopped me on the threshold.

'Mr. Ostalski,' he said, 'if I may give you a little piece of advice. If I were you, I would be much more careful with the American journalists, especially the ladies.'

He said it light-heartedly, with a playful smile on his face, as if he was joking or commenting on some frivolous matters.

It was actually a direct threat.

'Of course,' I replied. 'I'll draw the right conclusions!' As I walked out of the ministry, I was asking myself: whom did the general mean? Rita Nephew? Or Elaine Sciolino?

A few weeks later, after a suspicious car accident, I was lying in a cast in plaster at home, feverishly trying to organise my urgent and final departure from Iraq. And all of a sudden, I saw a report in the local newspapers about a new visit to Baghdad by a 'well-known American journalist and writer,' Rita Nephew, who was clearly getting VIP treatment from the Iraqi authorities and was granted audiences by the local bigwigs. Struggling with a painful fever, which prevented me from thinking clearly, I was trying to comprehend what that meant.

Before tackling the still distressing account of how my car crash happened, I should first say a little more about the new site I found for the Baghdad TASS office in late 1984, as it is relevant to what followed. The former premises that the bureau occupied looked grand but were definitely past their prime, quickly declining and becoming increasingly dilapidated and shabby. Big chunks of plaster were falling out of the walls and the ceiling, and flying cockroaches of incredible size were jumping at you from every corner. Besides, it was located far from the town centre, while the local antediluvian telephone exchanges were totally unable to provide adequate line connections.

It was quite a challenge to find an appropriate house in wartime Baghdad, and I had been looking high and low for many weeks before striking lucky. The beautiful *Al-Jadriya* felt like another planet. It was just a stone's throw from the riverbank with the fabulous palm grove on the other side. Here, I finally found exactly what I needed—a brand-new, cosy, and clean villa with a stunning garden. And, most importantly, in that privileged area of Baghdad, two new exchange stations provided excellent modern connections necessary for telephone and telex lines. The ongoing issue of reliable communication with Moscow and the local news agency was to be resolved.

The area was rich and clean, featuring stunningly beautiful villas, each decorated with intricate porches, fences, and stylish windows of strikingly diverse shapes. I wondered where this architectural tradition came from, and the locals told me it was mainly Italian in origin. It turned out that most of the leading Iraqi architects studied in Italy. I can't vouch for the truth of it, but one way or another, the fact was that the street looked very elegant and prosperous. Ah, blessed *Al-Jadriya*, what's left of you today, after all the bombings, shootings, explosions and social upheavals?

In comparison to the homes of the Iraqi bourgeoisie, the house I rented for the TASS office and as my temporary home looked very modest, with no frills and no piquant decorations – just a simple rectangular building, and that was it. But the rooms were bright and comfortable, and the house boasted a wonderful walled garden with 18 rose bushes of different colours, shapes, and scents.

There were also the obvious and significant economic benefits from moving to this location. Much shorter daily trips to the Information Ministry, Soviet Embassy, and other centrally located residences promised substantial savings on petrol, not to mention the correspondent's time. In addition to everything else, the rent for the new premises was significantly lower – it would have saved TASS tens of thousands of dollars per year.

And my new landlord was modest too - a wealthy farmer, who had not yet learned the art of squeezing exorbitant rents from foreigners. Everything was absolutely brilliant except just one thing: on the first floor, where the residential quarters of the correspondent and his family were situated, there was one surplus room that we didn't need but couldn't demolish or board up. That conundrum gave me a lot of headaches and revealed the essence of the Soviet system from a practical, economic perspective.

According to a Soviet Council of Ministers' decree, a TASS correspondent was entitled to a particular floor area of the living quarters, not a square metre more. Our two little bedrooms, the bathroom and the corridor fell inside that measure, but the damned extra room didn't.

If you exceeded the allowance in the size of your living area, you had to pay for every extra metre from your salary. In our case, we would have had to go hungry to meet those demands, as it would have cut our income nearly in half. To conceal the factual state of affairs would have implied a terrible risk of being sacked at best and possibly even being prosecuted for fraud. But there should be some logic and common sense in this life, I thought, and sent a letter to Moscow, to the TASS Financial department. If I move to *Al-Jadriya*, I pleaded, not only will my work become much more efficient and communications become much more reliable, but also serious sums of scarce hard currency would be saved for the Soviet state. I asked for an exception to be made, but received no response.

Next time I was in Moscow, I went to see the chief financial officer and asked him whether TASS wasn't interested in the huge savings that allowing an exception to the rule would bring.

'We are talking tens of thousands of US dollars per annum!' I said.

He looked me in the eye and said woefully: 'Thousands, millions, tens of millions – it makes no difference. This rule does not know exceptions; they are not allowed under any circumstances.'

'Well,' I said, 'sorry, then, I will have to stay in the old building with lousy communication lines, far away from the centre, but with flying cockroaches.'

The chief looked away and then muttered, as if talking to the wall:

'I heard you were smart. If you are, then think, use your brains, ok?'

I decided to justify my cool reputation. I thought and thought and came up with a plan. Back in Baghdad, I assured the landlord that TASS was willing to rent his house on a long-term basis, but there was one caveat: he would keep one upstairs room locked and forbid me from using it. And that had to be clearly stated in the contract. That suggestion visibly troubled my farmer. To begin with, he refused to believe his ears, thinking that he had misunderstood my excessively literary Arabic and called his better-educated son to interpret my words for him. But the son confirmed that I was clearly insisting on one room being permanently locked. The landlord suspected it was a convoluted bargaining tactic and angrily retorted that any further rent reduction was totally out of the question. When I assured him that TASS had agreed to pay the full asking price, provided that the damned room was made out of bounds to the tenants, he still hesitated. He was clearly wondering whether there was some clever ploy behind such a weird demand or whether I was mentally deranged. I could clearly see that thought in his eyes: it was not advisable to engage in any commercial dealings with a madman. But I pleaded with him, promising there would be no further complications, and in the end, he took pity on me, and the contract was signed. TASS was pleased with all its provisions.

Trying to make sense of that weird episode, I talked to friends and colleagues about it. I concluded that it was typical of how Soviet missions abroad, and indeed the USSR's economy, operated. In full accordance with the main principle of Soviet socialism, the benefits and privileges had to be strictly rationed according to the individual's place in the hierarchy. There was also a significant element of deception in how money worked in the USSR. Nominally, the difference between the salary of a high-ranking official and a simple worker was minimal. Still, one rouble in the pocket of a head of a department would buy much more than the same rouble in the labourer's purse. Many high-quality goods and services, along with health benefits, were available only to the privileged class of bureaucratic nomenclature. This class had its own shops, tailoring parlours, pharmacies, hospitals, spas, and the possibility of obtaining first-class travel tickets, among other amenities. The prices on all those items were kept artificially low, so, for instance, you could have an excellent lunch in the Central Committee's canteen for one-third of what a factory worker paid for his meal, which was of an inferior quality in comparison. Ministers and their deputies received even more for their bucks, and the absolute best was reserved for the Politburo members and Central Committee secretaries, whose living standards were on par with those of multi-millionaires in the capitalist West. The economy as a whole and common sense were readily sacrificed to preserve the pecking order that was absolutely central to the Soviet way of life. Losing thousands or even millions of dollars? No matter, as long as a correspondent (or any other functionary of the state) will not get even one square meter more than is prescribed to him or her according to their rank. That was the medieval, feudalist basis on which the Soviet state stood. To quote John Maynard Keynes once again, 'the mud was preferred to the fish'. From that episode, I inferred that such lunacy could not continue much longer. Even to an illiterate Iraqi peasant, it was clear that this was pure madness.

In the final analysis, the image of my country that had formed in my mind was as follows: in politics – alliance with murderous monsters, even if that meant total disregard and even betrayal of our own professed principles and values; in economy – blind hierarchical dogmatism, on the verge of idiocy, leading to inevitable ruin. Plus, the war in Afghanistan, which was totally unjustifiable both from a moral point of view and from the standpoint of elementary common sense. This was a war that the

USSR could never hope to win, and which would inevitably cause enormous harm to both the Soviet Union's international standing and its internal stability. And that was the country, or rather the political system, that I had to go on serving. It was a truly nauseous prospect.

And then something else happened.

Chapter Seven

A Clandestine Rendezvous

Soon after I moved to *Al-Jadriya*, I found I had another neighbour. Adjacent to the entrance into our cul-de-sac stood a high stone wall. It had steel gates guarded day and night by Iraqi soldiers. It took me a few weeks to learn what was hidden behind that wall. It was the residence of the Palestinian leader, the PLO chairman, Yasser Arafat. After he and his associates had been pushed out of Lebanon, their main headquarters were relocated to Tunisia, but they spent a significant amount of time in Iraq.

Saddam urged Arafat to consider Baghdad his 'second home'. He did it to score points in the eyes of the Arab public opinion, but also to spite the Syrian president Hafez Assad, whom Saddam wholeheartedly hated, and who had fallen out with Arafat in a big way. The quarrel was so fierce that all contacts between the PLO and Damascus were broken. Arafat and his acolytes were banned from even visiting Syria and Lebanon. The conflict led to serious armed clashes between the Syrian troops and Palestinian militia in the refugee camps, with many casualties on both sides.

I knew Arafat personally. I met him in Yemen, where I interviewed him for TASS. I now wanted to resume our acquaintance, primarily to find out what had gone wrong between him and the 'Syrian brothers' with whom he had been closely allied for many years. And there was another factor which further whetted my curiosity: the Soviet ambassador, for some reason, forbade me and other journalists from having any contact with the Palestinian leader. He refused to explain the order but hinted that Arafat was now in disgrace in Moscow.

The first English proverb I learned in early childhood was about a cat killed by its curiosity. But I particularly liked the ending, which came with a twist: satisfaction brought the feline life back. So once again, my nosiness prevailed over common sense, and I got drawn into yet another adventure and found myself in a nice pickle.

I also dragged my friend Dmitri Osipov, the *Novosti* bureau chief, into scrapes.

It happened almost by accident. One day, purely by chance, I ran into Arafat's spokesman, Ahmed, at the Information Ministry. I asked him to arrange a meeting with the PLO chairman for my colleague and me. I almost immediately forgot about it, thinking it was highly unlikely to really happen, given the stickiness of the political situation. Especially, as the Iraqis kept the Palestinians under strict control, not allowing them much freedom of movement or communication. Their residence abutting the rear wall of my garden was not only a fortress but also nearly a prison.

Apparently, Ahmed wasn't even allowed to phone me, and he couldn't provide me with a number to contact him either. But then one day, he just materialised without any warning at my door and told me that my request had been granted. Be ready with your friend at eight pm, he said.

That was an epic night. First came a long and unbearably boring dinner at a restaurant with Arafat's press attaché and his friend, accompanied by a rambling conversation about nothing in particular. Our hosts were clearly stalling for time, waiting for the sun to go down and darkness to fall. It was nearly midnight when we finally left the restaurant and got into a car. For half an hour, we were going around Baghdad in circles; the Palestinians, presumably, were checking whether we were being followed. Then, at some point, they suddenly told us to get down and hide. At that moment, I certainly started regretting my escapade, only now realising what a serious game it was turning into. It was a real clandestine operation, damn it. Deception and disguise were intended for Iraqi guards at the gate of the Palestinian residence, who apparently had orders not to allow any outside visitors in. The Palestinian leader found himself in a humiliating position: he could not even invite anyone without the Iraqi permission. And that permission was practically impossible to get. Therefore, the Palestinians acted by hook or by crook, smuggling a pair of Soviet journalists into the besieged fortress.

It was both scary and exhilarating: Arafat must have been truly desperate to tell us (or rather, Moscow) something if he was prepared to resort to such tricks. But what could that message be?

Security check at the residence's entrance was sloppy, and we were not found. But I have to admit: at the moment when the car was stopped at the gate, my heart did sink into my boots. No comparison, surely, with what double agents like Oleg Gordievsky must have felt when being smuggled by Western intelligence services out of the USSR through the heavily guarded border. They had their lives themselves at stake, a much scarier situation. In my case, I was anxious and excited in equal measure, and it was not an entirely unpleasant sensation, a bit like a good roller-coaster ride when your cabin is thrown into whirls and twirls and occasionally hangs upside down. Now I remember that love of thrills with a shrug, being a completely different person now. Am I even related to that reckless youngster?

It was a very long, never-ending night. To start with, you had to kiss Arafat, which, to put it mildly, I didn't enjoy doing, but it was a mandatory part of the ritual. Abu Ammar (as he was known to his comrades-in-arms) suddenly took off his famous *kufiyah*, which invariably covered his head whenever he was seen in public. This baring of his totally bald skull was surely meant as an intimate gesture of trust, but it did make the prospect of kissing his ugly, pockmarked and unshaved face even less appealing.

Many years later, my colleague at *Izvestia* and eventually the Soviet ambassador to Israel, Alexander (Sasha) Bovin, would boast that he was the only one who had managed to avoid Arafat's kisses. "I only smooch women", he allegedly told the PLO chairman to his face, and the latter had to grin and bear it, resigning himself to such an unprecedented rebuff. Some of my colleagues refused to believe Bovin's story, but I am sure he was capable of it. He was a daredevil and an absolutely brilliant journalist. I already mentioned that before being 'exiled' to *Izvestia* from the Central Committee apparatus, he was the favourite speech-writer of Leonid Brezhnev. The KGB, having intercepted some of Bovin's private correspondence, questioned his political loyalty and orthodoxy, and the Politburo got alarmed. Brezhnev half-heartedly agreed to sack him but was overheard muttering under his breath: 'With Sasha gone, who is going to write for me now, I wonder. None of these can string a sentence together.' The General Secretary meant other Politburo members and their assistants, most of whom were egregious ignoramuses. Brezhnev himself was not particularly better cultured, but he at least possessed some political cunning and was not totally devoid of common sense. Also, he was incredibly vainglorious, which proved to be a blessing in disguise. He liked to be treated as an equal by heads of other states and to speak at summits and international gatherings with some pretence at sophistication. For that, he needed well-educated and brainy individuals who would be crafty with words, so he allowed a few of those to reside in the Central Committee international departments and protected them from the rest of the party apparatchiks who, of course, hated the guts of those cerebral jackanapes calling them 'renegades' and 'Zionists' (some of those were in fact Jewish or half-Jewish by ethnic origin – a thing unheard of in other branches of the Central Committee, which was permeated by fierce anti-Semitism).

Bovin was a shining example of such an inter-party liberal, one of those who, wittingly or unwittingly, were paving the way for Perestroika and a new détente. I don't think that Gorbachev's reforms would have been possible without these people.

In 1985, I had no idea that, in a year, I would have the privilege of meeting Bovin personally and becoming a colleague of his at *Izvestia*. But first, I still had to survive Iraqi dictatorship and my own juvenile adventurism, not to mention Yasser Arafat's kisses, which, unlike Bovin, I was in no position to reject.

We sat, Bedouin-style, on a vast carpet and were treated to an all-night, endless meal. About 15 people were seated around - almost the entire praesidium of the PLO's Executive Committee. I knew some of the members by sight, but far from everyone. There was the bald Salah Khalaf (aka Abu Iyad), the intelligent Arafat's deputy, whom I had interviewed a couple of times. Mahmoud Abbas (Abu Mazen), the future leader who would succeed Arafat after his death, was also there, with his impressive full head of slightly greying hair. I noticed another figure sitting a little apart from the others and flinched: it seemed to me it was an internationally wanted terrorist, Abu Nidal, although on this score I could be wrong, as I had only seen pictures of him in the media and those of rather poor quality. Abu Nidal was responsible for terrorist attacks in twenty countries, in which more than 300 innocent people were killed and nearly 650 were injured. Could that silent man sitting there quietly munching on some food be the notorious terrorist about whom Abu Iyad said that his random cruelty 'made people of the world think that all Palestinians were criminals'? Arafat and Abu Nidal hated each other's guts. Still, at that point, the latter was considered a personal protégé of Saddam (he would later fall out of grace with the Iraqi dictator and would be murdered in 2002). It was easy to imagine that the Iraqis would impose his company on Arafat and try to make them reconcile, at the same time using Abu Nidal to spy on the PLO leader and his entourage. In this case, our nocturnal conversation will be reported to Saddam in every detail, I thought. However, there was no hope that our meeting could be kept secret from the Iraqis anyway, as there were bound to be other informants among that group, not to mention the inevitable eavesdropping equipment.

I don't remember what we ate or drank. Most of the time, the conversation was too vague. It was mostly small talk and mutual assurances of eternal friendship. I was getting annoyed with Arafat, but he was probably more aware than I was of the Iraqis listening to every word he uttered and had to tread carefully. And finally, something interesting began to emerge out of this vagueness.

Some cautiously worded grievance, more sorrow than indignation, was expressed about the position and actions of the 'Syrian brothers', about a 'disagreement' or rather 'misunderstanding' between the PLO and Damascus, which was sure to be resolved soon, especially if the Soviet brothers would help. Very soon, he was assuring us, the solidarity in the face of the 'Zionist-imperialist aggression' will be fully restored. 'The heroic Palestinian people extend warm greetings and heartfelt gratitude to the Soviet people for their ongoing assistance and support,' said Arafat. The emphasis on the steadfast Soviet support and its permanency was, it seemed to me, a confirmation of serious troubles in the Palestinians' relationship not only with Syria but with 'the Soviet brothers', too.

Arafat clearly hoped that we would not only convey his view to the Soviet government but also transform our all-night conversation into a press interview in some form, especially since we switched on a tape recorder at some point. Possibly the most sensational thing he said concerned the change in the PLO's stance vis-à-vis the suggestion of establishing Palestinian autonomy in the West Bank of the Jordan River and in Gaza. This could be a significant breakthrough, as the PLO's previous position had been reduced to a formula: all or nothing. When Israelis first suggested it with American support, Arafat rejected it out of hand as a poor substitute for a Palestinian independent state. Now, it seemed, he was prepared to accept that idea in principle as the basis for further negotiations. This change would make possible the Oslo Accords and Israeli withdrawal from most of the territories occupied in 1967. It was the first time we heard it from the horse's mouth.

When, at dawn, we were driven out of Arafat's headquarters in the same car, we were asked to duck again. But that was done solely to avoid open embarrassment, as our hosts knew only too well that our visit had not gone unnoticed by the Iraqis.

It was already quite light, and we decided to go to the embassy right away, to confess our sin to the ambassador. We agreed to be economical with the truth. To make it sound as if the Palestinian invitation came as a total surprise to us, and that we felt it was impossible to decline. I thought that the lie wasn't all that big, as my vague bid for an interview with Arafat happened *before* the ambassador's ban on communicating with him. I didn't see any point in withdrawing my request later, as I didn't believe it could ever come to anything. When Arafat suddenly agreed, it came as a complete surprise, even a shock. And it did seem impossibly rude to refuse his invite. Thus, the truth was 'edited' only ever so slightly.

The ambassador did not believe us, of course. But he did not want to call our bluff openly for some reason (perhaps he remembered my father-in-law's photograph with Gorbachev). Nevertheless, he frowned, looked at us in disgust and said darkly: 'You can easily lose your party membership for this'.

And I should remind the reader what being expelled from the party meant at that time. You would be doomed to live on puny

150 roubles a month or less your whole life without any prospect of promotion, never being allowed to travel abroad. And that would be the best-case scenario for you.

The ambassador had us write an explanatory note each in his presence and put the two documents into his personal safe. He made it clear that they might be brought into play if needed. He was clearly hedging his bets in case our adventure blew into an open scandal.

Meanwhile, we agreed to send the encoded telegrams to our Moscow bosses, describing what had happened (with the same minor edit), followed by the text of the interview transmitted via telex. We asked our superiors to offer at least part of it for open publication in the Soviet press, implying that Arafat would be gravely offended if none of it were to see the light of day. He might, we said, hold a grudge for a long time and refuse to have any dealings with TASS and *Novosti* in the future.

Since Stalin's days, the TASS correspondent had the right, in exceptional circumstances, to send his coded messages to his Moscow headquarters via the Trade Representative's cypher clerk, who was not obliged to disclose their content to the ambassador or the KGB. Stalin created this opportunity for TASS to circumvent the embassy in case the correspondents felt the need to supply Moscow with alternative important information. And that, as well as many other of Stalin's rules, remained in force until the end of the USSR.

It was the only time I took advantage of this right. But in the past, during my night shifts as the TASS copytaster, I occasionally had to deal with secret messages from my colleagues that came through the Ministry of Foreign Trade. The TASS correspondent in Warsaw was the first to learn about the coup against the Polish leader Edward Gierek in September 1980. It happened in the dead of night, and the official announcement about his forced resignation was, for some reason, postponed until the morning. Not having any open-source confirmation of Gierek's downfall, our Warsaw correspondent didn't dare to send his report by telex, but he clearly wanted to get ahead of both the diplomats and the spies and used the trade representative's cypher communication, bypassing the embassy (probably with the blessing of the Soviet Communist Party special advisor in

Warsaw). What our man in Warsaw couldn't foresee was that the duty official at the Ministry of Foreign Trade would be seriously intoxicated. As a result, I had to spend nearly two hours negotiating with him over the *vertushka* government communication line before he sobered up enough to understand what was required of him and sent the message to TASS via a courier.

Fast forward to Baghdad of 1985. A few days after sending encoded messages to our Moscow superiors, both Dmitry Osipov and I received identical putdowns by the same route, no doubt approved by the Central Committee's relevant department. We were told in no uncertain terms that we should never do anything like that again without first getting approval from Moscow. That in itself was a telling indication of some drastic changes in the Soviet attitude towards the Palestinian leader. After all, when I improvised three years earlier, interviewing the same Arafat in Yemen, I was commended for my initiative. Clearly, something was going on.

But the most striking proof of the disgrace in which Arafat was now held in Moscow was the incredible fact that not a single line from the interview got into print.

As a rule of thumb, whenever an important political figure granted an interview to a Soviet journalist, at least some of it would be published in the Soviet press as a courtesy, even if the correspondent was privately criticised for excessive zeal or putting inappropriate questions to the foreign personality. Arafat was clearly an exception. Nobody in Moscow seemed to care a damn if he would feel demeaned by this treatment.

Ahmed, the press attaché, wasn't even surprised when we apologised to him, explaining the absence of any publication as due to 'technical issues'. He knew that the apology was a white lie and that the problems were far from technical.

As a result of that adventure, the ambassador added another grudge against me to his ever-growing collection. More ominous, though, was the livid Iraqi reaction to my reckless behaviour.

Having returned from the embassy after the dressing-down I received there, I was greeted by an impossible sight: in the blind alley where only my landlord and I lived with our families, a military post had been set up. Precisely in front of my gates, there stood a soldier staring sternly into the entrance to my house with his Kalashnikov at the ready. The post stayed there for just a few days and then vanished as abruptly as it appeared. But the message was clear: the powers that be were seriously displeased with my actions. They were shaking their fingers at me: look, man, it is a war going on here, and *à la guerre comme à la guerre*, don't you dare to provoke us any further or else...

Only many years later did I learn the answer to the mysterious question of what Yasser Arafat had done to lose his status as Moscow's long-time favourite (that story will be told in chapter 10).

Meanwhile, the Iraqis were losing patience with me; the extent of their annoyance became clear soon enough.

It was a Friday, a day off, but I received a phone call from someone claiming to be a duty officer at the Information Ministry early in the morning. He told me there were extraordinary and sensational developments on the war front. In half an hour, a transport plane will take off from the military airfield near Baghdad, and, as a big favour, a few journalists, those of them who could be nimble enough to reach the airport in time, may be taken on board.

'But you have to hurry, because the plane will not wait,' he said.

I called a TANJUG correspondent who lived within a minute's drive from me, and he offered to go together. He also suggested that his friend, who was staying with him, could give us a lift so that we wouldn't have any problems with parking and leaving the car on the military base.

In two or three minutes, my Yugoslav colleague and his friend, who was driving, arrived at my gates. I leapt into the back seat of the car, and we drove off. Since it was a day off, the Tigris embankment was empty, so we quickly reached a speed of 100 miles per hour or more. The river was on our left, with some buildings on our right. And then all of a sudden, a car, a taxi, emerged in front of us from an inconspicuous alley between two houses, and it rolled out blocking our way. The driver was braking like mad, but it was clear that the collision was inevitable. 'That is how I am going to die,' I thought matter-of-factly before passing out.

The taxi driver must have managed to jump out of his car before the impact. Or maybe there was no one inside it to begin with, and the taxi was pushed into the road from outside.

When I came to, I found myself pinned to the ceiling of the car. The crash was so mighty that the front seat, the one next to the chauffeur, and behind which I sat, was torn from the floor and pressed together with me to the ceiling. But this, perhaps, saved me. Breaking my shoulder, the seat, however, prevented me from flying through the front window of the car and maybe even shielded me from other objects and debris.

That was practically a miracle.

The next thing I knew, strong hands were trying to get me out of the vehicle, but it took quite some time. How much exactly, I couldn't say, as I was drifting in and out of oblivion several times. At first, I didn't feel any pain, but when I finally regained full consciousness, the shoulder, the hand, and my badly bruised breast with a few broken ribs started aching unbearably. The world around me was billowing and flailing. Finally, the rescuers were able to break the seat which held me pinned to the ceiling and pulled me out. There were two of them, rather dour-looking young men in civilian clothes but with military bearing.

The police, for some reason, were not there. The usual crowd of onlookers did not gather around; only two or three characters did. I couldn't tell whether they were there by accident. I still had a chance to see what was left of the car we were travelling in. The front end, where the engine sits under the hood, was smashed and compressed into a tightly packed diaphragm. The most striking thing was that both my companions, including the one who was behind the wheel, also survived, getting off lightly, only with some bruises and cuts, concussions and broken bones, which I did not expect and until this day do not understand how it was possible. The two young men who pulled me out put me into their car and sped off at high speed. Well, that's it, I thought, now they are going to finish me off somewhere and throw my body into the Tigris. Still, in my strange state, having not fully returned from another world, I didn't feel frightened at all, as if observing somebody else's predicament with indifference. And then, suddenly, I discovered in the same car, next to me, the TANYUG correspondent – wounded, bloodied from head to foot, but quite alive. 'They're taking us to the hospital,' he told me. This gave hope: maybe they will not dare to kill two journalists at once?

I recall an eerie silence in the car as it sped through the deserted streets of Baghdad. Without saying a word, the two men brought us to the hospital, where we got first aid, were bandaged and X-rayed. We were served out of turn, like VIPs. Both our saviours sat self-effacingly on the side. And after all the medical procedures were done, they took us home.

What was it? An attempted murder that didn't go according to plan? In favour of this version spoke the fact that the supposed flight to the front from the military airfield on that day was cancelled. At least that was what we were told at the ministry. There was no flight. Allegedly, this is because none of the journalists managed to arrive in time. I questioned a few colleagues, and they said they knew nothing about the trip and hadn't received any calls. The alleged 'extraordinary developments' turned out to be a typical little 'victory' over Iranians, like the ones reported almost daily, and didn't alter anything in the war situation. But if it was a failed assassination attempt, why wasn't it followed through? Was it aborted because of the two Yugoslavs unexpectedly appearing on the scene? Or, maybe, the whole idea was to scare me rather than to kill, to give me one last warning, so to speak?

I still have no definite answers to these questions, but I do have a couple of hypotheses. In any case, from the wiretapping, *they* should have known that after the accident, I began to take measures to leave Iraq as soon as possible, under the pretext that I needed medical treatment in Moscow. Perhaps, such a turn of events suited *them* fine. But who exactly were *they*?

In Iraq at that time, there were approximately eight branches of secret services (some believed there were even more). They competed among themselves, and many other factions and centres of power fought for the ear and favour of Saddam. They may have had different opinions on how I should be dealt with. Under the dictatorship, the leader does not have time to decide everything. Without his final go-ahead, the security services often hesitate to act, especially when it comes to drastic actions involving a prominent figure, such as an official agency's correspondent representing an important country. It was also possible that what happened was another manifestation of the 'Thomas Becket syndrome' so typical of the authoritarian systems of government. The king said: Will no one rid me of this turbulent priest? And overzealous courtiers understood this as a command to kill Thomas Becket. Saddam could have said something in the same vein: Who will finally put this sucker in his place? The head of one of the special services could understand this as an order for 'liquidation', while another could interpret it as the instruction to give the 'sucker' the scare of his life.

I'm pretty sure that the two guys who so touchingly pulled me out of the car and drove me to the hospital belonged to the ordinary Field Surveillance, which should not have been necessarily aware of any plans that the department of 'wet affairs' (a term that refers to acts of violence, particularly assassinations) could have had for me. On several occasions in the past, colleagues of those sleuths made open contact with me. Once, they came to my rescue when I got lost on the way to the power plant near the city of Haditha, in the north of the country. Sick and tired of riding after me in circles, they decided to abandon their disguise and stepped in to show me the way.

But it's all guesswork, of course. Such operations born within opaque state mechanisms of authoritarian systems often appear entirely inexplicable to outsiders. However, for those on the inside, things are not always entirely clear either. The all-powerful head of the *Mukhabarat* Barzan at-Tikriti, Saddam's cousin and confidant for many years, was suddenly fired overnight and sent into honorary exile abroad. It happened around the same time my personal drama was unfolding. It was rumoured that he wasn't quite sure about the reason for his abrupt dismissal, but suspected that it was the doing of Saddam's eldest son, Uday. That young man was a vicious character with the murderous eyes of his father, who easily fell into a rage at the slightest provocation. Word of mouth had it that he could shoot a servant who didn't please him on the spot. Well, why not? He was the 'crown prince' after all. But, paradoxically, the association with that maniac might have saved Subhi. God (or fate) moves in mysterious ways, and my friend managed to get close to Uday after interviewing him. The 'prince' seemed to like the company of such a refined westernised hack and deigned to offer him his protection. It was the best security arrangement Subhi could hope for, though it was far from absolute; the capricious 'prince' could at any time shift from grace to anger. A relationship with him meant an additional and constant stress. Subhi introduced us. As if trying to disprove his fearsome reputation, Uday was courteous to me; he shook my hand, joked, smiled, and asked about Soviet achievements in sports (he headed the Iraqi Olympic Committee). Talking to him gave me the creeps, but I managed not to betray my apprehension. I told him a Russian joke in return, and even managed to elicit a semblance of laughter from him.

So I cannot rule out the possibility that Subhi, who was deeply disturbed by what had happened to me, pleaded with Uday to intervene — appealing to his sense of superiority and vanity, and perhaps suggesting that my troubles were the result of his uncle Barzan's scheming. I can easily imagine him saying to the 'prince': 'Remember, I introduced you to that Russian journalist? You said afterwards that you liked him. Well, he's got himself into some murky trouble, and there's been a strange car accident. Now something is seriously wrong with his hand — the plaster has been poorly set, it isn't healing, and he's running a high temperature. I'm afraid it could be the onset of gangrene.'

Or something to that effect.

It is a pretty wild guess, I admit, but it would have explained the fact that not only was I not finished off in the subsequent days, but a highly respected Iraqi surgeon appeared out of the blue and told me he was going to be treating me from now on. Subhi whispered in my ear: 'This is the personal physician of Saddam; all his family uses him.' When I then asked the doctor directly if that was true, he ducked the question. But later, I saw a bulky radiotelephone on his desk, a rare and costly device at the time. He said: 'Sorry, I am not allowed to turn off this machine even for a moment, day or night. Otherwise, I may go to jail.' So, it seems, Subhi didn't exaggerate. And, most importantly, the doctor was absolutely brilliant; he saved my hand and maybe even my life.

Today, when I reminisce about Iraq, I recollect a strange, tragic country that to a great extent defined my life. I sometimes feel as if I am reliving all that nightmare again, and it is a very sharp and unpleasant sensation. And all kinds of wild ideas and theories come to mind. Sometimes, during a sleepless night, the Devil's Advocate suddenly appears from somewhere in the darkness and asks me, 'Are you sure you understood what happened to you? What if you got it all wrong? What if things were not at all what they seemed? What if nobody arranged that car accident of yours, and it was just a stupid mishap? And it was Saddam (well, not directly, say, through an assistant) who kindly sent his doctor your way. Or maybe it was the General Charming of the Iraqi Intelligence, the one to whom you talked at the information ministry, who took good care of you. What if you misinterpreted the whole saga of Rita Nephew and her open letter, too, and the Iraqis were actually trying to knock some sense into you, and, satisfied that you had learned your lesson, wouldn't have any quarrel with you anymore?'

And finally, the most discouraging, frightening, blood-curdling question that the Devil's Advocate can offer: what if your dear friend Subhi was only a puppet in the hands of the Mukhabarat? There was only one ridiculously naïve and easily manipulated player in that deadly game, and it was you? What if all the horrors in which you so easily believed were just an invention? Imagine for a moment that no one was going to rape Subhi's wife; it was only his word after all that you had for it, didn't you? Maybe the *Mukhabarat* did exert a bit of pressure on him, gave him a mild beating, offered him some money, and that was all. He then agreed to everything demanded of him and became a dangerous provocateur. And your embassy was absolutely right to warn you about him and advise you to stay away. Yet, you, fool, did not listen and got into horrific trouble because of your own recklessness.

But then morning comes, my thoughts clear up, and I see that the probability of the Devil's Advocate's theory is extremely low. But the truly horrible and utterly repugnant thing is that it is still more than a zero, that such a revolting interpretation can't be entirely ruled out.

Closer to the end of Saddam's regime, Uday fell out of favour with his father, who didn't fully trust him anymore, and the many enemies of the 'crown prince' immediately took advantage of the new balance of power. Saddam, by the way, was wrong. Uday was one of the very few who remained faithful to him to the bitter end. He fought the Americans until the last bullet and died in the battle, while Saddam himself was hiding in some stinking hole. In the final months of the Ba'athist regime, Subhi found himself without a protector; he was arrested, thrown into the notorious Abu Ghraib prison and tortured there. The beatings were so severe that he nearly lost his sight, and his skull was fractured. He also had a massive heart attack and was sent home to die. But he miraculously survived, underwent a complex trepanning operation, and his heart was somehow patched.

After Saddam's defeat, Subhi came to England for a few days and stayed with us in Folkestone. I was relieved to see him alive, but it was quite a different person, a shadow of his former self. He was severely depressed and had some difficulty speaking. Not exactly a vegetable, but a long and difficult conversation was now beyond him. I noticed that the lights in his room were on all night. In the morning, he explained that he could no longer sleep in the dark.

He moved to Jordan but couldn't find a way to earn a living there, and later returned to Iraq, where I lost track of him. A familiar acquaintance told me he died of a second heart attack. If that is so, then this is not the worst death one could wish for, especially in Iraq.

The Iraqis have a saying similar to the Russian one: 'I've been begging God to grant me an easy life; I should have been asking for an easy death instead.'

Iraq's lot in the late 20th century and the beginning of a new millennium was one of the most tragic and horrifying in human history. A quick demise without prolonged pain and torture was a luxury here. Tons of human blood were spilt, and the suffering that befell its people is beyond imagination. First, all the horror of the revolutions and bloody coups, industrial-scale repressions undertaken by the Ba'athists against the Shiites, the Kurds, the Communists, anybody suspected of dissident thoughts. The massive slaughter of its own citizens and Iranians during the eight-year war, followed by the failed annexation of Kuwait and the first Gulf war. Later came the US invasion and a new war, and after that, the strife between the Sunnis and the Shiites that claimed hundreds of thousands of lives on top of everything that had preceded it. Were there at least a few days in recent decades when Iraq went without mass murder, bombings, shootings, executions and torture? I think the answer to that question is probably no. Not even one.

Tragedy can be contagious. Anyone who got too close was putting his or her welfare at risk. I was one of those, but escaped with a whole skin (and a few broken bones). My temporary replacement became an invalid for life, and my successor, Sasha Bolmatov, was killed.

In Chapter Three, I described the devastating effect the news of this tragedy had on me, spurring me into confrontation with Yevgeniy Primakov. Only much later did I manage to learn a fuller picture of what had happened.

Allegedly, it was a car accident (again!), but the official Iraqi version didn't hold any water. Sasha disappeared from his (our) home in *Al-Jadriya* at night, leaving the lights on and his glasses on the desk. He then purportedly drove to the outskirts of Baghdad, where his car collided with a heavy lorry. The incident looked like a thinly veiled murder; in fact, the veil was so thin as to make one wonder if that was not a deliberate message being sent to TASS and to Moscow by Saddam or his cohorts.

The reason Sasha was killed remains a mystery, but the prevailing theory links it to a particular publication in one of TASS's newsletters, BPI (*Billyuten Pochtovoy Informacii* – The Bulletin of the Postal Information). It used to be one of the less secret TASS periodicals, designated 'For Official Use,' but containing only translations of foreign articles deemed not too sensitive by the Soviet censors. With *Perestroika* and *Glasnost* in full swing, it was decided to gradually relax secrecy around TASS publications, as the Soviet press was now free to publish even harder-hitting material. The BPI was made available to subscribers, including the foreign diplomatic missions. One of the first to join that list was the Iraqi embassy. Among other reproduced articles, there was a piece from a French news magazine dealing with the deadliest subject an Iraqi could imagine – the private life of Saddam Hussein himself. Based on rumours and defectors' stories, it drew the picture of an unhappy and dysfunctional family headed by the callous tyrant who was a serial adulterer too. From my own experience, I knew only too well that in any authoritarian regime, personal attacks on the leader are always perceived as the ultimate offence, a terrible political crime. (I remembered from my copytaster's days that any criticism of Brezhnev was deemed the most sensitive material of all to be banned from distribution even among the politburo members). The reaction of Saddam's henchmen to any disclosures concerning the immoral shenanigans of the Great Leader was bound to be even more severe than to Elaine Sciolino's exposé. In their view, it couldn't go unpunished. And even if the source of the fateful article was French, the Soviet TASS was deemed at least complicit, as it did popularise the subject, circulating that piece widely and adding, in Baghdad's view, the stamp of its authority to the publication.

Blowing up the TASS headquarters in Moscow was probably judged a bit excessive, but taking the Ba'athists' anger out on the defenceless TASS correspondent and presenting it as a dodgy car accident was easy and safe: it would have sent a strong signal without necessarily imperilling bilateral relations. It might explain what happened to Sasha. Still, it is only a guess, but a pretty plausible one.

I tried to run the story of Sasha's tragic death in *Izvestia*, pointing the finger firmly at Saddam's regime. But the KGB became aware of those plans (the article was already typeset and ready for printing, but the editor was hesitant) and urged the Soviet ambassador in Baghdad to intervene. He sent an urgent telegram to *Izvestia*'s editor, claiming that such a publication would inflict tremendous damage on bilateral relations. The editor succumbed to the pressure and spiked the story. Meanwhile, TASS chose to shut down its Baghdad bureau. The puffed-up 'importance of bilateral relations' notwithstanding, the agency decided that it wouldn't put the lives of its correspondents at risk anymore. It was also a quiet gesture of defiance, a demonstration of its anger.

Chapter Eight

Quirks of the Chinese language
(or a super-spy from Beijing)

I first became aware of particular difficulties with the Chinese language in the autumn of 1985, while in Baghdad. It was there that I met a man whose name I still struggle to pronounce correctly. What began as a chance encounter with him soon turned into a hilarious, piquant, and somewhat risky misunderstanding.

As usual, the Soviet Embassy held a reception on the occasion of the national holiday, the Day of the October Revolution, celebrated on November 7. Embarrassingly, the Soviet ambassador had ordered me to work as a photographer at this do, demanding that I take pictures to commemorate that 'important event'. Probably, it was his petty vengeance for my waywardness. He wanted to cut me down to size, to humiliate me by equating me to the technical personnel who perform a subservient role at such official functions. In contrast, journalists normally participate in them alongside diplomats, as they are expected to use these occasions to establish and maintain contacts with their foreign colleagues.

The ambassador was clearly surprised that I didn't object. I merely shrugged. To hell with it, I thought — pride is a deadly sin. After all, it wouldn't be difficult for me to take a few photographs with my excellent semi-automatic Olympus. As for contacts, after all the traumatic events of that fateful autumn, I no longer cared for them. My only wish was to leave Iraq in one piece.

Nevertheless, I had a small 'guest quota', and I could invite several Iraqi and foreign journalists to the reception. Some of them did show up and were somewhat discouraged because, instead of chatting with them, I was running around the garden working as a photographer. Perversely, I began to enjoy the peculiar situation, deriving some pleasure from its absurdity. I was acting out my role with exaggerated zeal. I ran around with a solemn and enthused expression on my face, trying to take as many pictures of the ambassador as possible from every possible angle, some of them slightly ridiculous, so that finally he started to feel a bit embarrassed too. In other words, I was having fun.

But then events took an unexpected turn. Vadim, the GRU military intelligence resident in Baghdad, from whom I had always kept a safe distance, suddenly took me aside. We had met fleetingly in Beirut, where he was doing some spying under the Soviet Embassy cover, and he had always impressed me as a man of pleasant and modest demeanour. What a sharp contrast to the image I had of his KGB counterpart! Vassiliy Borisovich struck me as a self-important posturer, a tin-eared singer of old French songs who often had too much to drink. Interestingly, the KGB spies despised their GRU military intelligence colleagues, whom they disparagingly called 'the boots' behind their backs, but this contempt was not always well-grounded. At least Vadim clearly was a much more amiable human being among the two main Soviet spies in Baghdad. For a while, I employed his wife to fill a temporary vacancy in the TASS Baghdad office, allowing her to earn a little bit on the side. So, whenever we ran into each other with Vadim at the embassy or social events, we always smiled and said hello. But that was it until the day he suddenly turned to me with a strange request.

'Andrei, will you help me out, please!' he said. 'In a few moments, a person, a Chinese, will arrive here. Would you be so kind as to take a few shots of him from different angles, including a close-up if possible?'

I did not particularly like this request, and Vadim probably noticed my hesitation, but he insisted, and in the end, I agreed. 'It won't hurt me to do a few extra shots given the fact that I have to play a photographer anyway,' I thought.

And then the Chinese made his appearance. The GRU chief rushed to shake his hand, and I went on to snap the two of them together, then the Chinese alone, from close-up.

Vadim, for some reason, decided to make sure that his Chinese guest realised that I wasn't just a photographer.

'Andrei is not just a photographer, he is somebody much more important,' I heard Vadim saying. He went on to explain the role of TASS, noting that the agency I represented often issued important statements on behalf of the Soviet government while also providing it with urgent international information. It was a rather lengthy speech, likely intended to boost my ego (as a gesture of thanks) and also to provide a neutral starting point for a challenging conversation with a difficult interlocutor. The Chinese seemed duly impressed. He shook my hand vigorously and offered his visiting card, getting mine in return. After that, I quickly slipped away, leaving the two of them alone.

By the way, the Soviet-Chinese relations at that moment were still far from friendly, although already there had been some signs of a mutual desire to improve them, and both sides were cautiously looking for ways to establish contact with each other. The fact that the counsellor of the embassy (the title I noticed on his visiting card) attended the national day reception could already be seen as a positive gesture. As for me, I quickly forgot about my photographic endeavours and my small favour to the resident of the Soviet military intelligence.

But then, a few days later, I discovered on my answering machine a recording of a call from that same Chinese diplomat, whose name seemed to be 'Mr. Yu', and who was asking me to call him back as soon as possible. Okay, I thought, I have been brought up to be a man of good manners; why shouldn't I demonstrate my courtesy by calling the Chinese diplomat right away? I quickly dialled a phone number, the one that was printed on Mr Yu's visiting card.

'The embassy of the People's Republic of China,' a somewhat robotic voice with atrocious accent said in Arabic.

The conversation that followed went as follows:
'Will you please connect me to Mr Yu?'
'To whom?'
'To Mr Yu.'
'We do not have anybody with such a name here.'
'How is it possible? It's the Chinese Embassy, isn't it?'
'It is the embassy of the People's Republic of China.'
'But in this case, you must have Mr Yu there! I have his visiting card in front of me. It says in black and white, Mr Yu, Counsellor of the Chinese Embassy in Iraq.'

'Sorry, but we don't have such a counsellor or anyone else with such a name.'

And the damned duty officer, or whoever he was, hung up on me!

He probably took me for a prankster.

I was about to drop the matter, as I definitely had better things to do than to argue with those strange people. Still, I was curious: what the heck was going on? I called again, deciding to negotiate in English this time. The same robotic voice answered and then asked me to wait a moment while he searched for someone who spoke the language. This time, I introduced myself, making clear I wasn't a joker. However, the same dialogue then played out again.

'Please,' I said, 'I'd like to speak to Mr Yu.'

'To whom?'

'To Mr Yu. He is a senior diplomat, a counsellor at your embassy.'

'We do not have anybody with this name here.'

'But I have his visiting card!'

At this point, I got incensed, deciding that for some inexplicable reason the Chinese were playing games with me. I sharply raised the tone of my voice, practically shouting:

'Mr Yu! I'm telling you: I want to talk to your counsellor, Mr Yu!'

And then the miracle happened: the Chinese on the other end of the line became sweetness itself.

'Oh, you mean Mr Yu! Of course! I apologise for the confusion! Please wait a second!'

And indeed, after a few moments, I was speaking with Mr Yu himself, who invited my wife and me to dinner.

I soon learnt that one of the major problems Europeans face when learning Chinese is the presence of several tones, which can completely change the meaning of what you say. It turned out that Mr Yu's name had to be pronounced in a higher octave (or something like that). Or, as some people in the know put it, it is necessary to sharply raise the tone of one's voice as if squealing: Y-Yu! Otherwise, the Chinese may hear some other name.

Well, I thought, addressing the Chinese in my mind, you might be asking too much of those who don't have a perfect ear.

We went to dinner at the Chinese Embassy and were treated there as VIPs. The meal lasted a few hours, featuring a myriad of exquisite Chinese dishes served by the dashing, thoroughly schooled waiters. Especially good was the *Peking Duck*, I never tried better. The conversation with Mr Yu and a couple of his colleagues seemed to me utterly innocuous, at least I didn't register any probing questions, provocative subjects or dark hints, unless I wasn't au fait enough with those matters to notice. In the end, we could hardly breathe, as we had probably never in our lives eaten that much.

'What do you think, who are they taking me for?' I asked my wife on our way home. She just shrugged her shoulders: no idea. After all, it was clear from the utter deference with which he was treated at the Chinese embassy that Mr Yu was a very big shot indeed in their hierarchy, probably the head of one of their secret services in Iraq; I didn't know which. Or all of them at once? I wished I could put this question to the person responsible for our unexpected Chinese adventure – the GRU Baghdad chief. However, I knew I should avoid discussing it with him, as I was determined not to be seen as a mediator between the two intelligence services.

What was there for me to do? Elementary good manners demanded that we reciprocate by inviting Mr Yu to dinner at our place for a taste of vodka and Russian cuisine. Ideally, we would have preferred to take him to a restaurant, but the paltry hospitality funds of the TASS bureau could only buy a few bottles of mineral water and some tea and coffee. To treat the guests to a decent home meal still required purchasing quality food and paying for it out of my own pocket. Of course, had I asked the GRU chief for help in that matter, there would have been no shortage of funds and nice food. But, for obvious reasons, that was out of the question.

Incidentally, the surest way to detect spies among Soviet citizens abroad was to observe whether they could afford to invite foreign guests to a restaurant, as neither regular ('clean') diplomats nor journalists had sufficient hospitality funds.

To this day, I still do not know what caused the great misunderstanding in our surreal relationship with Mr Yu. Perhaps it was a matter of linguistics. Vadim, the GRU resident in Baghdad, spoke brilliant Arabic, but his English was at best mediocre. Conversely, Mr Yu preferred to communicate in English. Who misunderstood whom during that brief encounter at the reception at the Soviet embassy, when I played the role of a humble photographer? I have heard that miscommunication is generally commonplace in interactions between Europeans and the Chinese; the two races often have different perceptions of body language, gestures, postures, and head inclinations. Maybe the confusion arose from something I said or did, without realising it could have sent the wrong message. Did I talk to Vadim in too familiar a way, or did he excessively go out of his way to show his respect for me? Did Mr Yu take me for some particularly important and trusted assistant of the GRU resident, the channel for safe and confidential contacts? Mr Yu seemed to emphasise the equality of our status, which is a serious matter in the East. Did he think that I could be somehow instrumental in the continuing normalisation of Sino-Soviet contacts? Sounds utterly ridiculous, but stranger things have happened.

From time to time, Mr Yu started appearing at the TASS bureau, always arriving without warning or a phone call, as befits a spy. He would sit down in the living room, and I would offer him a cup of tea or water. After a minimal exchange of courtesies, he would solemnly inform me of something relatively sensitive, providing news that was not to be found in the press—for example, the details of a North Korean delegation's visit to Baghdad. I would pretend to be interested in what he was telling me. Then, without beating about the bush, right in my face, he would fire his questions at me, offering a frank quid pro quo. I usually didn't know the answers to his questions, but a few times I did have something to say, repeating what I had heard on the BBC World Service in English or Arabic. Once or twice, I may have repeated some small titbits of information I had heard from Subhi, which was probably a mistake; I should have been more careful not to create a false impression of my potential usefulness as a source. But I couldn't go against my upbringing, which required me to be polite at all times.

I also decided not to fill out a foreign contact card for Mr Yu, as I was wary of what the masters of those cards — the KGB station — might do if they discovered my Chinese connection.

They might well have tried to appropriate such a valuable channel of communication ('to hog the duvet', as the popular Russian saying goes), stealing it from the GRU, their rivals in military intelligence. As a result, I could have found myself in the position of a pawn in the dirty game of two rival intelligence services. That was surely the last thing I needed in my position, complicated as it was.

In the end, I made up my mind to ask Mr Yu to stop his strange visits. But then I got into a car accident. Mr Yu called in to visit me at my sickbed. He even brought some Chinese sweets with him. After that, I felt that it would be terribly rude not to invite him to my farewell party.

But that was a grave mistake. Possibly as a sign of reconciliation or due to the intervention of Subhi's benefactor, Uday (who, according to rumours, was mortally feared by the *Mukhabarat*'s new boss), a very rare concession was made. Almost all the Iraqis I had invited to my farewell soirée at the TASS bureau were allowed to attend. In my experience, the authorities usually permitted no more than half, and sometimes only a third, of those on the guest list. Accordingly, I had based my calculations for food and drink on an estimated attendance of about 50 per cent. I was horrified when 99 per cent turned up, almost all at once. Every inch of space on the ground floor of the villa, as well as in the garden, was packed to capacity. I panicked — but Mr Yu came to my rescue. He arrived late, yet immediately after his appearance, the Iraqis began leaving one by one, each offering some ridiculous excuse. Within fifteen minutes, the house was almost empty; only Soviet guests and colleagues from other socialist countries remained. It was only then that I realised what had happened: the Iraqis had been granted permission to socialise with me, but not with the chief of the Chinese intelligence service. How did my guests know who he was? Most likely, someone among them represented the *Mukhabarat* and had quietly given the signal for the others to leave at once.

Saying good-bye, Mr Yu suddenly amazed me by speaking Russian to me, albeit with a strong accent. It turned out that he was pretty fluent in my mother tongue, which left me thunderstruck. In parting, he gave me an unusual and strikingly beautiful farewell present: a handmade, bent-iron picture illustrating a Chinese folk story. But, alas, a casual acquaintance by the name of Kukushkin nicked it from us.

Many years later, it suddenly occurred to me: what if some secret message was concealed in one of the hollow iron tubes of that work of art? A microfilm, maybe? Now, only Mr Kukushkin, whom I have not seen since my time in Baghdad, may know the answer.

I still cannot bring myself to fully believe that, as a result of a ridiculous mix-up, Mr Yu really thought that I might have served as an intermediary between the Chinese and the Soviet spying organisations – at a time when their mutual hostility hadn't been fully overcome. But if it is true, then it is a story worthy of the Johnnie English series. Again and again, real life proves funnier and scarier than any fiction can be.

There are other, maybe less ominous, but still puzzling questions that remain unanswered about the Iraqi chapter of my life. One of them concerns a woman whose role, to this day, remains a mystery to me.

Chapter Nine

The Femme Fatale of Baghdad

I clearly remember the moment we first met, as well as the face and name of the Iraqi Information Ministry official who introduced us. Nazar, he was called. Officially, he was the ministry clerk responsible for issuing formal accreditation to foreign journalists, but his unmistakably military bearing clearly indicated his real place of employment.

In my first days in Baghdad, I was highly stressed. Everything around me seemed strange, incomprehensible, and disturbing. It was a country at war, and a police state with historic traditions of utter cruelty. I could sense it in how people behaved, spoke, and reacted to me. The country was showing me its cruel and hostile face.

Nazar, that son-of-a-bitch, pretended that he didn't quite understand my Arabic. It is true, though, that the Iraqi dialect is radically different from the language I was taught at university, and it took me some time to get used to it. And that's in addition to all the other 'joys' that Iraq had in store for me. My instinct was to cut and run, but there was no escape route from Iraq.

Once, Nazar suddenly asked me about my religion, probably knowing only too well that the Soviets were supposed to be atheists. It was surely a provocation aiming to embarrass me.

Even now, I find it difficult to define my faith (if any), something between a deist and an agnostic, probably. In those early days, I always tried to avoid any discussion on the subject of God. I did not know how to answer his question. But, in terms of cultural reference, I was definitely a Christian. So that's what I told Nazar, saying that I was a *masihi*. In my opinion, clearly enough. But he burst out laughing hysterically, shouting to his colleagues across the room:

'I have a Soviet journalist here who says that he is a musician (*mousiki*) by faith'.

Since that day, it became his favourite taunt.

At the end of yet another, again not very joyful, visit to the Ministry of Information, I was already on my way home when Nazar suddenly called after me.

'Hey, musician,' he said. 'Wait a moment, I want to introduce you to somebody.'

I turned around. I saw Nazar approaching me with a young woman in tow.

At that moment, something extraordinary happened: bright sunlight fell on her radiant face, playing in the golden, wavy hair. And her eyes shone with an incredible turquoise-green glow.

Perhaps it was simply the striking contrast: her lustrous face, bright eyes, and beautiful lips seemed utterly out of place in those sinister, shadowed surroundings — the only point of beauty amidst so much ugliness. With her warm, genial smile, she appeared to me as a delightful stranger from some other, wondrous world. For a few fleeting seconds, all the vile things around me faded away; they ceased to exist. All the Nazars and their ilk vanished, and we were left alone. I suspect I must have been gazing at her with such unguarded joy — my eyes openly drinking in her face and slender figure — that it somehow affected her. It was as though my delight at seeing her became contagious, and she, too, fell under its spell.

Katya began to appear regularly in my life, almost at every event I had to attend as a correspondent. That was not surprising, though; after all, she, too, was accredited at the Ministry of Information, and she was also a journalist, albeit representing an obscure regional radio station in one of the so-called socialist Eastern European countries. Therefore, I did not pay much attention to her constant appearances near me. I vaguely remember that her smile was pleasant. Once, while saying hello, she took my hand and, as if absent-mindedly, held it for quite a long time. I registered it indifferently, attaching little importance to it.

When my wife came from Moscow, Katya invited us to her place for dinner. It turned out that she had a husband, an engineer who worked as a major adviser and consultant at an Iraqi enterprise. She came to Iraq with him as an accompanying family member, her husband's wife, and was accredited as a journalist, working part-time as a freelancer. I liked her man; he was friendly, calm, and smiling, though perhaps not too sociable.

Then came the receptions, dinners, and cocktail parties; the intensity of our interactions gradually increased. More often than not, her husband was either absent or preoccupied with important matters, leaving Katya to attend our social gatherings on her own. Gradually, it dawned on me that she was definitely showing signs of affection; it had become impossible not to notice them. At times, she would touch me as if by accident — take my hand, hold my gaze for a moment. Yet she did it all with such care and subtlety that no one else would notice. To avoid drawing attention, she would quickly turn away and engage someone else in lively conversation, perhaps offering a playful compliment, chatting vivaciously about something, all the while carefully avoiding my eyes — only to touch my hand again discreetly when she was certain no one was watching.

She moved with a feline grace, and her figure was faultless. A beautiful picture is engraved in my mind: she sits in our garden against the background of the famous rose bushes, which really became her. She is dressed in a mini-skirt; it is clear how lovely her legs are.

'Is she flirting with you?' my wife once asked.

'I am not sure, but maybe she is,' I answered sincerely. 'But don't pay attention, it doesn't mean anything.'

I sincerely believed that these were all completely innocent games, a little entertainment and distraction from the horrors that surrounded us.

Once, Colonel Yurchenko, the Soviet military attaché in Baghdad mentioned in previous chapters, dropped by unexpectedly when Katya was visiting. It did look as though that was providence's plan: for him to appear at the scene in fateful moments of my life connected with mysterious women. I don't remember what brought him to us at that moment; perhaps it was again related to some nagging canine problems. This case, though, was different from the previous one because everyone was behaving. Katya came to see me, but we weren't alone; other people were around, including my wife, who was nearby, probably attending to our daughter. And Katya was dressed quite decently, not in some dubious dressing gown, as was the case with my strange American neighbour. In this incident, Yurchenko played a completely passive role, one might say, an illustrative one. And of which he, of course, had no idea.

I do not pretend for a moment to be a connoisseur of male beauty. Still, it always seemed to me that our military attaché could compete for the title of 'Mr Baghdad Diplomatic Corps' if such a competition were held. And, quite possibly, he would have won it. Tall, slender, with the figure of an athlete, with shining black eyes, thick black hair and regular facial features, he spoke in a low, strong baritone. He looked very manly and gallant, a proper colonel. Moreover, he was pretty young for such a high rank, about forty. In my humble opinion, women should have been falling head over heels for him in significant numbers.

When Yurchenko left us, I asked Katya, without any ulterior thought:

'What did you make of our military attaché? Didn't you like him?'

She hesitated for a moment and then said:

'How do you mean? I did not say a word to him.'

'Oh,' I said, 'I'm not talking about his intellect, nor about his talent of communication. But he's a handsome one, is he not?'

Katya reacted strangely. Looked away for a second. And then said in half-whisper, but distinctly: 'He is handsome, yes... but you're still more beautiful.'

And like a child, she blushed. Maybe she was afraid someone had overheard her. Or perhaps she was disconcerted by the way I reacted to her compliment. And I responded as if I was thunderstruck: my mouth opened with surprise, and I stood there lost for words. I did not know whether to turn this into a joke or tell her what she probably wanted to hear. Maybe it just was not easy for her to take the next step along the path that could lead us quite far. Perhaps, she had some qualms about it. And, finally, there is yet another explanation, the most unpleasant one, that leaves a bitter taste in the mouth.

Maybe she was just lying.

Katya quickly pulled herself together, said goodbye hurriedly and left. And I went to look at myself in the mirror. I studied my face.

Could it be true that in her eyes, I really outshone the colonel? I found it hard to believe. But even if that was so, what did it mean in practice? It was certainly pleasant to hear those words from possibly the most beautiful woman in Baghdad, who had practically professed her love to me. Thank you, Katya, that was really nice of you, and I was certainly flattered in a big way. But what now? Nothing, I presumed. But what if... What if... No, don't go there, that way disaster lies, I was telling myself. 'Come, say goodnight to your daughter,' my wife called me from the nursery.

Once, our colleague from the East German news agency ADN, called Hubert, suddenly decided to throw a party for the 'socialist camp' correspondents. It seemed that his bosses in East Berlin had instructed him to make some modest investment in strengthening ideological solidarity with journalists from 'brotherly countries'.

So, all of us, 'socialists', including Katya, gathered one night at his place. Hubert and his wife came up with a brilliant idea for an entertaining competition: they mixed different alcoholic beverages. They asked the guests to try to determine what was what in their glasses. The person who guessed the ingredients most accurately would be the winner and receive a prize (a bottle of some sort, I think). Quite incredibly, my wife, Sveta, who is practically a teetotaller, not only decided to make a rare exception but also won the competition, beating us all by a wide margin! To this day, she still recalls that episode with surprising pride. And on that occasion, perhaps, she got a little bit too excited (and maybe even a tad intoxicated) and lost her vigilance.

Having tried quite a few drinks, we all got, maybe, a bit too joyful. Then the hosts dimmed the lights, and in a rather intimate semidarkness, the dancing started. At first, I danced, if I remember correctly, with Hubert's wife, Sigrid. Then, probably with Marina, the wife of Dmitry of *Novosti*, but then came the moment of truth. I had nowhere to hide. It was Katya's turn.

We started well. Keeping a decent enough distance between us. But soon that distance began to shrink, and not on my initiative. Then Katya did an extraordinary thing. She raised her hands and joined them around the nape of my neck. I'm sure I've seen this dance mode in movies, and I recall witnessing some flamboyant couples engaging in it at least once. But it never occurred to me that I would one day experience it myself.

It was a stunningly intimate pose. Her arms were strong and hot. Something seemed to flow from them into my neck and then through my entire body, flooding it with a sweet, toxic, paralysing warmth. It was a completely new sensation. I'm sure I forgot, for a few minutes, where I was, and that my wife and colleagues were only a few metres away. That dance, if a dance it was, probably looked totally indecent if not obscene.

The turquoise-green eyes looked straight into mine, from a distance of a few centimetres. Something was happening to them, something terrifying yet wonderful. They were changing colour from turquoise to a dark blue and then getting darker still. They were going somewhere far, far away through some beautiful, tender fog, taking the whole of me with them.

And then suddenly the music stopped. And the spell was broken, too. She wouldn't let me go for a second or two, so I even had to – carefully and gently – tear her away from me.

I returned to this world. And was looking around in total bewilderment: how was it possible that I had flown to the Moon and back, that so much had happened during the flight, but that here everything remained as it was, and nobody seemed to have noticed my long absence.

I would not be writing about this intimate episode if not for what followed.

We were going on another war trip, this time to the southern sector of the front.

There was a fierce battle raging there for some time already around the region of Western Qurna, a very important area inside the Iraqi territory, rich in oil, which the Iranians managed to capture. And now the Iraqis were claiming they had won it back and wanted the foreign journalists to testify to their triumph.

On the eve of that trip, Katya called to cheerfully inform me that she would be joining us this time. It didn't seem like a good idea to me. Firstly, there was the risk. If the Iranians spotted, through their binoculars, the arrival of an entire convoy of cars, they were pretty likely to open fire. The larger the group, the more likely you are to be targeted. And it did look as if quite a horde was going this time. And secondly, these trips could cause nightmares. Once, somewhere in the south, not very far from Western Qurna, the Iraqis dragged us to an island inside a bottomless swamp. They wanted to show off how many Iranians they had killed there.

The causeway that we had to use to get to that island was entirely covered with dead bodies, so it was difficult to pass without stepping on one of them. It did happen to some members of our group, and I don't think they will forget it any time soon. All that was surely not for the faint-hearted, and even the strongest nervous systems can be shattered by those images. Why do it to a woman? I tried to dissuade Katya – fat chance.

After spending the whole day on the frontline, when we came back to the hotel, I felt drowsy, moving and speaking sluggishly, as if in a slow-motion film. I did not even realise that we left the restaurant together: the three of us, Dmitry, Katya and me. We entered the lift and found out that we had all been given rooms on the same floor – the seventh.

Iraqis had placed Dmitri and me in one room with two single beds, while the only lady in the group was lucky to get a chamber of her own. But - surprise, surprise! – it was located next door to us.

As soon as the lift began to move, Katya said to Dmitry, 'Dima, be a good boy, turn away, please. Andrei and I are going to kiss.'

My friend chuckled, thinking she was joking, while I, for my part, was completely taken aback. She had barely touched me with her beautiful lips when the lift stopped abruptly on the fifth floor, and in stepped a giant of a black man, formally dressed in a suit and tie. Katya's goose was cooked; she had to step back from me. The whole scene was surreal, especially the sudden appearance of a towering, impeccably dressed African man in wartime Basra, a city virtually on the front line. If memory serves me right, we greeted him politely in both English and Arabic, and he replied to us in French.

Getting out on the seventh floor, we reached Katya's room and began to say our goodbyes. Good night? Good night. Already with her hand on the door handle, she lingered for an extra second — just long enough to look into my eyes with such intensity that

I suddenly came to my senses, remembering vividly what had happened at Hubert's place.

Dmitry and I then moved to our room next door. Somewhat baffled, I looked at my friend, trying to guess whether he was truly oblivious to what was going on or was feigning it as another manifestation of his well-known tact and sensitivity.

At least he behaved as if no suspicion had crossed his mind.

We were both lying in our beds, talking, exchanging frontline impressions. Then Dima's voice grew increasingly unintelligible.

And then he fell asleep.

I lay with my eyes closed, but it seemed to me that I could clearly see what was happening in the next room.

I imagined myself rising quietly, sneaking soundlessly to the door so as not to wake my friend, stepping out unobtrusively, and closing the door behind me without even a click. Then I would gently scratch at the next door, ever so softly, and she would open it at once — for I knew she was waiting for me, standing there with her heart racing, straining to catch every faint sound. She would smile and press a finger to her lips — hush! Then, ever so tenderly, she would take my hand and draw me into her room. She would put on some beautiful, gentle music so that we could dance once more. And then—

Deep in my heart of hearts, I knew: of course, I would have done it—of course I would—if it weren't for fear, that most primitive, primordial human emotion. But you could also call it cowardice—or common sense, if you prefer.

I asked myself: could it be that I was being lured into a trap, that a camera had been set up in the next room? That a series of photographs would be taken, or a film made of whatever happened there, and then used for blackmail? I had to admit that this was a very real possibility.

Yes, but it's only a possibility, no way you can be sure about it, said another me, who was still hoping to get to the room next door somehow. Okay, said the first, more rational me, let's do some simple math: what's the probability that it's a honey trap rather than a case of a woman in love? Fifty per cent, sixty? What kind of heedless adventurer would take such high risks with his only life? And you are grown up enough to know exactly what will follow if the worst (and the likeliest) assumption is confirmed – those who organised that filming session would not forget to share the images they would get with the Soviet Embassy, and with your trusting wife, too.

The wife, though it may upset her, can be expected to forgive you in the end (yes, she is that kind and that loving). But the embassy wouldn't be kind, caring or forgiving; there was no chance of that. That will be the end of your career, and you will never be allowed to travel abroad again.

And it doesn't matter much who exactly may be behind this minor spying operation (if that's what it was). Theoretically, it may be the Americans for whom it would be a chance to get rid of you in a very neat way or some other intelligence service. Still, the Iraqi *Mukhabarat* was surely the most likely contender for that role, given that it was all happening deep inside its territory. In that case, you may be offered an alternative to being exposed as an adulterer: they may try to 'turn you' - '*zaverbovat*'! In fact, it is by far the most probable scenario; I did overhear somebody at the embassy talking about the Iraqi attempts to seek 'assets' among the Soviet citizens. But they would have been up for a bitter disappointment in that case. I firmly decided that under no circumstances would I succumb to Iraqi blackmailers and would rather do a Geoffrey Harrison (the British Ambassador to Moscow who, in 1968, was seduced by a beautiful chambermaid, but, when blackmailed by the KGB, reported his sins to the Foreign Office and was recalled in disgrace). Of course, I would have been punished much more severely than Sir Geoffrey, though, who went on to retire comfortably and even kept his knighthood.

Still, even a banishment to some small god-forgotten town in Siberia would be preferable to the prospect of becoming an Iraqi agent. That said, a lifelong career as a janitor in a freezing shithole was hardly an appealing prospect, either. Surely, I should try my best to avoid such a turn in my biography, shouldn't I? I asked myself. Apart from ruining my livelihood, the blackmail episode would be morally disgusting in itself, an utterly shameful and humiliating event.

But if these are the stakes, the clever me told the horny one, it wouldn't be just an act of adventurism but a sheer idiocy to take such risks. Pull yourself together and go to sleep. Take a look at

Dmitry; how peacefully and blissfully he is snoozing in his bed – that is undoubtedly an example to follow, I ordered myself.

I stayed in bed, but I didn't sleep a wink.

And I knew that the person behind the wall was sleepless too.

In the morning, at breakfast, Katya was impeccably polite with both of us, smiling mechanically. She no longer singled me out. No more fascinating turquoise sparkles for me. It was over; she was clearly hurt and offended.

All the way back – we were being dragged to Baghdad by coach for eight hours – all I could think about was her and what could have happened, but didn't. I was throwing stealthy glances at her now and then, but every time she would quickly turn away so as not to meet my eyes.

What strange beings we humans are: only now, when it was all over, I suddenly felt that I was truly in love. Gritting my teeth, tormented by the pain of jealousy, I watched woefully from a distance as she got into the car with her husband, who had come to pick her up.

The pain lasted for a few days and then gradually faded, muffled by the bustle of the correspondent's existence in a country at war, the chores of everyday life and family concerns.

Gone was the almost telepathic connection we had established after that love dance at Hubert's place — a bond that had seemed to let us read each other's thoughts and emotions. I could hear her thoughts loud and clear that night in Basra, knowing precisely why she felt insulted and humiliated. It wasn't merely the familiar syndrome of the rejected woman ('Hell hath no fury like a woman scorned'). She could read me, too, and so she knew exactly why I hadn't come. She knew whom I had taken her for — a 'swallow', as spies call those beauties used to ensnare a target, to lure him (or occasionally her) into a honey trap so that the victim can be blackmailed or publicly discredited. A vile, shameful role — far worse than prostitution. And yet, who are we to judge? Do we truly know what horrors those women endure to become the instruments of their unscrupulous and ruthless masters?

She knew that it was a mathematical calculation of the balance of probabilities. I preferred to rely on cold, rationality rather than on the instincts and intuition that were on her side. I still do not know if I guessed right.

And now I do not want to know. Katya must live in my memory as I saw her when we first met, so that she will remain a beautiful messenger from another world, a ray of light in the gloomy, fascist darkness of 1985 Iraq. A natural, beautiful feeling, in strident contrast to artificial pseudo-emotions engendered by the relentless propaganda machine, with its xenophobic hatred and the hysterical worshipping of the moustachioed killer.

Thank you, Katya, for those beautiful moments. I apologise if I offended you with a baseless suspicion. But even in the worst-case scenario — if you were, in fact, used by some malicious force — I still cannot bring myself to bear any resentment towards you. I hope that the nearly forty years that have passed since we last met have been kind to you, and that you have, in the end, found a love worthy of you.

…Katya came to look me up at home after I was caught in a suspicious car crash, most probably arranged by the Iraqi security service. I didn't like the idea of her seeing me the way I was then. I looked truly terrible: after my injuries and initially unsuccessful treatment, I was thinner than ever, a case of real scragginess. I was feverish and clammy with sweat, with ugly red rashes on my face and greasy hair sticking to the scalp. She looked at me with squeamish pity, at least so it seemed to me, but I could no longer know what was going on in her head.

After my return to Moscow, I've heard rumours that Katya left her husband, eloped with the manager of one of the Western hotels in Baghdad, and spent some time living with him in Southeast Asia. Then I lost track of her, and just recently I heard a rumour that she lived somewhere in the USA. I have no way of checking whether this is true.

Part Three

FORWARD TO THE PAST

Chapter Ten

Russian James Bond

(Or why Arafat fell out of grace with Moscow)

Having been dragged over the coals for my illicit contacts with Arafat in Baghdad, I was left in the dark over the big question: why did the Palestinian leader suddenly fall out of grace in Moscow in the first place? Many years later, I discovered the answer: it was to be found in Lebanon, my first love, the first foreign country I was allowed to visit in my Soviet life; it was so breathtakingly beautiful. I obtained firsthand information about Arafat's problems with the Soviet Union from a man I met briefly when, in 1978, I was sent for an internship at the TASS office in Beirut.

I will never forget the very first impression of that magical city that I got in the sky, on board the plane, looking down through the porthole and succumbing to the unknown feeling of something close to exultation. I literally could not believe my eyes. Nobody cared to tell me in Moscow to expect that kind of a fairy tale, a Hollywood scene, a mind-blowing beauty. They warned me about the civil war, about the dangers lurking around every corner, about the murders and kidnappings and artillery bombardments. But not a word about the way Beirut sparkled in the sun on a typically bright day, bathing in wondrous warm colours of peach, pink and yellow, set against the blue of the Mediterranean Sea. Living there for six months, I never tired of Beirut's dazzling, vibrant, multi-coloured architecture, a joyous antithesis to the war it was immersed in. When the military situation allowed, I enjoyed walking along the streets of Beirut and the famous Corniche promenade. At the peak of the civil fighting in 1975-76, there were serious battles in that area, and the famous palm trees on the embankment suffered badly.

They say that people can adapt to anything. But the Lebanese seem to be true masters of this art. It became commonplace for people to leave a restaurant or a party at a friend's house and return to a car riddled with bullets or damaged by shrapnel. I saw it happen myself. Half the night would be spent repairing the vehicle so that, by morning, they could go to work, or to the beach, or the mountains if it was a day off. The Lebanese learned how to work, eat, drink, raise children, make love under fire, and enjoy life in their beautiful country in the intervals between all sorts of calamities.

Of course, every day someone died, someone was crippled. They said the situation in the eastern, Christian, part of Beirut was much more dangerous. Still, in the western part of the city, life was far from peaceful either. Skirmishes of all kinds occurred regularly between paramilitary units, and civilians had to exercise maximum caution. They would get out of their shelters as soon as the fighting subsided and go to drink coffee or Pepsi-Cola, or green tea and smoke hookahs in their magnificent cafes – some of them no worse than the Paris ones. (The opportunity to compare presented itself to me only many years later). The Lebanese sat in those establishments, chatting, laughing, flirting, as if nothing frightening had been happening around. And so it would continue until a new flare-up occurred, at which point they would deftly hide in the nearest shelters. The hottest, the most popular district of the Lebanese intelligentsia in my time was Hamra, the Champs-Élysées of western Beirut. I had a favourite cafe there too, though it was a bit expensive for me. I was usually treated there by better-heeled friends or acquaintances. Glass walls, chrome surfaces, and elegant tables on the sidewalk, protected by bright canopies from the heat or rain, were a feast for the eyes, and what a pleasure it was to spend half an hour there. In the evenings, if there were no especially fierce flare-ups in the fighting, the restaurants were crammed. To the north, nearer the seashore along the Corniche embankment and the more openly glamorous (some might say sleazy) Phoenicia Street, the nightclubs beckoned — among them the Lebanese version of the Crazy Horse, a replica of the famous Parisian cabaret, though grander in scale; the establishment boasted hundreds of tables. During its heyday, before the onset of the Civil War, bankers, wealthy brokers, spies, Saudi sheikhs, disguised by European clothes, millionaires from all over the world and Hollywood stars burned the nights away there. Even young Osama bin Laden was rumoured to be among its clients occasionally until he had gone mad with the ideas of jihad and hatred of the infidels. In the late 1970s, it was still thriving, albeit on a smaller scale than before. I would have liked to go there too to take a peek, for knowledgeable people assured me that there was nowhere else in the whole world where such a concentration of unimaginably beautiful girls could be found. But the Crazy Horse was entirely beyond my means, and no one cared to invite me.

When I talked to the locals about their surreal existence, they, of course, cursed their misfortune and the world, for not only refusing to come to their rescue, but, on the contrary, often pouring oil on the fire. Each paramilitary group had its own foreign patrons.

But they learned to be philosophical about their fate. After all, the luckier people who live in other, peaceful countries enjoy life, although they know that every day a considerable number of them will die in a car accident or get cancer. The probability of getting into trouble in Lebanon was certainly higher, but maybe not by much. Life must go on, my interlocutors shrugged. If only those damned paramilitaries didn't shoot so loudly at night, depriving the city dwellers of decent sleep.

It was amusing to hear people discuss the military situation as if they were talking about the weather – if it was 'favourable' or not, whether one could go to the beach, and what time might be best to go.

Lebanon is a Phoenix bird with an incredible ability to regenerate. For so many years, the country had been pummelled, seemingly destroyed and devastated, only to be rebuilt again and again, each time rising from the ashes and ruins. Today, Martyrs' Square—which in my time had been reduced to something resembling Stalingrad in 1943, and from which I was firmly warned to keep away as it was a dangerous place—is now not only fully restored but gleams and sparkles as if brand new, along with the rest of the splendid Ras Beirut (Ras meaning 'head' in Arabic), which has regained its remarkable historical character.

But even in those darker times, I could enjoy the brighter side of my Lebanese life. The newest American and French films were shown here almost simultaneously with those in New York, Paris, and London. Never in my life have I sat in such deep, wide, comfortable chairs, with such a long distance between the rows, as in these luxurious underground palaces-cinemas. They also served as shelters so that you didn't have to interrupt the movie in the event of a military aggravation. The ticket cost a couple of dollars or something like that, peanuts even for a TASS trainee with his teeny-weeny salary. Regular trips to the seaside were a great pleasure. My TASS colleagues and I regularly went to these golden sandy beaches, at one of the clubs, about a few minutes' drive from the city centre. Dedicated staff constantly walked along the shore, removing all rocks, garbage, and other debris that the tide brought, thereby maintaining the beach in perfect condition. The cabins were very comfortable, equipped with excellent showers. You had to pay for the beach, but the ticket was easily affordable. And we drove there in comfortable, fast foreign cars, listening to local FM stations playing the latest French and British hits, rather than the exciting news from the Soviet kolkhoz fields.

I shouldn't pretend that all the other delights of consumer society didn't astonish me; they certainly did. Frankly, they came as a complete shock after spending the first twenty-five years of my life within the sealed cocoon of Soviet society, with its drabness and constant shortages of one thing or another. It was amazing, though, how quickly I got used to that material paradise and stopped paying special attention to the abundance of goods in the shops. You go into a store and buy whatever you need, a mundane thing, nothing special, taken for granted as the air, which you breathe but don't notice. A completely different psychological state than that of the inhabitants of the USSR who lived in constant tense expectation of the appearance of individual goods of 'increased demand'. And this category included almost everything outside the short list of 'first-necessity goods'. However, from time to time, some items disappeared even from that list, for example, toilet paper. And when it was 'thrown out' (that was the term used when some deficit goody would be unexpectedly offered in limited quantity at one or two shops), a huge queue would quickly assemble at the entrance to the store. But live for a little while in a society of abundance, even in a war-torn country like Lebanon, and it quickly becomes a new norm, the only possible and natural state of affairs when everything is always available, be it food, clothes, perfumes, appliances, movies, books, records, etc. There are tables at restaurants and cafes that you can book without special connections in the government or party apparatus. There is no need to bribe the doorman to get into some second-rate eatery, and the quality of both food and service in most average local restaurants is quite high. You suddenly realise that it is possible to have a decent meal outside the special Central Committee canteen, accessible only to the Communist Party's highest elite. It is not a dream, but the standard quality of life for the local middle class and urban intelligentsia. Compared to the local rates, my salary was ridiculously puny, but the housing came free, which helped. At the time, I still smoked and swapping Bulgarian cigarettes that smelled like a damp old cloth for Kent and Marlboro was a sensation in itself. Still, the nicotine addiction might have cost me my life. And not because of the tobacco's carcinogenic properties.

In October of 1978, Slava Korzelev, the chief of the TASS bureau in Beirut, left for Moscow for long holidays and asked me to act as his temporary, unofficial deputy. I even moved to the adjacent living quarters, just behind the wall, to the TASS office.

The only inconvenience was that in that part of the city, the fighting between different paramilitary groups had escalated, and in front of the house where I now lived and worked, fierce battles periodically broke out. The boss, though, had taken care of me by stocking up on gas canisters and various canned foods. Those were stacked in a special storage room together with a Kalashnikov assault rifle, a set of spare disks for it and a bundle of hand grenades. The weapons belonged to our security guard, who was attached to TASS by the Lebanese Communist Party's security. It was possible to withstand a siege here, provided it wasn't too long. Under no circumstances was I going to use the gun and grenades myself. Although, in theory, I was taught to deal with them at the military department of my MGIMO university, I, to put it mildly, didn't excel in those subjects. The guard came to visit me several times a week, but the rest of the time I was left to my own devices.

The food stock in the apartment was decent. The water was often cut off, but early in the morning, while the paramilitaries were still asleep after the night of fighting, a green tanker appeared in our street. An enterprising peasant brought it on a horse-driven cart, demonstrating once again that the Lebanese were indeed a nation of innate and intrepid businessmen. A long line formed in front of the cart right away, but I usually got the quantity of life-giving liquid I needed. Then some young men in green uniforms (indicating they had gone AWOL from their respective squads) dragged along a good supply of freshly baked, still warm, absolutely delicious flat village bread, *khubz markook*, and sold it at such exorbitant prices that they themselves couldn't help laughing at their own cheek. So, in the end, there was no problem with the bread either.

But I made a dumb mistake with cigarettes. I miscalculated and ran out of them at the worst possible moment. I had to do some urgent work writing about the military developments in the city, and had to endure a few hours without nicotine. But when I was through with my dispatch, the urge to smoke became intolerable. By that time, the fighting in our street had flared up, and a severe gunfight began. I waited and waited, yearning for a lull in the battle, occasionally crawling to the window, cautiously peeking out from under the solid blind, hoping that I wasn't seen from the street and that no stray bullet would find me. Then came the moment when it seemed to me that the gunfire stopped. I decided I could risk it and ran out of the building. I was hoping I would be able to dash to the corner, turn into the next street and there, right under the open sky, behind a tall pyramid of cigarette boxes sat my saviour, Amir, the merchant of the nicotine poison. Typical Beirut: there is a war all around, gunfighting, bangs and booms of artillery fire, offensives, retreats, hell on earth, and he sits in the middle of it all selling cigarettes. It is a special kind of fatalism driven by the commercial instinct which overpowers the fears. And, surprisingly, usually nothing ever happens to him, and people with or without guns run to him from every direction, from different sides of the civil war to buy a pack or a whole box. Amir sells with a significant surcharge, of course, but it's only fair considering that he delivers the goods to the front line (which happens to be everywhere around you in Beirut). And you can find such Amirs, by the way, in every district of the city.

In general, such an existence seemed utterly surreal to me. *À la guerre comme à la guerre*, but the communication lines, both telex and telephone, functioned most of the time; there were, of course, occasional hitches and interruptions, but such things happen now and then even in peaceful, prosperous countries. Water and electricity were also occasionally turned off during flare-ups, but the regular supply was restored quickly enough. That meant that somebody was working hard to keep the city's economy going. Garbage, damn it, was collected regularly! Sometimes you could see a phantasmagorical spectacle or an armoured vehicle making its way down the streets, with the garbage van trailing behind. Amazingly, there was no sense of the collapse of law and order. For many years, the country had been engulfed in a destructive strife with everybody fighting everybody, all kinds of paramilitary organisations, Christians, Sunnis, Shiites, and Palestinians being at war with each other, occasionally forming coalitions and temporary alliances which then would quickly collapse. There was also a heavy Syrian military presence, and Israel didn't remain indifferent to the conflict either. Meanwhile, there was no outrageous lawlessness. Courts functioned, the police didn't run away, and there was no epidemic of looting or rampant street crime, as one might expect. Apparently, each paramilitary group attempted to maintain some semblance of law and order within its designated area of control. In addition, the population was armed; nearly every family in our prosperous Sunni district possessed automatic weapons. Small-time burglars knew better than to try their luck here. On the other hand, if a major organised force decided to expropriate your wealth, then there would be no recourse, and resistance wasn't advisable. But then it should have counted not as a robbery, but a confiscation by the powers that be. In the six months that I spent in Lebanon, none of my friends were seriously robbed.

When I rushed out of the TASS office that day, I thought I only needed about two or three minutes to buy a pack of Kent and return. But I was out of luck, as an improvised checkpoint had been set up on the corner – a Palestinian one. They stopped me, demanded to see my ID, and asked me to explain where I was going. I did not have any documents on me. An obnoxious youngster who behaved like a commissar began acting out the role of a stern inquisitor, interrogating me as a potential spy. Perhaps he just wanted to show off, to demonstrate how cool he was. He repeated the same questions again and again, squinting contemptuously, showing that he didn't believe me.

I said: 'Listen, we are just a few meters from the entrance to my house, let me go back, and I will bring you my accreditation card issued by the Ministry of Information'.

The Commissar ignored my suggestion and went on with his interrogation:

'Why are you walking around without any documents? Don't you know there is a war going on here? It looks fishy to me.'

'I do apologise,' I answered. 'I was in a great hurry; I thought that it wouldn't take a moment. I wanted to buy some cigarettes from Amir, you probably know him, there he is, if you look around the corner, you'll see him right away.'

I did not convince him. He declared that I couldn't possibly be Russian, since everyone knows that Russians are fair-haired with blue eyes, not brown-haired and brown-eyed like me. I thought that I heard an ominous hint in his talk that didn't bode well for my immediate future; he was suspecting me of being a Jew or having some Jewish heritage, which could have easily meant a mandatory death sentence. I thought to myself: what about you, you little whippersnapper, you yob — you don't exactly look like a Palestinian yourself, do you? You're far too dark-skinned, too swarthy. Where do you come from? But of course, I didn't say any of this out loud. He began speaking rapidly, like a machine gun, in a semi-literate dialect to the others. From his tone and wild gestures, I gathered that the young, dark-skinned commissar was suggesting that I be shot, just in case, as I might be a suspicious character or a potential enemy spy. I knew he was probably bluffing. Still, these were mad times, and the man seemed tense—perhaps even unhinged—so anything could have happened. Also, I had to bear in mind that not all the Palestinians were necessarily friendly to the USSR. Still, this was western Beirut, where the Soviet influence was significant. So, my best hope was to invoke my country's political weight. And I had to seize the initiative anyway. I began discussing the Soviet role in the Middle East energetically, somewhat overstating the importance of my position as a TASS representative, while insisting on my right to contact the embassy and so on. There was a danger of overdoing it and giving my captors the idea of kidnapping me as a high-value bargaining chip. Nevertheless, my tactics seemed to work, as my inquisitor mumbled something not quite flattering about the USSR before turning away. It became clear that his authority in the unit was not absolute, suggesting he might have been temporarily filling in for someone. Another, older fighter started talking in a softer, soothing tone, even joking about the harm of smoking. He slapped me on the shoulder encouragingly and held out a cigarette from his pack of Marlboro. But I was insolent enough to suggest that I would still like to pay a flying visit to Amir. And, incredibly, two fighters armed with automatic rifles accompanied me on my way, patiently watching as I bought the long-desired packet, and then escorted me back to my house. But at the last moment, the swarthy commissar gave me such a dirty, menacing look that I shuddered.

Seven years later, I remembered that episode and asked myself: could it be that I had an encounter with none other than Imad Mughniyeh, aka Al-Hajj Ridwan or 'Hyena'?

Did fate bring me together with the world-famous terrorist at the dawn of his distinguished career? True, if you believe the date of his birth from Wikipedia, it doesn't add up: in October 1978, he wasn't even 16 yet. But should we fully trust such data, especially if the person concerned is somebody whose whole life was a complete deception and mystification? Such people populate the world of shadows, hidden in the dark depths of the terrorist underground, their existence consists of murders and sabotage, and between them of clandestine meetings and furtive movements under assumed names and often with changed appearance. Other sources say that in the second half of the 1970s, Mughniyeh was already a member of the youth detachment of the so-called 'Unit 17', the elite of Arafat's guards, his SS and KGB in one bottle. Just a few years later, in October 1983, Mughniyeh would become the main organiser of one of the most notorious atrocities in the history of mankind – attacks on barracks of American and French soldiers of international peacekeeping forces. As a result of the horrendously powerful explosions executed by suicide bombers, 241 Americans and 58 Frenchmen were killed. To reach such heights in this heinous business, it was necessary to have some previous practice – a running start. The mastermind behind it had to begin his career earlier. After all, terrorist attacks of this magnitude require a great deal of organisational experience and the ability to lead and bend people to your will. Later, 'Hyena' achieved even more notoriety. Hundreds of innocent people lost their lives as a result of his actions. The massive attack against a Jewish cultural centre in Buenos Aires alone killed 85 people; it was his doing. And incidentally, have you heard of many students who have killed the head of their own university? I haven't. 'Hyena' was the only one who achieved that, to the best of my knowledge. Before Osama bin Laden's advance, he was the most wanted terrorist in the world. American and Israeli special services had been hunting him for many years without much success; several times, he was almost caught, always slipping between the fingers of his pursuers at the last moment.

How likely is it that it really was Mughniyeh who came so close to ending my young life a little prematurely in 1978? Probably not very likely, as Lebanon was full of such self-styled, would-be 'Hyenas'. But I can't entirely rule it out either.

What is more certain is that it was he who organised the seizure in Beirut of four employees of the Soviet embassy in 1985. One of them was personally killed by 'Hyena'. He tried to blackmail Moscow, threatening to kill the rest of the hostages in case the embassy failed to comply with his demands. Without doubt, he would have done it as he loved to kill; he seemed to get great pleasure from it, if not for the resourcefulness and desperate, almost reckless courage of one person. His name was Yuri Perfiliyev. It was thanks to him that the three were saved.

In 1978, during my internship in Beirut, I met him, albeit fleetingly. He was an imposing figure, tall, handsome, athletically built. The then correspondent of *Izvestia* in Lebanon, Yevgeniy Korshunov, once called him in my presence 'our James Bond', and Perfiliyev did not deny it; on the contrary, he smiled with a seemingly proud expression on his face. For me, it was then a novelty; I thought that such things would have been a carefully kept secret from us, mere mortals. I was not yet accustomed to the fact that KGB men did not particularly conceal their departmental affiliation from their compatriots abroad.

Our paths rarely crossed; I saw him only at receptions and dinners, where we didn't have much chance to talk. So I was astonished when he took me aside one day and offered to smuggle into our homeland some forbidden fruits of my six-month stint in Beirut, i.e. books and vinyl records. And I was just wondering what to do about them. Knowledgeable people had warned me that at Sheremetyevo Airport, Soviet customs officers behaved harshly, ruthlessly confiscating all printed material and sound recordings. And there was no 'green corridor' in those days; each suitcase was carefully searched, and only persons with diplomatic passports could escape inspection. I remembered sharing my worry with a 'semi-colleague', who was supposedly a journalist but was actually a KGB intelligence officer (let's call him Tolya). He was an exceptionally kind and sympathetic man. I could never quite comprehend — and still don't — how someone with such a gentle disposition could serve in that organisation. It is hardly surprising that he achieved only limited success in his career there and never attained the heights he might have reached elsewhere. I suppose that he, without saying a word to me, asked Perfiliyev to help me. Anyway, suddenly there was such a generous offer coming from a stranger, moreover, a spy, and clearly not a junior one. A frightened thought flashed through my mind: what if it was a provocation, a trap? But then I dismissed this idea: no, a spy of a serious rank wouldn't bother to take part in settling up such petty ploys.

There was nothing overtly anti-Soviet among the books I planned to take with me back to Moscow. I bought and read with fascination Khrushchev's memoir, but didn't risk carrying it on me, and, regretfully, had to throw it away. I decided I could not entrust it to anyone. While the famous book by John Barron, *The Secret World of Soviet Secret Agents*, was available in a local bookstore, I did not dare even to buy it. I hid behind a spinning book-stand and feverishly leafed through it, performing this operation for several days in a row. I did buy, though, vinyl records of British and American rock bands, including *Breakfast in America*, the latest album of my favourite *Supertramp*, and I was desperate to keep them.

I also acquired a few popular thrillers and a stunning album of Salvador Dalí's paintings. Surrealism was another forbidden fruit for a Soviet, well, almost: it wasn't strictly speaking banned, but any interest in it was actively discouraged. The official line was to dismiss this artistic genre as a decadent perversion. The chief of the Central Committee Culture Department, Vassiliy Shauro, was once shown an album of Dalí's reproductions at a Soviet ambassador's residence and was shocked. He did not know what to say, and finally expressed his indignation at the artist's portrait of his Russian wife, Gala: 'How can you paint your wife naked!' he exclaimed.

I managed to buy Dalí's album at a significant discount because a bullet pierced its bottom. For me, this circumstance added an extra sentimental value to the album. All this was not very easy for me to afford; I had to save, putting away pennies from the small salary of the TASS trainee, although, paradoxically, in terms of the purchasing power of *Vneshtorgbank* certificates that hard currency could be converted into, I earned almost as much as a Soviet government minister. But this was due to the surreal perversions of the Soviet economic system.

I did not know what to do with all those goods. I was kicking myself: why had I spent my meagre earnings on something that would only enrich a customs officer at Sheremetyevo? The system, I was told, worked in the following way: if you insisted that the confiscation be officially documented, you risked being prosecuted for attempted smuggling, but if you didn't, the officer in question would more often than not just appropriate the forbidden goods, and you would be grateful to let him have it while letting you go.

I was racking my brains trying to find a solution to this problem when Perfiliyev surprised me by offering his help. Amazingly, he did not demand anything in return and showed no intention to recruit me or anything of that sort. He took the books and vinyl records through Soviet customs, then passed the whole lot back to me. I said thank you, and that was all. After that, we never met again and did not speak to each other until many years later, when he, having served his second stint in Lebanon – this time as the KGB's resident – retired as a colonel. I worked for the BBC at the time and interviewed him by phone from London.

He did not even seem to remember me; too much water had flowed under the bridge, and we were all inhabiting a different universe. I decided not to remind him of our previous encounter, just in case.

The subject of the interview was something that had never stopped intriguing me: what was it exactly that, for a brief period, made Yasser Arafat persona non grata for Moscow in 1985? Perfiliyev, it seemed, knew the answer.

He did not doubt that the chairman of the PLO Executive Committee himself was directly involved in the kidnapping of the Soviet diplomats. And the evidence wasn't confined to the fact that 'Hyena' had long served in the already mentioned Division 17, Arafat's Praetorian guard, or that he was personally on friendly terms with the Palestinian leader, even at some point acting as the head of his personal security. Some other incriminating circumstances had remained secret for a long time.

But first, a few words about the background against which it all happened. Having been elected General Secretary of the CPSU in the spring of 1985, Gorbachev immediately became engaged in foreign policy. His first steps, though, were cautious, and their direction was unclear. Initially, before the new foreign minister, Eduard Shevardnadze, got familiarised with the workings of the Soviet diplomatic service, the actors at every level remained the same; the hard-line Cold War warriors still ran the intelligence services. None of them had any idea what was now required of them. They proceeded from the same premises as before. The new order of the day was called

'*Uskoreniye*' ('Acceleration'). At first, it was the main slogan of the day that Gorbachev had put forward; later, it was complemented by '*Perestroika*' and '*Glasnost*'. As applied to foreign policy, the 'Acceleration' was interpreted in such a way that it was necessary to move faster, while still pursuing the same anti-American policy. In every field, whenever and wherever possible, do the utmost damage to the Yankees and look at all the local conflicts from this angle: how to exploit them to hurt the Americans most. It was being done in the spirit of the famous stratagem, as expounded at the Politburo by Foreign Minister Andrei Gromyko, when he explained to his colleagues in the early 1980s why the USSR shouldn't be concerned about the prospect of Saddam Hussein acquiring nuclear weapons. That's what he said: 'Can we imagine a situation in the Middle East when the Iraqi atomic bomb would be turned against us? I do not see such situations arising. But it will give the Americans and their ally Israel a tremendous headache.'

The fact that this 'headache' might lead to a regional nuclear war in which millions could die, or the fact that even the earth's atmosphere might get poisoned for years as a result, didn't worry the Soviet leadership as long as the hated Americans could be badly harmed. It was with this strategic goal in mind that the bloody war in Afghanistan was launched, and the Communists of Iraq were sacrificed, among many other reprehensible actions. All the Soviet foreign policy everywhere and all the time had been subordinated to this all-consuming, sacred hatred bequeathed to the Soviet Union by Stalin. That's why Arafat was loved. Every action breeds a counter-action. The American policy of the Cold War was also one-sided, as the containment of the USSR overshadowed all other considerations.

Brezhnev, however, at one time – in the early 1970s – tried to reduce the intensity of those dangerous passions, fraught with bringing the world to the brink of nuclear war. He initiated détente with the West, encouraged important arms control deals and even offered limited cultural and humanitarian cooperation to make the world safer. He supported the idea of the Helsinki Accords and similar agreements. The leading actors of the Soviet state machine didn't like it in the least but obeyed, albeit with a heavy heart. Deep in their minds, they considered it a betrayal of the ideals as formulated by 'Stalin the Great'; they thought it was a harmful indulgence, a whim of Brezhnev's. They whispered that this was the consequence of his vanity, excessive conceit, and burning desire to be accepted as an equal by the world leaders, which was partly true. I already mentioned in this book that Brezhnev was a very vain man who loved nothing better than to show off, to be seen as being on equal footing with the American president and other influential international figures. But why should it matter what the motive behind a good deed was? After all, Gorbachev was also driven by similar human foibles, at least initially.

Brezhnev had cultivated a group of bright and well-educated Central Committee staffers who supported his peaceful inclinations. The most important figure among them was Anatoliy Chernyaev, who later played a crucial role in opening the country to the world as Gorbachev's principal foreign policy adviser. But these 'young Turks' were in an absolute minority in the Central Committee apparatus. 90 per cent of its staff were poorly educated, primitive bureaucrats whose only merit was the blind loyalty to the simplistic Marxist dogmas.

Treading cautiously, Brezhnev nevertheless protected this group from the regular attacks of the haters while simultaneously presenting himself as the highest arbiter among the inner-party factions. He managed to maintain a semblance of a balance, but then, in the mid-1970s, he had a stroke, then another one; his brain could no longer fully function. The dogmatists among his advisers, as well as the unwavering hawks of the Politburo, Andrei Gromyko, Dmitriy Ustinov and Yuri Andropov (the heads of the Foreign and Defence Ministries and the KGB respectively), quickly moved to take advantage of Brezhnev's incapacity to return the Soviet foreign policy to the Stalinist track. They would have liked to do it much earlier, but were getting cold feet, remembering how ruthlessly and efficiently Brezhnev dealt with another ambitious grouping, headed by yet another 'hawk' – young and energetic Alexandr Shelepin, who, along with his acolytes, was demoted and then sent into early retirement.

Nevertheless, Andropov attempted to test the waters at least once. His favourite among the foreign intelligence spies was an anti-American fanatic, Boris Solomatin, who was the head of the KGB station in New-York. In 1975, he, with tacit encouragement from the KGB chairman himself, composed a memorandum calling for the immediate end of the détente and for the adoption of a much more aggressive policy towards 'the main enemy'. Andropov passed it to Brezhnev without comment. The latter was furious. 'Who has permitted the general line of the Party to be revised?' he wrote. Terrified Andropov had to shut up and sacrifice his favourite, whom he once described as 'a virtuoso of spycraft'. Solomatin was hastily recalled from New York.

But now, at the end of the 1970s, Andropov felt that his hour had come. The wrecking ram used to destroy détente was Afghanistan. Having enlisted the support of Gromyko and Ustinov, the KGB chairman tried to persuade Brezhnev to approve the invasion, claiming that otherwise this country would be seized by the Americans, who would then threaten the Soviet Central Asian republics and that the CIA had recruited the Afghan leader Hafizullah Amin. All of this was a complete lie, but why not lie in the name of the sacred goal? That was what Lenin and Stalin always maintained. Amazingly, Brezhnev suddenly showed common sense at that point. He firmly refused to endorse the invasion, saying: 'No, we do not need this, we don't need the war. This is dangerous, and the relationship with the world may be damaged.'

Clearly, it was a rare moment of remission in Brezhnev's mental state. But the knights of the Cold War did not give up: they waited for a more favourable moment, that is, a relapse of Brezhnev's deteriorating condition. The three of them came to see him again, cleverly exploiting his senile sentimentality, playing up the fact that Amin had killed his predecessor, Taraki, whom Brezhnev seemed to like. At the second attempt, they got what they wanted: the massive Soviet intervention in the war in Afghanistan was authorised. That was a total defeat for Brezhnev's former liberal advisors and the triumph of their enemies, as the last nail was driven into the coffin of the hated détente.

On December 24, 1979, I was working the evening shift at the TASS Eastern desk. I was already preparing to go home when the intercom rang. It was Sergei Losev, TASS Director

General, who summoned me urgently to his office. There and then, he told me in great confidence that in a few hours the Soviet troops would enter Afghanistan, and a big military operation in support of the Kabul government would commence. Losev ordered me to stay at work the whole night to help with the morning special news bulletin for the Soviet government bodies, focusing on the international reaction to Moscow's actions.

It came as a total surprise, even shock. But what Losev himself didn't know at that point was that the Soviet 'support' would turn into a fully-fledged invasion of the neighbouring country and that two days later the KGB commandoes would storm the presidential palace, murdering Hafizullah Amin, the president of Afghanistan. It was on his naïve, trusting invitation that the Soviet troops entered the country in the first place.

Comrade Andropov lived in a fantasy world, where the will of his KGB could quickly change a medieval country, one of the most troublesome and indomitable in the world, into a socialist ally of the Soviet Union. Andropov and other hawks in the Politburo didn't want to hear the expert advice, for they rightly guessed that every qualified expert on Afghanistan among their own subordinates would strongly advise against such a reckless adventure.

My position in TASS at the time was not too prominent, so I wasn't surprised to be told of what was going on at the very last moment, but I was astonished to learn much later from the memoirs of the chief analyst of the KGB Foreign Intelligence Service (the PGU) general Leonov that even he was kept in the dark about those plans. I have never met that general, but from what I read and heard, he was a very sophisticated and sharp operator. He had some experienced and well-informed Afghan hands working under him, who were all shocked by the news as well.

This extraordinary arrogance can be explained only by the KGB chief and his fellow conspirators' belief that they didn't need 'details' as they saw 'the big picture': the USSR had to snub the West and put an end to Brezhnev's détente, which in their eyes had gone too far.

On December 30, 1979, just a few days after the invasion, Anatoliy Chernyaev, who served at the time as deputy head of the Central Committee International Department, made the following entry in his secret diary: 'Our forces have entered Afghanistan and all our détente capital has been fucking wiped out... The Soviet people don't need this in the least; what they need is more meat and other goods and a bit more law and order.'

And a few weeks later, when the international backlash against the Soviet action became more evident, he added: 'The whole world has condemned us... what is especially ghastly about it is that a totally senile dotard has taken the decision (to invade Afghanistan), although it had been instigated and then executed by others... He (Brezhnev) appeared on television a week ago... what an abysmal spectacle.'

It so happened that I got myself into yet another sticky situation because of Afghanistan. Or, rather, because of my inexcusable naiveté. By that time, I had already come to fully understand that the information available to the general public in the USSR was heavily censored. But it still hadn't dawned on me that even the privileged party apparatchiks were often expected to believe the most primitive propaganda blindly.

It was pure chance that I happened to be on duty on that fateful Christmas night. Since the TASS Middle East team did not have any real specialists on Afghanistan at that moment, I had to fill that role for several weeks. This continued until journalists who spoke Dari and Pashto were brought in from abroad or from other departments. For a while, I had to follow all the information from various sources, including Western news agencies and very frank reports from our own correspondents in Kabul (which were designated for secret TASS government bulletins and never intended for publication in newspapers). Sometime in early February, I was asked to deliver a brief talk on the situation to a trusted audience of local party organisers in Moscow, specifically in the *Krasnopresnensky* district, which TASS also formerly served.

It proved to be a total disaster that nearly became my downfall. Having been instructed that the talk would be confidential, I didn't pull any punches describing the full 'complexity' of what was going on in that country. I told the shocked party functionaries that the ruling People's Democratic Party of Afghanistan, which had taken power through a military coup d'état, represented less than 3 per cent of the population, while more than 90 per cent saw it as an ungodly organisation, and many of those were prepared to fight to the death against its 'satanic rule'. The president of Afghanistan, Hafizullah Amin, led *Khalk*, by far the biggest and most important faction in the ruling party. At the same time, the small and feeble *Parcham*, headed by Babrak Karmal, couldn't hope to gain the loyalty of the party's rank and file, let alone the Afghan public at large. We placed our bets on a minority within an absolute minority and hoped to somehow prevail in the face of fierce opposition from almost all Afghans.

The party organisers listened to me in disbelief: what I was telling them totally contradicted the rosy reports in the Soviet press. The unease gradually gave way to protest and condemnation. I was jeered at and booed. 'This is an outrageous lie! Who are you working for?' somebody shouted, and the rest of the 'trusted' audience hissed in agreement. I had to cut myself short and ran – literally to the TASS party secretary who had sent me on this mission in the first place. I knew that I had to be the first to tell him about the debacle, as written denunciations to higher party bodies and the KGB ideological police departments would inevitably follow.

To his credit, the TASS party secretary didn't sell me down the river and came forcefully in my defence. He also enlisted the support of a deputy director general. My ass was saved, but just in case, I was immediately taken off editing the Afghan news. Which, of course, was a great relief.

Andropov used the Afghan war to consolidate his power as the éminence grise. Arguably, from that moment in late 1979, he was practically running the Soviet Union, although he would be formally anointed as the country's leader only after Brezhnev's death three years later.

When Andropov and then his successor Konstantin Chernenko died one after another, Gorbachev came to power with the thought that 'something has to be done about Afghanistan', i.e. a way must be found to extricate the Soviet Union out of that country, while, at the same time, somehow saving face. It proved difficult because the Central Committee's departments and apparatus resisted; the party was reluctant to admit mistakes. At least thirteen thousand Soviet soldiers died to satisfy the geopolitical fantasies of the ruling gerontocrats. How many Afghans were killed, nobody could really know. According to some estimates, up to two million. Even if this figure is overstated, it is still clear that the Afghan society had suffered irreparable damage, not to mention the economic destitution caused by the Soviet intervention. This is where the roots of the civil war that continues to this day are. For quite some time, the détente with the West couldn't be restarted because of the senseless slaughter that went on for three more years, and in which, furthermore, a modern jihadist movement was born. Later it became Al-Qaeda and then gave birth to the so-called 'Islamic State'. To a great extent, the latter owes its existence to the senile Soviet leaders' senseless belligerence.

One of the very first novelties of Gorbachev's 'new thinking' was an unexpected turn in the Soviet Middle East policy: Yasser Arafat was suddenly demoted from the ranks of untouchable sacred cows. And it happened because of certain events in Lebanon.

Having been pushed out of southern Lebanon in 1982, Arafat's armed forces moved to the north of Lebanon, settling in the camps around the ancient city of Tripoli. They lived by their own law, ignoring both the Lebanese and the Syrian authorities. In 1976, Syria occupied Lebanon, supposedly with a noble goal of stopping the devastating civil war, but mainly with the view of restoring the borders of the ancient Levant under its auspices. In the end, it didn't happen; Lebanon proved too tough a cookie for Damascus to devour. I will not delve into details; this story is far too long, but the fact was that a brutal conflict flared up between Arafat's forces and the pro-Syrian Palestinian rebels supported by Damascus. Ferocious battles were fought using heavy weapons. Syrian President Hafez al-Assad (the father of the now-deposed dictator Bashar al-Assad) declared Arafat an enemy and was looking for ways to replace him as Palestinian leader with a more pliable figure, preferably a puppet who would always toe the Damascus line. Gorbachev had no understanding of Middle East politics. Still, some of his advisers and Foreign Ministry experts persuaded him that Assad was a much more important and reliable ally for the USSR. The KGB, which supervised Arafat, lost that round for some reason, or perhaps its chairman, Vladimir Kryuchkov, decided to give up on his ward, ruling that he wasn't trustworthy. One way or another, but Moscow clearly chose to take the Syrian side. Arafat was offended.

Many years later, I had the opportunity to discuss those events in great detail with a well-informed former diplomat who, at the time, held a senior position in the Middle Eastern department of the Soviet Foreign Ministry. This diplomat directly dealt with regional settlement issues, including relations with the Palestinians. Here's what he told me:

'Despite the arrival of Gorbachev, initially, we continued a tough course of confrontation with the US and Israel in the Middle East. Our main ally was Syria. In the reports sent to the Central Committee of the CPSU, the Foreign Ministry always used the customary phrase: 'we consider it expedient to consult our Syrian friends'. At that time, the very idea of the two-state solution of the Middle Eastern conflict was anathema to Damascus, as it might mean the loss of its influence in the region. Arafat, meanwhile, had softened his stance and was sending out signals that he was ready for a historic compromise. That was the main reason for the collision, and we decided to support the Syrian side against Arafat.'

When I heard this, I understood why the Soviet ambassador in Baghdad tried to ban communications with Arafat. But there was another, exacerbating factor, the suspicious role that the Palestinian leader had played in the abduction of the Soviet diplomats in Beirut. The accusations of his complicity in that kidnapping fell on fertile ground.

In the interview I recorded with him for the BBC, Yuri Perfiliyev said that it was he and his subordinates who conducted indirect talks with the kidnappers. He had an additional incentive to succeed in them, as two of the abductees were his KGB colleagues. (The wayward fate: one of those two will later defect to the Americans).

Initially, some progress seemed to be made in the negotiations, but at some point, they stalled. The Lebanese counter-intelligence service bugged Arafat's telephone conversation with someone, in which he asked not to release the

Soviet hostages until certain guarantees were obtained. According to one version, the Lebanese themselves enjoyed providing this recording to Soviet intelligence to show Moscow the true face of the Palestinian leader. This information was reported to Gorbachev and the Politburo in Moscow, and they were furious. Arafat, for a while, fell into total disgrace.

Still, he was relatively soon 'forgiven' by the Soviet government as Moscow's priorities were rapidly changing. Assad was losing his influence and could no longer dictate the Soviet policy in the Middle East. Understandably, though, Arafat never again had the Kremlin's full trust.

This story demonstrated an elementary lack of intelligence, as well as an astonishing short-sightedness and narrow-mindedness on the part of the PLO chairman. He had shown himself a practised master of intrigue, managing to survive and hold to power in the parochial world of bickering and back-biting Palestinian factions, but, as it turned out, had no idea how to navigate the ocean of serious international politics. He foolishly tried to rely on methods of gangster vendettas – the only ones he was familiar with. On top of everything else, he failed to grasp the evolving nature of regional rivalries and loyalties. He missed the fact that his former bodyguard, Imad Mughniyeh, was no longer working for him but for the Iranians, who at the time were not getting along with the Syrians either. In the 1980s, pro-Iranian Hezbollah, along with the Palestinians, fought against the Syrians. Later, they became close allies of Assad Jr. and remained so until the day he was overthrown. That's how things are changing and turning around in this troubled world.

I don't think that Arafat was the initiator of the operation, but he did not object when he learned about 'Hyena's plan. Did he seriously believe that Gorbachev would let himself be bent in this way? His idea was, apparently, to act as an intermediary, to secure the release of the hostages in the hope of earning Moscow's gratitude.

But in the meantime, all attempts to secure the release of the hostages failed, and Arafat's duplicity had exacerbated the situation. Perfiliyev felt that he had only a few days, if not hours, left before 'Hyena' would start killing the surviving hostages. Mughniyeh also threatened to organise a massive shelling of the Soviet embassy. The threat was taken seriously, and most of the embassy's employees and their families were urgently evacuated.

That's when Perfiliyev went for broke, playing poker with the Hezbollah leadership at his own peril. He paid a visit to the spiritual leader of the movement, the most influential Shiite cleric in Lebanon, Ayatollah Fadlallah. He presented him with a clear threat, albeit expressed in an ornate oriental style. The Moscow Centre would have never authorised such an incredibly daring bluff.

'You may have heard,' Perfiliyev told the ayatollah, 'that the Soviet armed forces are currently conducting military exercises in the south, testing new missiles with powerful warheads. Our military, of course, is doing its best to ensure that the missiles fall in safe places on Soviet territory. But after all, with new, previously untested armaments, anything can happen. Accidents cannot be ruled out entirely. Some of those missiles can unexpectedly deviate from the set course and unintentionally hit the Iranian territory. For example, they may, God forbid, fall on the holy city of Qom, the centre of the theological thought of the entire Shiite world. Oh, what a mishap, what a dreadful disaster it would be, if something like that were to happen!'

A few days later, all three of the remaining hostages were driven to the embassy neighbourhood and released there. 'Hyena' was deprived of the pleasure of shooting them.

Apparently, Perfiliyev played his hand supremely; his bluff sounded convincing, and he managed to sway the Shiite clergy. And most importantly, he correctly defined the target of his threat, understanding that the real masters of 'Hyena' were in Tehran.

When this story is heard by Western journalists who have faced the problem of terrorist hostage taking, they roll their eyes in envy. If only we had such a 'Perfiliyev' in our secret services, who could scare those rascals, they say. But in the Western system of responsible politics, such a brazen and risky bluff would not be possible. Everything has its flip side. But the fact remains: Western hostages often die, and the survivors, as a rule, spend years in captivity. It took only about a month to secure the release of three Soviet prisoners.

A tough professional like Perfiliyev certainly deserves the grudging respect of his Western colleagues. Russian James Bond indeed. It's another matter that his professionalism served a rotten system. Well, for a while, so did I. I served the Soviet Union in my own way, as a rank-and-file journo. Though I may try to console myself with the fact that my 'achievements' in that respect were hardly significant and that the service I rendered had been at a much lower, unimportant level, the moral difference is not so great. You can repent as much as you like, but you cannot change the past.

But at that moment in the 1980s, Perfiliyev saved lives, resisting the monster. And, by the by, he managed to show the Soviet leaders Arafat's true colours. Of course, I also heard other versions of that story. Some people maintain that Perfiliyev greatly exaggerated his role in that episode, while others claim he is a shameless self-promoter, excessively ambitious, and boastful. But if there is any truth to this criticism, it is most likely an integral part of a real spy's character, one of their typical traits. The ability to bluff with a blank face and the penchant for taking enormous risks are at the top of the list of talents required of an accomplished spy. He (or she) has to be a natural adventurer. And this, probably, manifests itself in the big, as well as in the small. A minor episode involving the not-quite-legal transportation of my 'prohibited goods' across the Soviet border could have been a telling sign. Perfiliyev did it without batting an eyelid. In a psychological battle with 'Hyena' and his Iranian patrons, he also neglected the rules; otherwise, he would not have won. Rules and laws for such people are not written.

There is another episode I remember from my Iraqi days that, to my mind, confirms this conclusion. It happened during my trip to neighbouring Kuwait in 1984. For me, it was a rare opportunity to escape, at least for a short while, the totalitarian police state of Saddam. It was like a breath of fresh air after breaking out of a fetid dungeon. Kuwait is not a democratic country by any stretch of the imagination. Still, you crossed that border, and suddenly it felt as if you had landed on a different, much happier planet. You were not followed all the time, nor were you eavesdropped upon. People in the streets were not afraid to talk with foreigners; they were, by and large, hospitable and welcoming. The atmosphere was incomparably lighter, and the heavy gloom and doom that had permeated the air in Iraq was suddenly gone. You felt it physically – with your skin. In addition to everything else, the abundance of food and goods in the shops was comparable to that of Western Europe (although the prices were significantly lower), a sharp contrast to the ascetic shops of Baghdad. In one respect, though, Iraq was freer than Kuwait - the emirate had a 'dry law', a total ban on alcohol, while in Saddam's kingdom, wine and spirits, while pricey, were freely available. Among the Soviet citizens based in Iraq, only the fortunate few had the chance to escape its suffocating atmosphere occasionally, spending a few days and a pile of saved greenbacks in the neighbouring consumer paradise. Some of these fortunate individuals were involved in a very unusual sport — competing to see who could smuggle the largest quantity of strictly prohibited alcohol into Kuwait. It seemed the intelligence officers were clearly in the lead.

In most cases, the only penalty they could face was the confiscation of the illicit liquid, especially if the individuals involved were protected by diplomatic passports. It would be a different matter if you were caught consuming alcohol or selling it inside the country, which would have meant a guaranteed prison term for ordinary citizens and expulsion with a big scandal for diplomats. Under international conventions, the latter were not to be searched under any circumstances. However, occasionally, Kuwaiti customs officers brazenly violated international law if they had reason to suspect an attempt to smuggle alcohol into the country. The story was circulating in the Soviet colony about a diplomat, the first secretary of the embassy, and, presumably, an intelligence officer, who employed cunning psychological techniques to outwit the customs authorities. For example, he once put a bottle of cognac on the front seat next to him in his car. The customs officer noticed the bottle through the car's window and was flabbergasted: he had never encountered such impudence in his career. He tried to remove the bottle, but the diplomat resisted. A major pandemonium arose, and all the officers, including the director of the customs office, rushed to witness an imminent confrontation. The Soviet diplomat then delivered an impassioned speech, stating that the bottle in question was not contraband at all; it was not hidden away but held openly for everybody to see. It was intended for strictly medical purposes.

'I am being successfully treated for my alcoholism; the daily doses are being gradually but steadily reduced, but my doctors strongly advise against the abrupt termination of alcohol consumption as it may inflict damage to my metabolism. That is why I need this bottle for my trip, it is a medical necessity,' he claimed.

The din continued for a long time until the diplomat, almost with tears in his eyes, handed over the coveted bottle, which was then ceremoniously smashed. The head of the customs office, who was delighted that the strange episode had been safely resolved, waved his hand. His subordinates immediately lifted the barrier, and the happy diplomat headed into Kuwaiti territory, bringing a whole box of vodka in the trunk of his car. I do not know how true this legend was, but I saw with my own eyes a KGB officer smuggling seven or eight bottles of vodka, which he managed to fit around his waist with the help of improvised rope loops. He hid the contraption under an oversized cloak, which turned him into a ridiculous fatty. If I were a customs officer, such an unnaturally portly figure would have definitely drawn my suspicions. As it happened, the Kuwaitis didn't pay attention.

I was part of a group of Soviets driving to Kuwait together. It was much safer to travel with the company than to go alone, especially since the journey was long and tiring, lasting the entire day. It required passing through not entirely secure southern areas where criminality, including road banditry, was rife. At our last stop before the border, our 'smuggler' confided in all of us, proudly demonstrating how cleverly he arranged his subterfuge. He probably wanted to show off a bit and also make us all fret together with him, while admiring his iron nerves and dexterity. He enjoyed diplomatic immunity, which made a personal search highly unlikely. Still, it couldn't be entirely ruled out. But in the end, everything went smoothly. But why did he need these bottles? Well, he probably made himself very popular with his colleagues at the KGB Kuwait station. Also, he treated us, his fellow travellers, to a few drinks taken clandestinely before dinner at the restaurant. He would say, 'Hey, everybody, come quickly, wash your hands!' And we knew it was a signal to go to his hotel room, where he would pour everyone a small aperitif.

But was it worth this risk? The man was far from stupid and knew perfectly well that he would be sent back to the Soviet Union and probably fired from the KGB if caught. Was the game worth the candle? Definitely not, but he wanted the excitement, the rush of adrenaline, because he was a real spy.

A great deal of official contempt has been directed at Dmitry Polyakov, a GRU general who spied for the United States for more than twenty years. According to KGB accounts, during that time he betrayed nearly five hundred Soviet intelligence officers, along with their 'HUMINT assets' (recruited agents). He provided the CIA with twenty-five boxes of photographs of top-secret documents, among them materials exposing the system the USSR had created to circumvent US sanctions and procure prohibited goods with military applications. He is alleged to have inflicted immense damage on his homeland, with losses running into billions of dollars.

When Aldrich Ames — another traitor, this time within the CIA — exposed Polyakov, leading to his arrest, Soviet investigators were unable to provide a convincing explanation for the latter's actions. After all, Polyakov had been a hero of the Second World War; he had fought on the front lines and was decorated many times for exceptional bravery, later becoming a renowned master of espionage. His career had been remarkable — he was a favourite of fortune and his superiors alike. What, then, could have driven him to take such immense risks, effectively placing his life on the line?

It was clear he was not motivated by money, as he accepted only modest gifts from his American handlers. He drank in moderation, took no drugs, and was an exemplary family man, devoted to his wife. Soviet investigators searched but could not uncover the usual weaknesses that recruiters seek to exploit. After his arrest, he continued to toy with his interrogators, offering conflicting accounts of his motives to confuse them, while astonishing them with his composure and self-control.

At times, he claimed that his motive had been to 'help democratic countries contain Soviet expansionism' — the explanation the CIA preferred to believe. On other occasions, he recalled his disgust at the disgraceful behaviour of Soviet leaders abroad, asserting that he had volunteered to spy for the Americans in 1961 after witnessing Nikita Khrushchev and his aide Andrei Gromyko banging on the table at a UN conference, hurling absurd insults and threats.

He also recounted how, while stationed at the GRU office in New York, he had been denied funds for a crucial operation his gravely ill son required — and how the boy had later died as a result of his superiors' heartlessness. Revenge seemed a plausible motive, yet many years had passed between his son's death and his decision to contact the Americans.

Another detail that perplexed KGB investigators was Polyakov's complete lack of fear during interrogation, as though he had no concern whatsoever for the retribution that surely awaited him. One investigator suggested that perhaps he hoped to be spared by agreeing to play a double game against the CIA. But that was a flimsy hypothesis: Polyakov, more than anyone, understood the true nature of the Soviet political system and its intelligence apparatus — and could not possibly have entertained any illusions about his fate.

Since the Second World War, there had been no traitor in the Soviet armed forces holding the rank of full general; it was almost unthinkable. Polyakov knew that the authorities would undoubtedly prefer to make an example of such a senior turncoat rather than pursue any theoretical advantage from elaborate spy games in which a professional like him had every chance of outwitting them. No, the system would almost certainly want not merely to kill him but to tear him apart, quarter him or break him on the wheel, or to inflict some other equally excruciating punishment. Had it happened in the 'good old days' rather than in the 'vegetarian times' of Gorbachev's *Perestroika*, some very special way to execute Polyakov would have been found. In fact, it was rumoured that the GRU bosses tried to push for permission to burn him alive in a crematorium in front of the staff of the military intelligence, but Gorbachev refused to authorise it.

When saying good-bye in America to his CIA handler, Polyakov suggested that he was likely to end up in a 'mass grave'. He declined asylum in the USA, which was offered to him, demonstrating a strange fatalism. Come what may, he said, one should die where one was born.

The death of his son and a grudge he held against his bosses could have played a role in his decision to betray the GRU and the Soviet political system. Yet there was another factor in Polyakov's life, a 'drug' that determined his behaviour. Once, during an interrogation, he let slip that his brain craved risk, that he constantly needed an adrenaline rush, and that he enjoyed the thrill of danger. The usual routine work, conducted under the safe cover of Soviet diplomatic missions abroad, no longer brought satisfaction; it seemed tedious and boring.

I think this is the main explanation: Polyakov loved a deadly game with enormous stakes. That's what made his life worth living.

I wouldn't be surprised if all truly accomplished spies worldwide understood what drove Polyakov, though the Russian ones would likely pretend to condemn him. There are numerous similar stories to be told from all over the world, the latest one that has come to my attention related to the extraordinary life of a fearless and brilliant spy, Krystyna Skarbek, who was one of the most efficient British agents in Nazi occupied France. Winston Churchill even called her 'his favourite spy'. She certainly made a significant contribution to the success of the British military campaign, saving countless lives. Her numerous breath-taking adventures took her across mountains, with deadly secrets hidden in her gloves, and at other times, she miraculously escaped from prisons. She once even persuaded an entire German garrison to defect. As a half-Polish, half-Jewish woman, she naturally hated Hitler and the Nazis, but people who knew her well always suspected that she took those incredible risks mainly for kicks. One of the British senior diplomats once officially complained about her 'pathological love of danger'. I suspect that the same could be said about many other successful spies. Otherwise, why else do those people choose this onerous and exhausting occupation with its constant tensions and hazards, which isn't particularly rewarding materially? The spies' remuneration is usually modest in comparison with many other professions; those going into business can hope to earn much more, and even Foreign Ministry officials and other bureaucrats are often paid better. These individuals are not motivated by financial gain. They are risk takers and adventurers. I'm not saying that all of them are necessarily potential traitors, but many probably are. At least during Soviet times, KGB operatives defected to the enemy more frequently than regular diplomats or journalists. I have met a couple of successful spies, who, I thought, would probably have become high-calibre professional criminals if they hadn't been enlisted into intelligence services, as they couldn't bear an ordinary, boring life devoid of adventure.

And isn't a spy, in essence, a criminal in the country on which he is assigned to spy? Of course, he (or she) is. I suspect that those who serve in intelligence services and don't understand the allure of such games have chosen the wrong profession.

I have read in somebody's memoirs a story of a KGB foreign intelligence officer who wanted to get rid of a rival. He managed to insert a forged denunciation into that officer's personnel file, accusing him of misconduct, which was entirely fabricated. When the forgery was discovered, the culprit was, of course, reprimanded. But his chiefs could not hide their admiration: what dexterity! What an accomplished professional! How skilfully the personnel manager's attention had been distracted so that the forged document could be placed into the file. Soon, everything was forgiven, and the operative's career proceeded smoothly.

What a telling story, what a weird world.

I would have perished there quickly, I am sure. Although I have — or rather had, in my youth — an adventurous streak, it is certainly underdeveloped. Paradoxically, on the one hand, I had an excessively short temper, a quality wholly incompatible with a career in intelligence. On the other hand, once I had calmed down after an outburst, I would invariably begin to imagine all sorts of alarming consequences arising from my own intemperance. This is also not very good for a potential spy. Then, lying is a serious problem for me; my grandfather, Porfiriy, had instilled in me a strong subconscious aversion to it. That is why I struggle with it. Another problem is empathy for living beings, which again switches on without any conscious control of my brain and very often in the most inopportune moments; it is another unforgivable flaw in the spying profession. So, I never get tired of thanking my guardian angel (or the vicissitudes of fate) for the serious, life-threatening ailment that struck me in my last university year. An injury provoked the rupture of the aneurysm that was hiding inside one of my internal organs. I underwent a four-hour surgery and, for a while, feared that I might be permanently disabled. Soon after that, the KGB foreign intelligence offered me a job, which would have meant, had I accepted it, attending their special spying school for a year and then becoming an officer. Looking back now, I find it absolutely incomprehensible that I could have been so naïve and foolish as to seriously consider that offer, seeing it as a big adventure. Without any doubt, it would have ended in tears rather quickly. Luckily, because of my surgery, the KGB medical commission rejected me. The price for this salvation – my health never fully recovered – was high. But even that was worth it to avoid losing my freedom and the inevitable personal disaster that would have followed. I clearly remember how surprised I was not to feel any disappointment after the KGB rejected me. I felt only relief: deep down, I knew that this job was not for me.

At that point in my life, I still did not fully understand myself and had not realised that by nature I was a yarn-spinner, someone for whom telling the story was much more important than living through it. On the other hand, without exciting experiences, there would have been nothing to tell. That is probably why adventures and misadventures have followed me all my life. And in the end, I got pretty tired of them, desperately yearning for peace and quiet.

... Having returned from Lebanon in December 1978, I made up my mind to marry my university mate Svetlana (Sveta) Vdovina. It wasn't a sudden or unexpected decision. We had been good friends for many years, having met at MGIMO in September 1971. I had visited her place, though never alone, but in the company of other students and acquaintances. We very often met on the way to the university, chatting about this and that. I always enjoyed our conversations and found her attractive, although my romantic interests lay elsewhere at that time. I really liked the way she talked, with love and tenderness, about her father. I remember thinking, 'It shows that she will make a perfect wife.'

At the graduation ceremony, Sveta looked sad and subdued with blue melancholy oozing from her large, beautiful eyes. Her mood struck a chord with me as I felt strangely forlorn, too. Nearly a year after my surgery, I was still suffering from the attacks of existential angst. Sveta made it clear that she was unhappy in her marriage. My love life was also at a low ebb. I broke up with my girlfriend, though she was quite handsome and a nice person. But I discovered that I didn't know what to talk to her about—suspecting, though, that the alienation was my own fault. I started courting another young woman but only half-heartedly, and generally felt dejected and lonely.

We danced and then went to a friend's place. Certain that we were lovers, he gave us a small room where we spent the whole night talking about everything. Lying side by side, fully clothed, on a sofa, we didn't even kiss—though at one point I gently pressed my cheek against hers. I thought it was the most wonderful cheek in the world, so smooth, soft, and warm. Strangely enough, nothing else happened between us that night.

First, I didn't want to get ahead of myself, trying to understand what I really felt about Sveta and whether we could be happy together. And secondly, strange as it may seem, to seduce another man's wife for me was, if not a matter of total taboo, then still not a very noble act, to put it mildly. By the time of our graduation, Sveta was no longer Vdovina; she had a different name, having taken her husband's surname. It took her nearly two more years before she concluded that her marriage could not be salvaged. Meanwhile, I also felt more confident about our prospects together. All that time, I thought I missed that velvet cheek, those blue eyes, and our conversations, and I could tell myself that I was undoubtedly in love. Sveta left her husband, even though he was working in clean, tidy Western Europe, while I could only offer her the prospect of accompanying me to the hot, dangerous places in the Middle East. I made a point of warning her about this possibility, but to my surprise, it did not deter her; she accepted my proposal without much hesitation.

The path to her divorce, though, proved thorny; at some point, I was even physically assaulted by her husband. I had trouble at work, too; my TASS career was nearly derailed. It was all due to Sveta's husband's job. You have probably guessed it by now: he was a spy, a KGB officer, who also had influential connections through his father. Luckily, I received strong support from some TASS bosses, though I only learnt about their benign involvement in my affairs many years later. But the main thing was that Sveta and I firmly stood by each other and survived it all. And her ex-husband, too, I hear, is quite happy in his new marriage. So, all turned for the better in the end.

In Lebanon, besides the two stunningly beautiful Italian golden rings, I bought a joyful cream-coloured cotton dress in the oriental style. It was ankle-length, with bright embroidery on the chest. Astonishingly, it wasn't too expensive but looked festive and exotic in a very warm way. I showed the dress to my temporary bodyguard, Hamdi, who expressed doubt whether it was luxurious enough. I said, 'Let the bride decide: if she doesn't like it, I'll buy her something more traditional.'

The bride actually liked it a lot and decided it would be her wedding dress. Surely, it was unusual and original. And then, suddenly, a few days before the wedding, the phone rang on my desk in TASS. It was the Moscow correspondent of the Egyptian newspaper *Al-Ahram*. He said that he had just come from Lebanon, where he had run into Hamdi, who persuaded him to take along a wedding gift for me.

I was terrified. You are no longer in Beirut, I kept telling myself, for an unauthorised contact with a foreigner, you could easily be blacklisted. Moreover, I had overheard something very worrying about the Egyptian journalist: he was in the Soviet authorities' bad books. This suggested that he was probably seen as a spy, even if he was not. Therefore, meeting him would likely make me a suspect. The surveillance team had to report the target's activities, and a copy of it would surely end up in my file. I would have been a marked man.

What made the system particularly insidious was that these unsubstantiated reports became a kind of virus, lying dormant in your KGB file for a time. Not the foreign intelligence department, but the secret police. You could know nothing about it, feel normal and healthy, be more or less successful in your career, even get promotions and small bonuses from time to time. No one suspects anything, but then your boss decides to send you for an assignment abroad. This could only happen with the approval of a so-called '*Instantsiya*', the coded name for the CPSU Central Committee Foreign Travel board. This organ, in its turn, requests the opinion of the KGB, and that is when that virus in your file springs to life. And you find yourself sick. Terminally ill. You walk, talk, laugh, eat, drink, like other normal and healthy people. But no, you're not the same as them; you have a fatal flaw, you are a leper.

The name of the disease may never be revealed. Nobody will openly say anything. TASS, for example, or any other organisation with offices abroad, will receive a curt message from the Central Committee stating, 'There will be no *Instantsiya*'s decision on CITIZEN X'. This means that you are not allowed to cross the border. You have been stamped as untrustworthy without any clarification. In rare cases, the head of TASS or an influential relative of the would-be culprit can ask a contact in the Central Committee apparatus to explain the problem. But in most cases, the hapless Citizen X. will be left in the dark, trying to guess what crime he had committed. Perhaps his in-laws informed on him, revealing that he occasionally told anti-Soviet jokes? Or maybe in-laws have nothing to do with it at all. It was the doing of a neighbour, that vindictive scum, with whom he had fallen out after a disagreement over the water leak? Or could it be the dumped lover's revenge? Or maybe the problem stems from his correspondence with an English schoolboy many years ago, when he received the black mark.

Often, there wouldn't be enough compromising evidence to arrest Citizen X. or demand his dismissal from his position at work or expulsion from Moscow, but allowing a person to go abroad was considered an enormous prize, of which only the totally loyal with impeccable record and reputation were worthy. A shadow of doubt or an adverse rumour could be grounds for withholding the entitlement to foreign travel as a preventive measure. But for Citizen X. it's a real tragedy, if not the end of the world. Not only would he be deprived of the only chance to significantly improve the living standards of his family, but he would forever feel humiliated, an inferior, damaged specimen, behind whose back his colleagues would be whispering: 'Have you heard? Citizen X. is *'nevyezdnoy'* (banned from travelling)'.

Take the typical case of one of my favourite university professors, brilliant Arabist and historian Georgiy Mirsky. He seemed very successful in his career, teaching at the most prestigious university in the land and admired by students and colleagues. He regularly spoke at authoritative academic conferences inside the USSR, with many high-profile books and publications to his name.

Despite it all, his applications to travel abroad, even in a private capacity or as a tourist, were routinely refused. Every time, he would get the same response: 'No decision of the *Instantsiya*'. And never offered any explanation for this contemptuous rejection. It was only many years later, when the Soviet Union came to its natural end, that he found out what it was all about. His file contained a few libellous denunciations, mainly vague suspicions of KGB informants. His biggest sin seemed to be that one of his post-graduate students joined an unofficial Social-Democratic discussion group. Nothing serious, even by Soviet standards. But Mirsky didn't have a chance to defend himself as he couldn't know what the charges against him were in the first place. He had been convicted without trial.

I was afraid that I could share the same fate. In fact, receiving a strange object from a foreigner suspected of espionage was a much more serious matter that could have ruined my life without giving me a chance to explain myself.

I went to my superiors for advice: what shall I do? To my surprise, they didn't send me away in horror, but offered to accompany me to this risky rendezvous. The names of these two decent and gutsy gentlemen were Georgiy Kuvaldin and Igor Bereznikosky. The three of us went to meet the Egyptian near the TASS building. Having thanked my saviours, I insisted on showing them the contents of the package. I wanted them to be sure that there was no spyware equipment, no radio receivers, no secret photographing devices. Only one thing was there: a posh, apparently expensive, dark-green, ankle-length handmade Lebanese dress, embroidered with silver and gold threads. Hamdi thought it would be more appropriate for my wedding. But it proved to be one size too big for the skinny bride, and only a few years later, having gained a tiny bit of weight, Sveta managed to flaunt it at a New Year's party in Baghdad.

I am terribly ashamed that I didn't dare send Hamdi a letter of thanks, fearing that it would also end up in my file.

By association, I recalled two Palestinian fighters, escorting and guarding me during my cigarette excursion in war-torn Beirut. There was something remotely in common between the two situations. And I keep in my heart gratitude to all those acquaintances and strangers who so often came to my rescue without expecting anything in return.

I have visited over sixty countries. I have lived in some for a time, travelled to others once or twice, and returned to a few so often that I have lost count. But I have never been back to Lebanon, and that is sad. Perhaps, just perhaps, I may return there one day. They say it is now absolutely stunning.

Chapter Eleven

Exile into The Middle Ages

After returning from Beirut, I was promoted to the position of senior sub-editor on the TASS Middle Eastern desk, which entailed regularly leading the late-night shifts. In that capacity, I was unexpectedly noticed by the TASS éminence grise, Sergei Solovyov. I am not even sure what it was that allowed me to win his favour. Perhaps, he was positively impressed with my clear answers to his occasional editorial queries. Or, maybe, he liked the little essay I had written for the internal publication called *Tassovets*, in which I described my impressions of the war-torn Lebanon. The piece had a rather daring title for that time: *'Ag-rr-ression with the three "r"*. Its central theme was the sad impotence of a journalist clutching at the familiar, emasculated clichés in a feeble attempt to truly render the sense of horror of the ongoing civil war and human suffering amid that nightmare. The piece proved popular and was widely discussed in TASS corridors; Solovyov couldn't help noticing it. Some other accidental episodes might have played a role, as I aligned with Solovyov's ideas about a new generation of journalists who, he later told me, could potentially introduce a more creative streak to TASS's ways. Anyhow, I was suddenly moved from the Middle Eastern desk's editorial office and offered a job on the so-called Main News Desk. It was the headquarters of TASS International News department (the GRII – *Glavnaya Redakciya Inostrannoy Infromacii*), where all the materials prepared in the regional editorial offices were approved or declined, given a final touch and released for publication. In a sense, I suddenly became my colleagues' superior, which inevitably sparked some envy. Initially, my task was to oversee the publication of short news items. Conflicts arose, some of them were very revealing. I will cite two examples. Once, the Latin American editorial team brought me an item —just a few lines —about Pinochet's repression in Chile. It was the usual baloney. That is not to say that the real massacres and atrocities did not really occur in that tragic country regularly; they did. But the Soviet press was turning the reports about them into tedious propagandistic pabulum. Our own 'Latinos' produced such news stories every day, and all those news reports looked as though they were carbon copies of the same piece, only with different dates, figures and the topographical names inserted. More often than not, the language was wooden and primitive.

I dreaded the idea of having to engage in lengthy, dreary negotiations with the Latin America desk, trying to explain what I didn't like about their news item. I knew that, after taking my criticism as a personal affront, they would take a long time to rewrite it, resulting in a version that differed very little from the original. As it was, I was already being bad-mouthed behind my back, with some colleagues grumbling aloud about my alleged high-handedness. 'I will be much better off rewriting the damned thing myself,' I thought and rushed to a free room, assigned to our group. I sat down at the typewriter, and – hey presto! – five minutes later, the piece was ready. It wasn't a masterpiece of modern journalism, but at least it was shorter and more to the point. But, being under pressure and in a great hurry, I made a silly mistake: instead of the word 'three', I typed 'four', accidentally increasing the number of the Communists shot by Pinochet's hit squads. This gave my detractors an excellent excuse to protest against my alleged imperiousness. With their complaint, they bypassed Sergei Solovyov and went directly to the Editor-in-Chief, Gennady Shishkin. He spent a few minutes trying to grasp what it was that they wanted from him as my accusers tried to generalise, to use this example to prove that 'this whippersnapper' was taking too many liberties. Finally, Shishkin said, 'I do not see a big problem here. Had Andrei, on the contrary, downplayed the number of victims of repression, that would have been a political mistake. As it is, this is just a minor error.'

Shishkin was neither an idiot nor a scoundrel, but he knew the rules of the game. Of course, the episode had underlined the boundless cynicism of the Soviet propaganda, but Shishkin was also taking the mickey. In his deadpan voice, I heard a trace of irony, even sarcasm: three or four, what does it matter how many were really killed if we must maintain the daily flow of this crap.

The second case was much more annoying. One early December morning, a bright and quick-witted journalist, a leading light of the North American desk who would eventually make a successful career and with whom we would work at some point in *Izvestia*, brought me a poorly edited news report from the USA. Above the text sent by a TASS New-York correspondent, a handwritten phrase had been hurriedly added. It said, 'Crime rate in the streets of American cities is soaring'. And then the text of the report itself followed: 'John Lennon, the famous leader of the Beatles rock band, was shot dead today at the entrance to the Dakota residential compound'.

I was astonished that an experienced journalist did not seem to understand that this tragic, sensational news was important in itself, and not just as an illustration for our favourite propagandistic assertion about the growth of criminality in the country of 'the main enemy'. John Lennon was already well-known and even revered by many as a living rock icon, not only in the West but also in our country. The North American colleague apparently had no inkling that his editing of this historic report might well go down in history as a shocking example of the crassness of the Soviet style of propaganda. I tried to put it to my colleague in the politest way, but he got angry, waving his hand at me as if to say, 'Do whatever you want, since it is you who is in control today.' I quickly crossed out the shameful add-on, put my initials under the text, and rushed to the teletype hall window, asking the girls there to transmit the item urgently.

Later in the day, I informed Solovyov about what had happened, and he supported my position, promising to protect me against any attempts to turn our disagreement with the North American editor into an ideological issue.

There were many similar episodes, and at some point, it dawned on me that this work did not satisfy me. In the end, I could only mitigate the idiocies of propaganda to some extent, but the essence remained unchanged. Moreover, thanks to my diligence, these materials, often misleading and sometimes outright deceitful, became somewhat more acceptable and convincing. My initials marked dozens of short news items each day, which were later published by newspapers and broadcast on the radio and television, but I wasn't proud of them. Instinctively, it felt wrong, even though I was still in denial about the source of that unease. That is why I was delighted when Solovyov offered me a further promotion and appointed me a copytaster.

This is an essential position in all serious news agencies; its holder is responsible for assessing news stories immediately upon receipt, rating their importance and urgency.

As one of the four TASS copytasters (we had to do 12-hours shifts providing a round the clock service) I had to be the first person to read through the entire flow of information coming to the agency, both from TASS own correspondents and from all other sources, instantly deciding what had to be done with it, i.e. whether to forward the items for subediting to the regional or to other, specialised desks, including the one that was publishing secret or semi-secret bulletins designated entirely for the government consumption. Many things were happening in the world that the Soviet population at large was not allowed to learn about. That secrecy, though, was something much more than just a form of censorship. I already mentioned in one of the previous chapters that the main feature and the cementing principle of the system was the strictly hierarchical rationing. Through the intricate mechanism of exclusive shops, which were inaccessible to the general public, as well as medical clinics, spas, in-shop canteens, and other facilities, the government was rationing scarce material resources, food, clothing, white goods, and medical services. Most importantly, all entitlements were defined strictly according to an individual's place in the hierarchy. The higher the place, the more and better goods and services a person could obtain for their rouble. But the same principle applied to information. TASS published many different categories of news bulletins designated 'for official use only'. The most 'secret' ones were intended for the Politburo and the ministers, who needed to see the full picture of world events to govern. There were also more widely circulated, but partially expurgated, bulletins for the use of middle- and lower-ranking state officials. At the same time, the 'plebs' were fed the potage of heavily censored news and primitive propaganda.

A good copytaster needed to know what stories were so important that the TASS bosses had to be urgently notified, sometimes at ungodly hours. But if you made a mistake of waking up a big chief with something that wouldn't be judged as weighty enough, you might be forgiven for it only so many times; after that, you could easily lose your job. Conversely, failing to inform top executives promptly about significant international developments was an even greater offence.

The copytaster was supposed to work closely with the Urgent Official Use Information Desk. That was by far the most important of all TASS departments and perhaps the main reason for the agency's existence. Headed by a legendary editor (and functioning alcoholic) Sergei Ivanov, its main task was to supply the Politburo, the Central Committee and the leadership of major governmental departments with the regular bulletins of urgent international news called *Svodka* (The Summary), or 'White TASS' in professional jargon. *Svodka* was issued several times a day and sent with special Kremlin couriers (for good measure, dressed in military uniform) to Brezhnev and other members of the Politburo. Moreover, at the discretion of the relevant TASS department, additional special and urgent bulletins could be issued at any time of day or night and had to be forwarded to recipients immediately. If it happened at odd hours, the Politburo members could theoretically be woken up even at night. But it happened very rarely and only in extreme cases – such as a coup d'état in an important country, or a massive terrorist attack, or an assault on a Soviet embassy, etc. Apart from *Svodka*, the same department also published daily important news bulletins 'A' meant for middle-rank bureaucrats as well as more secret and restricted bulletins 'AD', which contained news reports deemed 'anti-Soviet'.

This intricate and convoluted system of news rationing existed to compensate for the absence of press freedom in a country where there was no truth in the newspaper called *The Truth* (*Pravda*) and no news in *The News (Izvestia)* daily. It would only change with *Perestroika*. The press dealt almost exclusively with propaganda, brainwashing the public. The worldview presented by the official media was so distorted that it bore little resemblance to reality. However, those who ran the country had to be aware of what was happening so that they could navigate the world.

In this complex system, TASS served as a vital channel of international information for the government, alongside the KGB, GRU, and the Foreign Ministry. Moreover, in certain situations, at the time of unexpected, dramatic developments, TASS acquired special importance, as the agency drew its material from open sources around the globe and didn't have to lose time encoding and then decrypting its reports, and thus inevitably was often ahead of everyone else in the Soviet information supply chain. So, contrary to widespread opinion, far from serving only as a cover for KGB and GRU agents (although it did have that function too), TASS played a distinctive, in fact, crucial role in the USSR's state machinery. About half of the agency's correspondents abroad were indeed spies posing as journalists, but someone had to do the serious TASS work as well.

Not immediately, but quickly enough, I started to learn the ropes. One of the main rules was to inform *Svodka* editors in the room next door if anything overwhelmingly important happened anywhere in the world: it was a matter of minutes, because it was vital to stay a jump ahead of the competition – the KGB, the GRU and the Ministry of Foreign Affairs – and be the first to inform the powers that be.

But the main test for a copytaster came on the night shifts. In the evening and at night, the flow of information was noticeably weaker, allowing the copytaster to produce, by early morning, a summary of the main international events of the last 12 hours (usually not more than one page). Its quality had a significant bearing on your reputation in the eyes of not only the TASS bosses but also many influential people outside the agency. It was initially conceived as a purely domestic intra-TASS product, a kind of rough draft, devised to help the editors of the morning shifts quickly grasp the flavour of the day's news agenda. But gradually it became something much more important.

Inside the TASS building, there was a small unit that occupied a room on the fifth floor. It was totally independent, as all its personnel belonged to the Defence Ministry or to the GRU, the military intelligence (nobody seemed to know for sure which). The function of that unit was to use TASS technical facilities to keep the military brass informed about international developments. They produced their own bulletins, which were transmitted to their bosses via telex. But they didn't work at night, and soon enough it occurred to them that they might as well make use of the copytaster's summary first thing in the morning. Every time, they would grab a copy of it and send it to their customers, almost unchanged. I was amazed when I started receiving early-morning calls from the CPSU Central Committee, querying points in the copytaster's summary. How did the party apparatchiks know what had been included in it? It turned out that they found a way to receive a copy of the bulletin prepared by the military, while also knowing what it was based on. Thus, you suddenly found yourself responsible for shaping the morning news agenda inside the most powerful organisation in the USSR.

During the night shifts, I had a *vertushka*, the government line secret communication telephone, sitting on my desk, which could theoretically allow me to call the duty officers of major ministries, the KGB, the GRU, and the CPSU Central Committee directly. With a few notable exceptions, I never used it on my own initiative but was regularly on the receiving end of their queries.

I referred to one such exceptional episode earlier in this book, which occurred in September 1980, when the TASS correspondent in Warsaw was the first to learn about the overthrow of Polish leader Edward Gierek (the coup was likely carried out with the secret blessing of the Soviet Union).

Most of the people who phoned me using the *vertushka* at night and early in the morning were impeccably civil, if demanding. The top Foreign Affairs advisor to Brezhnev, Andrei Alexandrov-Agentov, called a couple of times. The first deputy head of the Socialist Countries department, Oleg Rakhmanin, once called a duty secretary of the TASS Director General (the poor girl was peacefully asleep on a makeshift sofa constructed from two armchairs, hoping that nobody would disturb her), solely to find out my first name and patronymic so that he could address me in the politest of ways. This manifestation of good manners touched me, but I immediately checked myself: there was nothing to be particularly proud of. Sometimes the copytaster began to feel close to the centre of decision-making, communicating directly with some of the most influential figures in the Soviet system. Still, by and large, it was an illusion. Servants, that's what we were. Well-bred masters do, in fact, speak courteously to their valets.

It had been generally assumed that Soloviev, indeed a gifted man and a highly efficient manager, was soon to become the Foreign Editor of TASS and Deputy Director General. A protégé of his could also hope for a spectacular career in the agency. But nothing of this came to pass. Rumour had it that Sergei Solovyov belonged to a certain 'mafia', a networking group which was ultimately defeated in the power fight. Apparently, Solovyov had his own patrons at the top, but they must have lost their influence; something went wrong, the storm blew, and his carefully constructed pyramid was momentarily destroyed. Soloviev was suddenly dismissed from his high office and appointed TASS correspondent in Australia, an honourable but certainly irrelevant position. I, too, was banished – to North Yemen.

Only recently, I was at the centre of things, feeling like one of the TASS seniors, communicating with the high and mighty of the land and supplying them with important information. To find myself after that in the godforsaken medieval city of Sana'a was a rather sobering experience.

Nothing of note ever seemed to happen there. Of course, rumours reached me about the power fighting, which was going on under the wraps, the slow-burning conflict with the communist Southern Yemen and troubles with the desert and mountain tribes, as well as the tensions between the Sunnis and the Shiites (Houthis). However, there was no mention of any of this in the heavily censored local press, and officials refused to discuss those forbidden subjects. The TASS correspondent, unlike the spies, was not supposed to base his reports on rumours. As a result, I had never had so much free time in my life. In fact, I was bored rigid. And there were practically no leisure facilities available.

In the evenings, the medieval town of Sana'a was utterly deserted, with no theatres, cinemas, or nightclubs. More or less normal (but boring) restaurants were typically found only in hotels, and in any case, I couldn't afford to eat there.

Only the embassy offered some recreation for Soviet citizens: there was a private park on its vast grounds, where you could at least take a nice walk with your kids. Soviet films were regularly shown in an improvised outdoor cinema. But that was all. Out of boredom, my wife and I started regularly watching American movies on VHS. A whole new world suddenly opened for us; from then on, we couldn't even imagine our lives without the forbidden fruits of Western culture.

It took us some time, though, to save enough money to buy our own video recorder. However, a sympathetic embassy attaché invited us to join him and his wife at their place. As I understood it, Zakhar was a KGB officer, but his work was purely technical. He was a highly qualified engineer by training and had never been involved in human intelligence (HUMINT), so he did not exude the sinister energy typically associated with those who manipulate people and lure them into traps. By an uncanny coincidence, Sveta knew him from early childhood as their families shared a communal flat in Moscow at some point. That attracted Zakhar to us in the first place; he was also desperately keen to find a soul-mate whom he could trust with his little secret: the unquenchable passion for Western pop music (Rod Stewart and Shirley Bassey were his favourites) and American movies. He wisely refrained from flaunting those ideologically suspect pursuits among his KGB colleagues, but in Sveta and me, he found trustworthy partners in crime. Besides, Zakhar and his wife spoke very little English, so I had to serve as a simultaneous interpreter for those cinematic sessions. Together, we had watched dozens of films. Besides, Zakhar had a sardonic sense of humour and, I felt, slightly despised his spying colleagues for their political rigidity and narrow-mindedness, although, of course, he never spelt it out in so many words. Gradually, our relations developed into an unlikely friendship which proved very important to me. It is one of the sores in my conscience that I had to abruptly sever all relationships with Zakhar when I moved to live in Britain in 1992, feeling very strongly that in my new life there was no place for any kind of contacts, including the purely personal ones, with any Russian intelligence officers, even the retired ones. Zakhar probably thinks of me as a traitor – if not of Mother Russia, then of our friendship. Meanwhile, in the Soviet reality of the 1980s, he proved to be a true thick-and-thin friend, becoming a vital source of information, helping me to navigate the shark-infested waters of the Soviet colony in Yemen, a few times giving me crucially important early warnings about the machinations which could affect my family and me in one way or another. So he has probably every right to think of me as an ungrateful son of a bitch.

Despite Zakhar's support, my situation was far from safe. The ambassador strongly disliked me for some reason, and there were also issues with the KGB that I will describe further on. Having learnt of my fretting and worrying for my and his daughter's safety, my father-in-law managed to resume his university days' friendship with one of Brezhnev's assistants, Yevgeniy Samoteykin, who, to my total amazement, one day dropped a note to the Soviet ambassador in Sana'a hinting at his interest in the well-being of my family. From that moment on, I had no problems whatsoever with the ambassador, and I suspect that the KGB resident (the chief of station) in Sana'a was also duly informed of that association. I vaguely remember the latter as a calm, outwardly friendly and polite man, but one of his deputies, the so-called 'security officer', aptly nicknamed '*Khmuriy*' (meaning 'Glum') because of his perpetual angry scowl, caused me and my close friend Alexander (Sasha) Ivanov-Galitsin a great deal of distress. Sasha, who later gained fame for condemning the attempted putsch in August 1991 as a counsellor of the USSR Embassy in London, was at that time the second-in-command at the Soviet Embassy in Sana'a and often stood in for the ambassador in his absence. In the capacity of Chargé d'Affaires, he had frequently experienced the full horror of dealing with this obnoxious character. 'Glum' was brusque, grim and arrogant. He looked at everyone with hostile suspicion and, ever since his arrival in Sana'a, had been energetically and purposefully trying to recreate in the embassy and in the Soviet colony as a whole the nightmarish atmosphere of Stalin's purges. He didn't have firing squads at his disposal, but his substitute for 'capital punishment' was the deportation of 'guilty' Soviet citizens to their homeland. It was a major weapon in his hands, as it took away their only chance to improve their living standards by saving up for an apartment or a car. Some of the desperate Soviet technicians found an ingenious formula, retorting to his threats with the phrase: 'You can't frighten me with life in my motherland!'. In reality, however, the vast majority were terrified by the prospect of losing the privilege of working overseas and earning hard currency. Perhaps those Russians who today feel nostalgic for 'good old Soviet times' (and there are many) should be enlightened that the people of the USSR were divided into two unequal groups: the fortunate minority who could, at least once in their lifetime, get an employment abroad, and the unlucky majority who could only envy the former. That was the way that society lived and functioned.

Therefore, 'Glum' had in his hands an instrument of blackmail, with which he could recruit informers. As a result, he quickly managed to create a climate of moral terror inside the Soviet colony, with everybody suspecting everybody.

'Glum' ordered a duty commandant (the official title for junior officers who guard the embassy) to build a fence around his office window, ensuring that no one could accidentally see or overhear what was happening there, including how he was communicating with his informers, both actual and potential. As a result, walking around the embassy building took much longer.

After that, the secretary of the Embassy's Communist party organisation, whom, according to the absurd rules of Soviet secrecy, we were obliged to call Secretary of the Trade Union Committee, decided to intervene. He tried to explain to the Stalinist that the times had changed somewhat, and he couldn't inconvenience everybody in such a way without getting the consent of other senior officials. If I remember correctly, the ambassador was away. My friend Sasha Ivanov-Galitsin, as the Chargé d'Affaires, tried to reason with 'Glum' but was rudely rebuffed, while the chief of the KGB station, who, in theory, was 'Glum's boss, preferred to take a neutral position in that conflict. After all, the political police part of the KGB had always been more powerful than the foreign intelligence branch.

The heated conversation between the party chief and 'Glum' took place in the latter's office, and it was so loud that even through the thick upholstery of the cabinet door, we could hear muffled shouts and screams.

Then the party secretary popped out of 'Glum's office like a scalded cat and rushed to his flat in the embassy compound, where he apparently had to lie down right away. It soon became known that he had developed a heart problem and had to stay home for nearly a week. 'Glum', meanwhile, having learnt the details from the embassy doctor, openly boasted of his triumph, saying as if to himself but so that many people could hear it: 'What a sissy your Party secretary has proved to be!'

But he miscalculated. Unlike Stalin, Brezhnev and his Party deputy, Mikhail Suslov, did not like it when the KGB tried to put itself above the party. The most famous case involved Yuri Andropov's attempt to dismiss Alexander Yakovlev, the future architect of *Glasnost*, who was serving as the Soviet ambassador to Canada in the mid-1970s. When at a meeting of the Politburo the chairman of the KGB began to complain that the ambassador was hostile to the KGB operatives in Ottawa and got too close to Prime Minister Trudeau, Suslov snapped, uttering a phrase that the party apparatus would quote with gusto again and again: 'It wasn't the KGB that had appointed ambassador Yakovlev, and it's not for the KGB to decide whether he should be relieved of his post'. Andropov fell silent and never returned to this subject. It had proved a pivotal moment: had Yakovlev been fired then, *Glasnost* and *Perestroika* might not have happened in the late 1980s.

Rumour had it that 'Glum', while in Moscow for his vacation, was summoned to the Central Committee along with the embassy's party secretary. They were both reprimanded for arguing in public, and cooperation and mutual respect were emphasised.

But judging from the smug look on 'Glum's face on his arrival back in Sana'a, he didn't consider himself a loser. On the contrary, he somehow drew the wrong conclusion from the whole episode, feeling he could act with impunity. He clearly had some protectors in high places. But in the end, they either were not influential enough or didn't want to stick their necks too far out for him. His overconfidence became his downfall. When he started digging up dirt on the amorous Soviet ambassador, he was promptly recalled to Moscow and sacked from the KGB.

For a while, though, 'Glum' seemed unsinkable. My friend Sasha and I were wondering whether he represented a general political trend: whether a new version of Stalinism was emerging in our motherland. In official propaganda, cinema and literature, we could clearly see persistent attempts to rehabilitate the moustached mass murderer. Stalin's 'rating' has always been (and still is) the surest measure of socio-political temperature in Russia. Whenever attitudes towards Stalin become more positive, when he is praised more often or, at least, vigorously defended against so-called 'demonisation' (as Stalinists call attempts to reveal the extent of his crimes against humanity), it means that the barometer is pointing to a harsher crackdown and new powers for the secret police.

All this was clearly happening in the Soviet Union. KGB chairman Yuri Andropov was growing more powerful by the day. We were at times despairing, but I was indeed fortunate to have Sasha on my side.

The most memorable clash with 'Glum' occurred around my interactions with a helicopter pilot, Volodya Mikhailov. I no longer remember how or where I met him. He was a lovely man, friendly, agreeable, sympathetic, always ready to help. Unfortunately, I unwittingly caused him serious trouble, making another careless mistake. Bored rigid by the absence of serious work in Sana'a, where nothing ever seemed to be happening, I asked Mikhailov to introduce me to the Palestinian pilots who were working with him, teaching Yemenis to fly those machines. Mikhailov got us together, and we had a nice dinner at one of those Palestinian places. We discussed the situation in the Middle East and their personal dramatic stories. My wife enjoyed chatting with their wives and playing with the host's baby. Not a very exciting event, but in the dull tedium of our medieval existence, even that could pass for a pleasant diversion.

But someone (I have no idea who) informed 'Glum'.

He decided not to touch me: after all, the head of the TASS bureau was the Central Committee nomenclature, also the influence of my father-in-law had to be taken into consideration, so 'Glum' probably thought that he needed to collect more compromising material before going into attack against me (I did not doubt that he was planning to do it at a later stage, but my time had not come yet). But Mikhailov was a smaller fish, and 'Glum' decided to blackmail and recruit him as yet another informer. And that was what he tried to do, accusing him of violating the rules of conduct for Soviet citizens abroad, according to which Mikhailov didn't have the right to socialise informally with foreigners without explicit permission from the embassy (in this case, from 'Glum' himself).

But Mikhailov stood up to blackmail. The fact that he was so friendly and soft-spoken didn't mean he was spineless. He absolutely hated the idea of becoming a snitch.

'Glum' then, as was his usual method, threatened Mikhailov with termination of his contract and sending him back to his native Novosibirsk.

When the helicopter pilot informed me of what had happened, I was taken aback and horrified. Once again, I had forgotten what kind of country I belonged to, even when thousands of kilometres away, in the Arabian Peninsula. Luckily, the ambassador was away, and my friend Sasha Ivanov-Galitsin was the acting head of the embassy. In my desperation, I rushed to see him, pleading to save Mikhailov and my guilty conscience. After all, it was because of me that the honest man found himself in such a pernicious situation.

Sasha wasn't pleased about the whole episode, but he decided to help, not only out of friendship but also because of his deep aversion to the disgusting practices of 'Glum' and everything he stood for.

Sasha summoned him to his office and demanded that he leave Mikhailov alone.

'It was I who asked comrade Ostalski to contact the Palestinians,' he said, 'as the Ministry of Foreign Affairs has an interest in what is happening in relations between Yemen and the PLO.' (Which, incidentally, was true, and, to provide an alibi, I even went so far as to quickly concoct a short report for Sasha on the subject).

'I was aware of Mikhailov's role in establishing that contact,' added the Chargé d'Affaires.

That, of course, was a white lie, and 'Glum' did not believe it for a second. He reacted in a very rude, insulting and threatening way, promising to settle scores with Sasha one day. But there was nothing he could do to Mikhailov now. The pilot was saved. Or so I thought. He was indeed left alone until the end of his one-year contract, which, as was the norm, should have been almost automatically extended for another year or two, especially as the Yemeni hosts were very happy with his work. But Mikhailov didn't get an extension and had to go home without any explanation. I had no doubt whose trickery was behind it.

'Glum' summoned me to his creepy office, too. I don't think I ever experienced such a dressing down: nobody ever yelled at me like that. I'll give him his due: he knew how to insult and frighten without resorting to the world-famous Russian 'mat' (foul language). The general sense, minus the threats and insults of what he said, was to the effect that he long ago could have destroyed me, but he showed goodwill, turned a blind eye to some of my misdemeanours and unauthorised contacts with foreigners. He let me be, not interfering in my work, but how did I dare to interfere in his?

I came out red in the face, feeling trampled and humiliated. I could easily imagine that at a more advanced age, I would have got myself heart trouble as the party secretary did. Sasha also felt insulted, and we started plotting revenge together.

Or rather, not revenge as such, it would have been totally pointless; we just felt we had to do something, to teach the KGB goon a lesson once in his life, to let him taste the same bitter medicine which he was used to pour into others' throats.

To start, we decided to drink vodka. And it was one of the rarest occasions in my life (I can count them on the fingers of one hand), when I overcame the resistance of my body and drank much more than I was usually able to endure, and ended up pretty drunk. This, of course, was the direct result of the stress inflicted on me by 'Glum', or that was the way I justified it to myself.

I can see it clearly in my memory as if it happened yesterday. Sasha Ivanov-Galitsin solemnly declares:

'Pierre Smirnoff welcomes Mr and Mrs Ostalski!'

And with these words, another glass is poured for me.

Having got seriously drunk, we started planning our operation. The idea was to play on 'Glum's interminable paranoia. Knowing that every morning he was served a cup of tea in his office, we conceived an ingenious plot: to write on a tiny piece of paper in clumsy block letters the phrase: 'Your tea has been tampered with' and slip it under the door of his apartment. He would then, we thought, go totally mental, suspecting all and everyone of an attempt on his life. It would have been exciting to see whether he stopped taking hot drinks altogether or devised a test to determine whether his tea was indeed poisoned.

Because of the amount of alcohol consumed, my recall of events is vague. If I remember correctly, the scheme was almost ready for implementation. The note had been prepared, and Sasha and I even went down to the floor where 'Glum' had his living quarters. We probably even shoved that scrap of paper under his door, but then one of us came to his senses, retrieved the note, and destroyed it. Had we fully implemented our little plan, the consequences could have been rather dramatic. It's easy to imagine that 'Glum' would have initiated a full-blown investigation, mobilising all the forensic resources of the KGB station in Sana'a, presenting our hoax as a major anti-Soviet sabotage action. In that case, we would have most probably been found out and severely punished. But, on the other hand, it was entirely possible that he would have preferred to hush up the case, so as not to look stupid. In any case, we have had a lot of unforgettable fun, taking the piss out of 'Glum', visualising the enraged expression on his choleric, stern face as he read that note. Sometimes, just imagining things is nearly as good as the real thing.

But something much more ominous happened to me in Yemen. This truly spine-chilling episode occurred one day after my wife and I returned from a short trip to the Red Sea with our small daughter.

We arrived in Sana'a after midnight. The streets of the capital were deserted. Silence and darkness fell on the city, and in the failing light of rare electric streetlamps, the mud houses looked dead, more like crypts than human dwellings. Our daughter, tired after a long trip through the mountain ridge, was sleeping in the back seat of the car. When we arrived at the gates of our house, Sveta immediately came out, carrying the little girl in her arms, and hurried inside. I had to go out, too, to fully open the gate to drive my little green Mazda into the yard.

And then, out of nowhere, a jeep appeared, like the ones used by the Yemeni military, blocking my way. The driver was a man in uniform.

'Show me your ID,' he barked. I walked over to his car's window to get a closer look at the man behind the wheel. Judging by his insignia, he was a major in airborne troops.

'Can I first have a look at your document?' I asked, politely but firmly.

'Sure,' he said, 'here it is.'

With those words, he took out a gun and pointed it at me. My determination to stand up to the bully somehow evaporated. I silently handed him an ID card issued by the local Ministry of Foreign Affairs. I must say that I had been bestowed with it without any request on my part, and it was probably a mistake, a misunderstanding. According to the rules, I was entitled only to a journalistic accreditation card, which I also obtained. I used one or the other, depending on the circumstance. To the major I handed, of course, the Foreign Ministry one, saying: 'See, I am a Soviet diplomat.'

'Fine,' replied the Major, and nonchalantly put the coveted card in his pocket.

'Hey, you can't do it, please, give me my document back!' I panicked, but he just drew the muzzle of his gun closer to my head, and I went silent. Then he started interrogating me, deliberately and unhurriedly spitting out his questions. It turned out that he was primarily interested not in my work or status but in my dwelling arrangements, how many people lived in my house, what I knew about my neighbours, etc.

Generally, I am not always capable of thinking on my feet; quite often, acting under duress and provocation, I take too long to gather my wits and decide on the right move. But in this case, instinct dictated the entirely correct course of action to me. Looking into the barrel of a black gun, I told the major that the house was full of people. It was true that the landlord and his family did indeed live on the top floor, while my family occupied the ground floor with a separate entrance, a private courtyard, and a small garden. The landlord was a rather prominent figure, well known in Sana'a. He was a Sayyid (a direct descendant of the Prophet Muhammad) and a popular London-trained dentist who occasionally treated government officials, including the president's relatives. I spelt it all out, slightly exaggerating the importance of my landlord and insisting that he had a rather large, extended family, all of whom resided together with him (while in reality he, unusually, had only one wife and two little children). I insisted that the dentist's numerous relatives were all at home.

'Are you sure?' asked the major suspiciously. 'Why then are the windows on the upper floor dark?'

In fact, I had no idea who was in the house and who was not. But I was inspired to suggest that perhaps we could only see the children's bedrooms from our side of the house, while the landlord and others were surely in the sitting room, which overlooked the other side.

'They go to bed late, so probably are still awake,' I said. I lied, well knowing that my landlord was, in fact, an early bird who would most probably be deeply asleep at this ungodly hour.

I saw that the major was hesitating, as if he could not quite decide what to do. I took advantage of his vacillation and said: 'Excuse me, sir, but can I, finally, move my car into the bay?' 'Okay, do,' he allowed haughtily, lowering his gun, 'but hurry.'

And hurry I did. Having driven my Mazda around his jeep and through the open gates into my yard, I leapt out of the car, jumped head over heels onto the porch and slipped inside through the door left open by Sveta and then, standing on my knees, quickly locked it behind me. While I was running and jumping, I was fully expecting to be shot at. However, I wasn't; instead, I heard what sounded like the engine working and the jeep moving. But where to? It was not clear at all what was happening. Was the major gone? Or did he just move his car into a better shooting position? Or maybe he was trying to see the other side of the house, to find out whether there was really light on in my landlord's living quarters. I crawled to the telephone and dialled the Soviet embassy's number.

The duty guard told me that he would immediately inform the Soviet consul and the security officer about my predicament. Ten minutes later, the consul (a KGB officer, of course) called back and gave me instructions: all the lights should be off, all doors and windows shut, we should keep low and never stand up to full height.

'Hold on, we will be there soon,' he said.

The 'soon' stretched to forty minutes. Forty minutes of tension, spent crawling and crouching in expectation of an attack. Finally, I heard the noise of engines and the loud voices of many people outside the house. His Majesty the Consul arrived - but not alone. A whole platoon of Yemeni gunmen accompanied him. Well, maybe not a platoon, rather, a detachment of ten men or so, armed with Kalashnikovs and led by a brave captain.

'These are members of the President's own security guard,' the consul told me proudly. I felt flattered, but I would have much preferred it if a couple of regular armed policemen had come right away. In the forty minutes that had passed, we all stood a good chance of being killed many times over. Couldn't they come earlier? I asked the consul. He began explaining in great detail how long it had taken him to raise President Saleh's security chief, who then ordered this unit to be dispatched to defend me from the assault. It all now sounded quite farcical, as the culprit was long gone. The entire episode could have unfolded very differently, with tragic consequences. I felt vexed, thinking to myself that the embassy was, in fact, packed with dashing officers exuding proud KGB machismo, with 'Glum' and his sidekicks allegedly making sure the Soviet colony was safe. But in reality, they were very good at gathering compromising material on Soviet citizens and catching them violating one instruction or another. But when it came to actual physical danger, all this macho power was somehow absent, and a desperate 'tovarisch' would expect in vain to get real protection from them. When I still tried to tactfully find out whether it was, after all, possible to do something before the arrival of the Yemeni soldiers, I was assured that the consul was acting in strict accordance with existing regulations.

But that was not the end of the story, oh no.

The next morning, I was taking out the rubbish as I did every day. To reach a large refuse skip, I had to saunter into the nearest commercial street with its pathetic, small shops, in which, occasionally, one could nevertheless find amazing things. For example, I once bought my wife a fantastic birthday present at a very reasonable price. It was an original golden necklace—a small, handmade masterpiece by an unknown Arab artist of remarkable talent. Shaped like a snake, it looked breathtaking as it coiled gracefully around Sveta's long, beautiful neck. When it was later stolen from us during a burglary in Britain, I was more upset than by any other material loss, for it held immense sentimental value and was utterly irreplaceable.

Europeans walking on foot were a rare sight in Sana'a, and every time I stepped out into that street, I felt I was stared at with a mix of curiosity and occasional hostility. Luckily, it was only a short walk, no more than thirty meters. A few years later, the wife of my successor as the Sana'a TASS correspondent would be lashed across her face with a whip, most probably for not wearing a hijab in public.

Nothing ever happened to me during those journeys, though. That is, until that morning, the day after the sinister encounter at the gates of our house. While I was walking back home with an empty bucket in my hand, I suddenly noticed a car very slowly moving alongside me in my peripheral vision. I stopped. The vehicle stopped too, and the driver dressed in a white traditional gallabiyah leant out the window and addressed me in Russian:

'Hello, how are you? I am a neighbour of yours. Last night I saw some strange things happening near your house.'

I was stunned.

'May I ask, who are you?' I said.

'My name is Mahmoud. I work as a pilot for *Yemenia Airlines*. I was trained in the USSR, which is why I speak Russian. And I live near here,' he answered.

I said, very nice to meet you and all that.

'Tell me what happened yesterday?'

While we talked, I started moving toward a small lane leading to my house, and he drove alongside me.

After I briefly described the events of that night, Mahmoud said:

'I would like to help you, Andrei. I happen to be good friends with the director of the central prison, and I think the person who attacked you yesterday may be incarcerated there now. Why don't we go there and have a look? What do you say?'

I hesitated, wondering whether it was such a good idea to get into the car with a stranger, even if he was (or claimed to be) a neighbour and a fluent Russian speaker. Shall I check with the embassy first? I thought. But, after what happened the day before, I no longer believed in the effectiveness of the Soviet security services. Aloud, I said:

'Well, surely I shouldn't be going anywhere with an empty bucket in my hands?'

Mahmoud agreed that a bucket was not a good item to carry around. I persuaded him to come with me to my place for a moment. I gave him something to drink and introduced him to Sveta. It seemed to me that after that, I could feel somewhat safer in the neighbour's company. My wife was still worried, but I decided to take the risk. I got into the car with Mahmoud, and we were off.

Sana'a's Central Prison is really something: a proper fortress. Tall stone walls, towers, and formidable gates could probably withstand a full-blown military assault for many days. Upon our arrival, we were led directly to the director's office. He treated us to very sweet and strong tea in small glasses and, after engaging in some small talk, asked:

'Shall we start?'

'Start what exactly?' I felt disconcerted.

In reply, he used a strange Arabic expression that I did not recognise.

'He is going to show you all those who were detained last night,' explained Mahmoud. And so it began.

It was a depressing sight: ragged, dishevelled men, many of them clearly recently beaten. All wore chains—the so-called legcuffs—on their feet. It was the first and last time in my life that I saw people treated in such a way. Yet, perhaps, the regime in that jail was not as brutal as in the notorious Abu Ghraib prison in Baghdad. At least two of the prisoners were not afraid to come to me and ask for a cigarette. I looked at the director: will it be all right if I oblige them? He nodded. It's okay if that is your wish.

All in all, about forty people, maybe more, passed in front of me in that sad procession. I thought: could it be true that they had all been arrested in the course of one night? I guessed that the head of the prison decided, just in case, to demonstrate to me the entire 'catch' of the last week. But subsequent discoveries led me to doubt that explanation, and begin to suspect something much worse: that I had been played for a sucker.

In any case, the attacker was not among the prisoners shown to me. My new friend Mahmoud was very disappointed and kept asking me, 'Are you sure?'. I was sure.

Mahmoud visited us at home a couple of times after that. Once he came to dinner, drank the forbidden vodka with relish, confessing that he had been taught this vice while studying in the Soviet Union. He was a strong, slender man with a military bearing. Both Sveta and I immediately concluded that the *Yemenia Airline* was his cover story. It was apparent, though, that he had been indeed trained in Russia, but most probably as a military rather than civil aviation pilot. He somehow managed to get into either the President's Guard or, more likely, the Yemeni intelligence service, where he now held a significant position, judging by the reverence shown to him by the head of the Sana'a central prison. This was not so surprising, considering that my night-time adventure had attracted the personal attention of the commander-in-chief of the guard, if not the president himself.

The day came, and our 'neighbour' came again, this time to show me a military ID, which sported a picture of my attacker. But what stunned me was the name printed on it.

'Is it him?' Mahmoud asked me.

'It is, no doubt about that,' I answered. 'But what about the name? Surely, it can't be his real one!'

'Why not? It is a fairly common combination,' said Mahmoud, but I didn't hear much conviction in his voice.

The ID bore the name *Ali Nasser Muhammad* — the very same name as that of the ruler of South Yemen, officially known as the *People's Democratic Republic of Yemen*. That country, inhabited by the same people, was regarded as an enemy — a land unfairly severed from the North by the Soviet Union and its communist puppets. The two Yemens did not recognise each other and had no diplomatic relations. It was a situation much like that of divided Germany or Korea.

Nevertheless, despite the mistrust and hostility, some trade still took place between the North and the South, and *Yemenia Airlines* even operated a regular passenger flight to the southern capital, Aden. After the collapse of the Soviet Union, the Aden government lost Moscow's support, and the two countries were reunited under the authority of the North. However, during my time there, relations were so tense they stood on the brink of war. Back then, no one could have imagined that the despised and marginalised Houthis would one day become the rulers of the country.

I felt that in his heart of hearts, Mahmoud did not believe in the coincidence of the two names. It was most probably a mockery. Somebody was taking the piss.

When Sveta excused herself to attend to our daughter's needs, our 'pilot' began speaking more frankly - as much as he could allow himself to.

For a moment, I was offered a rare glimpse into the complex internal politics of Yemen, about which neither I nor TASS cared much. Mahmoud said that President Ali Abdallah Saleh was forced to constantly balance between different clans, factions, tribes, between Sunnis and Shiites and that he didn't want to shed blood. If the delicate balance was disturbed, it could lead to a terrible civil war. And then there were the Communists, the agents of the South, and behind the South stood Moscow (I did not react to this, refusing to see it as a taunt). The state's intelligence services had to combat the southern threat and, in the process, sometimes competed against each other. For example, this so-called Ali Nasser Muhammad pretended to be a major in the Air Force, but he wasn't. In reality, he worked in the counterintelligence department of the Army's General Staff. This department was a very important and influential organisation. Notably, it was at the forefront of the fight against communist penetration. It was possible to imagine that in his eyes, I, as a Soviet representative, was an abettor of those enemies. In the end, he was really detained in the middle of the night and held in the central prison. But in the morning, he had somehow disappeared from there. Only this ID of his had been left behind.

I remembered the prison, the poor wretches in chains. Nobody could escape from there unless someone inside, who had access to the keys, helped by removing the legcuffs and unlocking the doors.

Mahmoud stopped, and I was trying to digest what had been said.

'So, this department of his, military intelligence, was behind it...'

'No,' he interrupted me. 'I do not think that he had an official authorisation to attack you. This man was doing something illegal near your home. And he thought that you had noticed what was going on. He most probably wanted to kill you. Liquidate a witness. But you managed to scare him off, impressing on him that you live in the house of a very influential person, who, by the way, treats the teeth of the Chief of the General Staff, and he believed you that the landlord could have been at home and awake. I think you have saved your life, telling him that.'

'But what was it– what was he doing near my house?' I asked.

Mahmoud shrugged, 'I don't know. We, too, have corruption. For example, there are suspicions that some of the officers of that department may be engaged in drug trafficking under the guise of fighting the southern agents. Who knows, possibly they were delivering their consignment of heroin... Are you sure you hadn't seen anything like that when driving up to the house?'

'Absolutely nothing,' I replied. 'Nothing like that at all. It seemed to me that everybody was fast asleep; the streets looked empty.'

Sveta came back, and our candid conversation ended right then and there. I was left with the feeling that Mahmoud had another hypothesis to explain the weird episode. He had omitted essential details or maybe stopped himself short of saying something else. I cannot rule out the version that his task from the very start was to confuse and mislead me. Why? What for? Today I am none the wiser.

In any case, I have never seen either Mahmoud or the so-called Ali Nasser Muhammad again in my life.

After that, I was, in a sense, 'demoted', as the Yemeni secret service had clearly been ordered from above to keep a close eye on me, appointing a much less prominent officer for that task. Abdallah, his name was, and he was rather uncouth in comparison to Mahmoud. He didn't even speak any Russian or English.

Introduced by a mutual acquaintance, he appeared in my life rather abruptly and invited us to dinner at his place.

His residence was a typical mud hut. We had to sit on the carpeted floor. Despite the presence of Sveta, his wife wasn't allowed to eat with us and just fussed around like a servant. But, as a gesture to us, she was given permission not to cover her face, only her hair. Sinking his hardened, blackish hands into a large pot of boiled lamb, our hospitable host was kindly selecting the best cuts of meat for his guests and placing them on our soup plates. His hands, I think, were not necessarily dirty; they just seemed so. But Sveta got almost sick at the sight of it. I was nervous, too, as I had previously suffered from a nasty case of dysentery in Yemen, from which I have never fully recovered, and getting another one could have easily killed me.

Now, sitting on the floor of Abdullah's house, I was warily looking around, trying to assess the level of sanitation. In the end, I decided that the actual risk of catching another severe infection wasn't all that great, but some precautions wouldn't have been out of place. Luckily, Abdullah provided one himself (albeit for all the wrong reasons), proudly producing a bottle of Scotch. He looked at us triumphantly: what? Didn't expect it here? After all, in the country of strict prohibition, where consumption of alcohol was officially deemed a serious criminal offence, that forbidden product cost a fortune on the black market.

I presumed the bottle had been sourced from the operational fund of confiscated goods intended for loosening tongues. Anyway, that Johnny Walker came in very useful. 'Drink!' I whispered into my practically teetotal wife's ear as she was sitting on that carpet pale with fear, and in the end, she did swig a big gulp of the Scottish national drink.

We had to invite Abdullah back and treat him to a bottle of authentic Russian vodka, which he apparently liked much more than whiskey. He also looked as if he were in awe of our house, and it was pretty clear that he couldn't even dream of ever getting a dwelling like that. I am ashamed to say that at some point, Sveta and I worried that he might be driven by envy to do us some harm, in one way or another. But we were unfair to Abdullah; nothing like that happened.

Our home was indeed truly exceptional by local standards. And we were fortunate to find it. Our landlord indeed belonged to the upper echelons of the local nobility and was a dentist, trained in London. In Sana'a, he served the upper echelons of society. Therefore, he was both wealthy and influential. The house itself was built in the local traditional style, but with all modern amenities. When I stumbled on it after several months of fruitless search, my delight knew no bounds. By that time, we were close to despair, thinking that nothing more or less acceptable could ever be found. We had been living at the embassy hotel for months and, in the end, felt exhausted by that existence. The building itself, however, was palatial, a fine example of Yemeni medieval architecture. Besides, it was surrounded by a lovely park within the embassy's grounds, a rare sight in Sana'a. However, there were no separate living quarters available, so we had to live in a communal apartment with strangers. This could be quite an ordeal, even with the nicest people as neighbours, which was not always the case.

At one point, we shared the kitchen and the only bathroom with two KGB translators who, for some reason, had been temporarily seconded to Sana'a. I had no idea why their presence was required there, but after a few glasses of Armenian brandy, they freely admitted who they were working for. They did not, however, volunteer any details about the exact purpose of their assignment in the Yemen Arab Republic — and we knew better than to ask.

One of them was consistently well-mannered, impeccably polite and proper, while the other, a middle-aged Armenian with greying hair, could at times be overly familiar and a little insolent. Still, I thought he was harmless enough and was willing to make allowances for his extroverted nature. But before long, his mask slipped.

Once, he came rushing to me in a panic, begging for help to translate a text from Arabic into Russian. His difficulty, he explained, was that although he was completely fluent in the spoken dialect, he sometimes struggled to fully comprehend texts written in *al-fusha* — classical literary Arabic. He was terrified that his superiors might discover the limits of his linguistic ability.

For understandable reasons, he did not wish to turn to his colleagues for assistance and instead decided to take a serious risk by illegally showing me the classified material. My brilliant mentor, Vladimir Segal, had trained me to navigate the twists and turns of classical Arabic and to unravel its intricate puzzles, so it did not take me long to translate the relatively short report.

I had to read it from a photograph of a handwritten note using a diascope — a simple device, rather like the one I had used as a child to view coloured filmstrips. The text appeared to be an agent's secret report from Aden describing a visit by a Chinese delegation to South Yemen. Yet there was nothing special or exclusive in it that could have justified a 'secret' classification. It might just as well have been copied from a newspaper article or a news agency bulletin.

For a moment, I even suspected that the KGB translator was pulling my leg. 'What kind of spy report is this?' I asked him. But he assured me he was not joking. That left me to conclude that the KGB was wasting both its time and money on utterly useless sources.

Then another thought occurred to me — could this be some test? Perhaps they wanted to see whether I would reveal the classified information I had been shown to others, such as the Western journalists I occasionally met. But if that were the case, surely, they would have used something more substantial as bait. This so-called 'intelligence' was of no interest to anyone. Either way, it seemed an exercise in sheer bureaucratic stupidity.

In the end, I merely shrugged, completed the KGB translator's task for him, and promised to keep the entire incident secret to protect his professional reputation.

He repaid me with utter ingratitude: a couple of weeks later, he caught my wife alone in the shared kitchen, while I was in town on business, and started grabbing and molesting her with the explicit intention of forcing sexual intercourse on her. Sveta managed to defend herself with a saucepan. I had a strong urge, which lasted only a few seconds, to report the swine to his KGB bosses, telling them about his behaviour in the kitchen and maybe mentioning his recklessness with state secrets. But then I cooled down and decided against it: my highly experienced father-in-law strongly advised me to make a concerted effort to stay away from the KGB.

'Who knows what that viper could do in retaliation?' I thought. But also, I hated the idea of contributing to the atmosphere of Stalinist denunciations and talebearing that the Soviet colony in Sana'a had become mired in. For the time being, a bump on the attacker's head and a good-sized bruise that the saucepan in Sveta's hands had given him would suffice, I thought. I curtly told him face-to-face that if anything like that were to happen again, I would stop at nothing to ensure he was punished.

He was apologetic, saying that the whole episode was a misunderstanding—a silly joke that had gone wrong. But I could see hatred in his eyes and knew that he would try to find a way to make me pay for his humiliation.

Luckily, he was very soon recalled to Moscow, and meanwhile, I had a happy breakthrough finding the dentist's house. We had a separate little garden and a yard with its own gate. The entire villa was protected on all sides by a high stone wall, featuring sharp, cemented glass shards and iron blades at the top for added security. I've never seen anything like this before or since.

The dentist kept peacocks in his garden to entertain his children. My advice to everyone is: never live anywhere near these beautiful birds. Believe me, they produce disgusting, loud shrieks from early morning to late at night.

Having settled down in the new, nice house, I could concentrate on organising the proper functioning of the TASS Sana'a office, only to discover very soon that my work in North Yemen was as useful to my employer as a fifth leg to a dog (the English equivalent of this Russian expression is 'like a hole in the head'). There was nothing of political interest happening there that could be reported, as the heavily censored local press carried very little news. I wrote brief items about exciting developments, such as fluctuations in regional gas prices, among other mundane topics, which were published by one of TASS's less important news bulletins. From time to time (but not too often), I was also expected to craft disingenuously upbeat stories about joint economic projects and the exemplary work of Soviet technical advisers at local enterprises, intended for publication in the Soviet press. Generally, I felt like a temp, a stand-in (and that was indeed my position). After all, I was promised that my stint in Sana'a would be limited to one year. As it happened, it lasted twice as long.

I may have been bored to death, but the true, passionate Arabists were jealous of me. More than six thousand 'skyscrapers' built in ancient times literally cram the central districts of Sana'a.

Medieval builders developed a unique technique, using layers of loam mixed with lime mortar. These houses have stood for centuries, surviving earthquakes, fires, and wars, while more modern buildings have vanished from the face of the earth. The typical 'skyscrapers' of this kind rise to six or seven, and sometimes even eight storeys; their façades are decorated with geometric patterns made from clinker — a dense ceramic material — and white plaster. They are further adorned with yellow ochre, reflecting the lush greenery of the surrounding mountains.

Sana'a lies in a gorge at an altitude of almost two and a half thousand metres above sea level (2,300, to be precise) and has existed for roughly the same number of years. The oldest part of the city has been designated a UNESCO World Heritage Site, but this has not spared Sana'a from the severe damage inflicted by the relentless bombardments it has suffered in recent years during the brutal civil war.

But in my time, Sana'a was relatively peaceful. The high altitude shielded us from the summer heat, despite the city being located near the equatorial latitudes. It was chilly in winter, but mild enough so that we could do without heating. But for everything in life, we have to pay: in exchange for this subjective climate comfort, we had to adapt to a 30 per cent lack of oxygen in the air, experiencing shortness of breath when climbing to the third or fourth floor. The solar radiation was also significantly higher than normal. Even in our fabulous house, the cleaner was sweeping out the corners, young, white-skinned baby scorpions. We had to check our children's beds before bedtime to ensure they were free from any dangerous insects. I once caught a fearsome scolopendra in my office.

The local men wore white dishdashas, ankle-length garments with long sleeves, and carried rather scary, curved daggers called *jambiyas* on their belts. Women went out into the street dressed in niqabs, and, as far as I was concerned, it was a shame, for the Yemeni women are gorgeous. How do I know that? Well, I've had my moments. A few times, local beauties, when meeting me somewhere in a secluded place, opened their faces for a second, smiling at me and even winking. Clearly, they were driven to this mischief by utter boredom.

I also had a chance to talk to a few Russian women who had come to live in Sana'a after marrying Yemeni men. Finding themselves suddenly in this medieval tribal society must have been a terrible cultural shock. There were cases of severe nervous breakdowns and even suicides. Many fled back to the Soviet Union. But amazingly, the majority stayed put. Larisa, a 26-year-old from Ryazan, told me that, like the others, she was driven by desperation. She preferred living in a medieval mudbrick house to the oppressive atmosphere and the squalor of Soviet provincial existence.

'What was there for me to expect in my hometown? Fighting to make ends meet, queuing for hours to buy at least some basic, unhealthy food, and being regularly beaten up by a drunkard of a husband. No, seriously, all my potential suitors were heavy drinkers, without exception. And all my schoolmates, who stayed home, suffer from abuse and violence all the time. And they can't even move to Moscow or another big city, as the '*Propiska*' (mandatory residence permit) practically nails you to the place where you are registered. And there was no hope, no light at the end of the tunnel. Here I feel safer, my local hubby takes good care of me, and we can even sometimes travel to Europe.'

When I arrived in Sana'a in 1981, I was initially captivated by this exotic, medieval country with its ancient architecture, authentic culture and customs. But soon I felt I'd had enough. It was a completely alien, surreal environment, and I began to experience bouts of ennui. 'Why am I here?' I was asking myself, silently howling in response.

On May 6, 1983, I received an encoded telegram from the Director General of TASS, demanding my immediate and urgent departure to Moscow. It said: 'You have been appointed the TASS correspondent in Iraq. You should arrive in Moscow by May 9 to receive the travel documents and fly to Baghdad immediately. Losev'.

I did not doubt that it would be a challenging job, but I was still glad, as there was clearly no use for my energy, skills, and knowledge in Yemen. Maybe, I thought, my life in Iraq would be 'more exciting' (if only I knew what kind of 'fun' my Iraqi epic would turn out to be).

It was the first official encoded cable I ever got. Before that, the ambassador sometimes signed other such telegrams for me to peruse; those were typically directives coming from the Central Committee or the Ministry of Foreign Affairs, concerning journalistic affairs, and I went to read them in the so-called '*referentura*' – a soundproof bunker inside the embassy, protected from all kinds of eavesdropping. But this time it was different: the telegram was addressed to me personally, and I may have taken it too literally, too seriously, as if it were a state decree, obligatory for execution at any cost. Aeroflot flew to Sana'a only once a week, and it was not possible to return to Moscow on a direct flight by the dates indicated in the official missive. Therefore, I flew to Aden with a local airline, and there I boarded the Soviet plane.

The funniest thing, though, happened on my arrival at Sheremetyevo Airport in Moscow: it transpired that my blue 'service' passport was invalid, as it had expired. Neither Sana'a's nor Aden's border guards noticed this as I was waved through the controls. Neither *Yemenia* nor Aeroflot paid any attention to my passport when issuing my boarding passes.

In line with the Soviet rules, my passport had been kept in the Soviet consulate in Sana'a until the very last moment (to make it more difficult to defect, I presume), and I got hold of it only on my way to the airport. The document was handed to me personally by the same *courageous* Soviet consul, a KGB officer, who took more than forty minutes to respond to my distress call during the nighttime attack at the gates of my house. Remarkably, this presumably highly trained intelligence agent failed to notice that the passport was invalid. Moreover, it was he who marked the passport with the *'Vyezd do'* ('the departure before the date...') stamp, which indicated the last day I would have been allowed to leave the USSR again.

Thank God, the new generation of Russian citizens has no idea what this stamp was for. It was actually a Soviet exit visa, a significant and poignant symbol of our lives at that time. It was another instrument of control: what if the holder of the document lost the authorities' trust during his travels? It was a clear case of belt-and-braces policy, as the passport was always taken away from you immediately upon arrival, making it impossible to hold on to it until only a couple of days remained before your approved departure. Meanwhile, the need to get this exit visa every time you had to travel on official business created a lot of inconvenience. I recall what a feat it was when journalists specialising in international affairs were allowed to obtain multi-year exit visas during the years of *Perestroika*. Now it was possible, in case of some urgent development abroad, to fly there quickly, without spending several days or even weeks waiting for the cherished stamp in your passport.

Luckily, I wasn't arrested, just reprimanded by stern and scary Soviet border guards who warned me that I could come to serious grief if something like that ever happened again. In the end, it didn't take them too long to confirm my identity.

Back at TASS, I was issued a new passport, already stamped with the Soviet exit and Iraqi entry visas. Thus began the toughest and most challenging period of my life — the most difficult test I ever had to endure.

Later, I would think of it as a leap into a whirlpool in which I nearly drowned. The Iraqi experience dazed and abraded me so profoundly that I emerged from it a different person — more mature, perhaps, but also somewhat damaged.

I have already written about those events in some detail in the previous chapters. I would like to add, however, that the genre of this book could probably be described by the fashionable term 'coming-of-age' — the drama of growing up. My favourite writer, Yuri Trifonov, believed that ageing is a gradual loss of the capacity to be surprised. I was so overwhelmed by my Iraqi experience that, by the end of it, I felt as though I had lived through decades, becoming a much older and far sadder human being — truly, much less capable of being surprised by anything.

Still, what happened to me, to *Izvestia*, to the country, and to the world at the end of 1991 and the beginning of 1992 could not have failed to astonish even the most omniscient and utterly cynical observer.

Chapter Twelve

Return to the Promised Land

It's amusing how great historic events can sometimes produce unexpected personal consequences. It was due to the failure of the August 1991 coup d'état that I found myself in October of the same year at the legendary King David Hotel in Jerusalem. I wouldn't have been there if the putschists had prevailed. Just two months ago, I was sadly saying goodbye to my beloved *Izvestia* and preparing to move to an American agency. But those three days in August upended everything most incredibly. The putsch faded away, the Communist Party dissolved into thin air, and the KGB also temporarily disappeared, hiding itself in deep cracks. A peaceful revolution took place in my favourite newspaper, too. The informal leader of our liberal grouping, Igor Golembiovsky, became the editor-in-chief, and I was appointed the paper's Foreign Editor. While the newspaper was undergoing a restructuring, I accepted an invitation from the new Soviet Foreign Minister, Boris Pankin, to witness a historic event: the restoration of diplomatic relations with Israel. Jerusalem gave me quite a shock. In psychiatry, there is a term known as 'Jerusalem syndrome'. Many people suffer from it. Once there, they feel as though some energy field influences them; under its impact, they become feverish, their heart rate quickens, they feel dizzy, and in extreme cases, they may even experience hallucinations. I did not quite reach such a state. Still, as I looked at Jerusalem from the Mount of Olives – where, according to biblical legend, the Ascension of Christ is said to have taken place – I couldn't help but feel excited. It was as if the view had been permanently imprinted on my memory, and from that moment on, I could always close my eyes and see it again whenever I wished. You cannot help but be moved when you realise that Christ, Pontius Pilate, and Joseph Caiaphas, the high priest of the Jews, all once looked upon almost the same landscape. Later, I visited the Holy Land many times and once even had the opportunity to stay in Bethlehem, the birthplace of Christ, in the luxurious villa of a

Palestinian Orthodox grandee, who was the landlord of a vast estate. I came to him in a state of severe fatigue, with a serious heart problem. He sent for an Arab doctor, who, however, graduated from the medical faculty of an Israeli university. He quickly put my arrhythmia under control and, most importantly, explained the problem and how to avoid the recurrence of this unpleasant and dangerous condition that had been haunting me for years.

While staying in Bethlehem, we visited one of the most famous and ancient churches in the world – the Basilica of the Nativity of Christ. The one built above the cave where Jesus was born. In its original form, it was constructed between 327 and 330 under the Roman Emperor Constantine the Great and his mother, Elena. This is the same emperor who ended the persecution of Christians, converted to Christianity himself, and effectively founded Byzantium by relocating his residence to the East.

There is an interesting version explaining his choice. According to some sources, the main reason was the fear of the gods' punishment for the murder he committed. The gods of the Roman and the Greek pantheons did not forgive such a thing. But Christianity, people in the know told him, was the only religion that allowed you to repent and get forgiveness for any sin. Perhaps one of the acts of repentance was the construction of a temple over the birthplace of Christ.

Paradoxically, if not for the mortal sin of the emperor, the fate of Christianity could have been very different. And it might not have prevailed in Byzantium, and therefore Russia would not necessarily be a Christian country or, at least, hardly Orthodox ...

But these are all subjunctive inclinations that neither historians nor theologians are willing to tolerate.

The basilica survived all the wars, assaults, earthquakes and fires, weathering the Arab, Persian and Ottoman conquests. Muslims, who consider Jesus a minor prophet compared to Mohammed, did not destroy the church, but turned a part of it into a mosque for a while. Later, however, under the Ottomans, the whole building was returned to the Christian church. Nevertheless, after the fire of 529, it had to be rebuilt, but some parts of the original edifice remained; the most stunning of these are the mosaic floors, carefully covered with wooden slabs.

But since then – that is, for a thousand and a half years, imagine it! – the basilica has remained intact. Kingdoms have risen and fallen, cities have been built and destroyed, nations have come and gone, vanishing forever into the mists of history — yet the basilica has withstood it all. The interior of the temple is austere and authentic, reflecting the original appearance of early churches. But you can spot a phenomenal icon on one of the walls. It was painted in Russia, in violation of the canon. They say it is the only one in the world that depicts the Mother of God smiling.

In October 1991, however, I did not have time for sightseeing. At night, I slept at the King David, while during the day I moved quickly, running after Pankin, writing reports on what was happening, and then sending them to *Izvestia*. Most of the time, I would dictate my texts to the stenographers over the phone. It was also possible to use telex; as a former TASS employee, I didn't find punching the paper tape difficult. Nowadays, such methods of communication seem ridiculous, archaic, the stuff of museums. None of us could have imagined at the time that the world was on the threshold of an information revolution that would change it unrecognizably in just a few years.

That was my second trip to Israel. I managed to visit the country earlier, in 1988. That was a much more relaxed and unhurried journey, during which I could enjoy the views, speak with priests, monks, and nuns, and take in every detail at a leisurely pace as I wandered through the Church of the Holy Sepulchre.

My first trip to the Holy Land was considered a sensation in the USSR. As for me, it wouldn't be an exaggeration to say that it was one of my life's main discoveries. I had long dreamt of it. *Izvestia* was also very interested in getting journalistic reports from Israel. But the country was still something like a forbidden land; it wasn't possible to send a correspondent there, the Central Committee's permission was still required. My super-influential colleague Alexander Bovin, with his phenomenal connections at the top, somehow managed to make his way there a couple of times. But officially, he went there not as a journalist, but as a member of some public delegation.

Suddenly, a plausible pretext presented itself: the Palestinian newspaper *Al-Quds*, published in East Jerusalem, invited journalists from *Izvestia* and *Novosti* to visit its headquarters. The Arabs, of course, had their own propagandistic motives. In East Jerusalem and across the West Bank, the so-called *Intifada* — a Palestinian campaign of civil disobedience — was underway. However, it had already gone far beyond the boundaries of a purely civil movement, resulting in frequent outbreaks of violence.

The pattern was always the same: groups of Arab boys would commit acts of vandalism, and when the police arrived, the boys would begin throwing stones at them. In response, law enforcement officers would fire rubber bullets and use tear gas. Soon, adult Palestinians would join the clashes, and inevitably there would be injuries — sometimes even deaths — on both sides. The Palestinians would then present these incidents to the world as 'atrocities of the occupiers', sparking a fierce international information war. In reality, as is often the case in such conflicts, it was not always easy to distinguish between victims and aggressors.

The newspaper that had invited us hoped to use our visit to promote its version of events. Not long ago, the Palestinians would never have felt the need to spend energy or resources convincing their 'Soviet friends', who had always unconditionally supported their cause. But times were changing. Although the Soviet Union still had no formal diplomatic relations with Israel, a Soviet consular group was now operating in Tel Aviv within the Finnish embassy. Moscow also maintained contacts with Arafat, who had returned from the political cold after a period of ostracism, though he could only look back with nostalgia on the hugs and kisses he had once shared with Brezhnev.

In this context, someone at *Al-Quds* evidently thought it worthwhile to invite a pair of Russian journalists to Jerusalem, hoping they could be persuaded to see events through Palestinian eyes.

I felt a little guilty in advance, assuming that I would probably disappoint the expectations of the hospitable hosts. I was trying to find some comfort in promising myself that I would try to be as honest and objective as possible in everything I was going to write as a result of the trip, always being on the side of the suffering human beings, be they Jews or Palestinians. On the other hand, I thought it was high time for our colleagues from *Al-Quds* to understand the profound changes occurring in the USSR and to recognise that *Izvestia* had become a very different newspaper from what it used to be, and that we were no longer thoughtless Soviet propagandists.

To give our Arab hosts credit, they did not object when my colleague, Volodya Kedrov of *Novosti*, and I suggested we spend at least one day in Tel Aviv as well, talking to Soviet diplomats and Israelis there. They did not show us their frustration, and they even agreed to take us there. We also had planned a visit to the Israeli Foreign Ministry in Jerusalem, which the Palestinians also had to accept.

In the not-so-distant past, this would have caused an enormous scandal. But now I was discovering that not everyone at *Al-Quds* was a stubborn fanatic. There were also some thinking people there who understood that the Palestinians had to get rid of illusions that with the help of the USSR and China, it would be possible one day to break the Israelis and make them accept all the demands of the PLO, meaning the end of the Jewish state. These people realised that sooner or later they would have to recognise the right of Israel to exist, and only then would they be able to count on the creation of an Arab state alongside it.

But that first evening, our hosts' hospitality was put to the test.

We landed at Ben-Gurion Airport in the late afternoon. The welcoming party consisted of two *Al-Quds* staffers who drove us to Jerusalem in a car. I was looking out of the vehicle's window excitedly. Everything was interesting: the houses, the vegetation, and even the colour of the soil along the highway seemed unusual, glowing with a hint of deep red. On the left-hand side, we could clearly see the triumphant victory humans had achieved over the insidious desert, as the land had been lovingly and painstakingly cultivated here. Volodya and I were both astonished as we had been fed an obvious myth that the Jews were hopeless city dwellers and poor farmers, a myth which was being disproved in front of our own eyes.

The landscape should have been familiar, I told myself, since this was still the Middle East. The Lebanon that I knew pretty well was just a few hours' drive away. Yet everything around us seemed somehow different, special, extraordinary — perhaps because of the thrilling realisation that this was the Promised Land, made all the more mysterious for the Soviet journalists by the fact that, for us, it was also a Forbidden Land. It was an off-limits destination, practically another planet, another dimension. It was a vortex into which some of our fellow countrymen would occasionally vanish, disappearing from our lives forever — compatriots in whom just enough Jewish blood had been found, and whom the ever-vigilant KGB had, astonishingly, permitted to leave the Soviet fortress.

It was already dusk when we reached Jerusalem. Our Palestinian hosts felt obliged to offer us a welcoming dinner. But where? One of the features of the *intifada* was constant strikes, in which shopkeepers and traders participated. Some of them, in fact, nearly all of them, worked only in the mornings. In the evenings, Arab East Jerusalem looked dead. In vain, our hosts drove long distances in their old Toyota — one moment squeezing through narrow medieval streets, the next heading out into the wilderness, through semi-pastoral areas. They were becoming increasingly desperate as every place they thought of turned out to be closed.

'What about Abu Khalil?' one of them would suggest. 'Or that Egyptian place, *Al-Qahirah* — perhaps it's still open?' But no such luck. One hope after another was dashed; there was absolutely nowhere to eat. Even grocery stores and other food shops were closed.

Then one of the hosts had an idea: why not go to the hotel where the rooms for the Soviet guests had been booked? Apparently, there was a small restaurant there — surely it would still be serving meals for the residents. The choice might not be great, but it would certainly be better than nothing. 'We won't let you go hungry, insha'Allah!' ('With God's help,' literally, 'if Allah allows it.').

But Allah did not allow it. The hotel restaurant was also closed. 'Please, do us a favour and open it for our guests from faraway Russia. Give them anything that might be left in the kitchen,' our hosts pleaded. But the hotel attendants only shook their heads in reply. 'We would be glad to help, but we can't. The chef has gone, the restaurant is locked, and nothing can be done.'

The faces of our Palestinian colleagues have become an expression of despair. Volodya Kedrov and I felt sorry for them; we tried to assure them, not quite sincerely, that we were not hungry, that we had been well fed on a Cyprus Airways plane (in the absence of diplomatic relations, there were no direct flights from Moscow at the time and we had to make a transfer in Larnaca). No, no, that's out of the question! This was the reply we received from our hosts.

They started whispering to each other, and we guessed they were discussing the possibility of inviting us home for a meal. However, that was clearly ruled out, too, as there were crying kids, pregnant wives, and sick relatives that made it an impossible proposition. But then our hosts suddenly had another idea, prompting them to assume facial expressions of heroic determination.

'Come what may, we will have dinner in half an hour!' one of them solemnly declared. And off we went – across the invisible border between the two worlds. In a surreal contrast to the empty, bleak part of the town we had been criss-crossing for the last two hours, this Jerusalem was full of life, buzzing and bubbling. The streets were full of people and cars, with the lights of advertising and restaurant signs shining all around us. We could even hear music coming from somewhere. Kedrov and I didn't believe our eyes: we ended up in western, Jewish Jerusalem!

The duty of hospitality prevailed over politics and deep-rooted hard feelings towards the Israelis. Our Palestinians clearly were not happy with the prospect of seeking 'enemy's food', but from the two evils, they chose the lesser one, as leaving their guests hungry was deemed the worst. Just so.

But the first place they considered didn't suit them. Nor the second one. The third and fourth were rejected as well. What exactly are they looking for? We were wondering, but didn't dare to ask because we didn't want to embarrass them further. Sitting in the back seat of that Toyota, we could only exchange puzzled glances. Even discussing our predicament aloud didn't seem like a good idea, as one of our hosts was a graduate of a Soviet university and understood Russian quite well.

Only in hindsight did we guess what it was that our Palestinian friends were looking for: they were desperately trying to find an eatery which would look the least obviously Jewish.

They found what they were seeking – or so it seemed. It was a restaurant called *Bangkok*, and it surely specialised in Thai cuisine. At the entrance, we were met by a man of a pronounced Mongoloid appearance; he may have been Thai, Korean, or Chinese, but clearly not Jewish. Inside, every single waiter had also originated from Southeast Asia. Our Palestinian hosts seemed relieved. I don't remember what Volodya chose, but I was ready to eat anything, as long as it wasn't too fiery hot. The waiters brought metal pails with a fire burning inside, heating the grill at the top. A rather attractive smell of chicken emanated from those contraptions, although maybe anything would have seemed appetising to me at that moment. At least it all looked spectacular. Our hosts didn't order any alcohol, nor did it occur to us to ask for it.

No sooner had we had a chance to try anything than we saw an apparition coming into sight from the service corridor. He was a large, red-haired man in his forties. He had a large Semitic nose, and there was no hint of anything Mongoloid in his appearance.

'Probably, this is the owner,' I said in Russian. One of our escorts turned around and stared at the redhead without any pleasure while the latter was examining the hall. His glance stopped at our table. He looked astonished. Clearly, our strange party could not fail to provoke surprise. To begin with, two obvious Palestinians – what were they doing in the midst of the *intifada* in the depths of the Jewish part of Jerusalem? Were they really so desperate for a bite of oriental cuisine at night? Secondly, and this seemed even more weird – what are those two Europeans, quite formally dressed, doing in their company? We didn't look like repatriates.

The restaurant's owner made a decisive move towards our table. It turned out that he had heard me speak and understood what I was saying.

'I am sorry,' he said with a strong Georgian accent, 'did I hear wrong, or did you speak Russian?'

He told us he was a Jew, a native of Kutaisi, Georgia's third-most-populous city, who emigrated to Israel fifteen years ago. The fact that we had just arrived from Moscow, but not as part of the Jewish repatriation, that we were Soviet journalists, seemed absolutely incredible to him.

'I can't believe it, I simply can't!' he was saying joyfully, ardently gesticulating in a typically Georgian way. He was not sure about *Novosti*, but he knew the word *Izvestia*.

'My father used to read *Izvestia*, we were subscribed to it, yes!' he exclaimed. 'Do you really work there? I can't believe it, I will tell my wife, she won't believe it either!'

He then quickly assessed the choice of dishes on our table and said:

'Pooh! You ordered everything wrong. I know what you would really like.'

With those words, he called the waiters and started giving out some incomprehensible commands, spouting unpronounceable names of unknown dishes. An incredible fuss ensued around our table; the chicken and iron pails were taken away – I followed them with wistful eyes. Something else, exotic and mysterious, was brought in its place. The food was too spicy for me, but I managed to eat something nonetheless. Then, the moment of high drama arrived: the owner brought out a bottle of Johnny Walker and placed it on our table.

He disappeared for a while, then returned, waving his hands and laughing — delighted like an excited boy. He asked questions about Moscow, which he had visited only once, in early childhood. He hinted that he would be genuinely pleased if his restaurant were mentioned in *Izvestia*. I tried to politely sidestep the suggestion. The story, in truth, was more than worthy of publication, but I felt uneasy about causing our Palestinian hosts any further embarrassment. As it was, they sat there with stony expressions, eating almost nothing. Kedrov and I had a little whisky, but our companions, as I recall, didn't touch it. They were clearly eager to bring the awkward meal to an end, and my colleague and I were only too glad to oblige.

'Can we have the bill, please?' one of the Palestinians said. But the red-haired Jew was firm — there would be no bill.

'You are my guests,' he declared.

'Please, we insist... we want to pay,' the Palestinians protested, growing increasingly agitated. But the owner refused to hear of it.

To sum up what happened: on our first day in Palestine, we were treated to a free meal by a Jew, an Israeli; moreover, our Arab companions had to accept his hospitality against their will. They felt humiliated. They quickly exchanged several phrases with each other, discussing, I guessed, the suggestion to throw money on the table. Fortunately, in the end, they decided against it, realising that such an offensive gesture would have been highly embarrassing for us, their guests. We thanked the redhead, shook his hand and wished him good luck. While we were saying good-byes, the Palestinians were sulking, waiting for us outside the restaurant.

In total silence, they drove us back to the hotel, only to wish us goodnight at the last moment.

While discussing the events of the day, Volodya and I concluded that the phrases 'We have just come from Moscow' and 'We are Russian journalists' could have a magical impact on some owners of Israeli restaurants and snack bars. We took advantage of this discovery only once more. It happened in Tel Aviv, at lunchtime, when we accidentally found ourselves at a small place where the owner was another redheaded Georgian Jew. We talked to him in Russian, and the same thing happened again: he treated us to a good meal and categorically refused to take any money. Now, with visa-free tourism between Russia and Israel and vast numbers of people moving daily in both directions, it's hard to imagine that there were times when the appearance of Moscow correspondents could cause a sensation and excitement. And it wasn't just about restaurateurs of Georgian origin; our visit to the Israeli Foreign Ministry and other official organisations was clearly perceived as an important event. So, we might have also made a small contribution to the restoration of bilateral relations.

A series of articles I published in *Izvestia* upon my return was well received by Israeli diplomats in Moscow who worked under the Dutch Embassy's roof. The head of the group called me to express approval. This is an impartial publication, she said. I was very pleased to hear it, as it demonstrated the Israelis' objectivity, among other things. I didn't try to please anybody in my pieces. I wrote in some detail about my meetings with the Palestinians, some of whom I thought were quite sensible people. I conveyed conversations with representatives of the left-wing Zionist movement, genuine liberals for whom human rights were a fundamental principle and who were prepared to defend Palestinian Arabs, including their right to self-determination. For Volodya and me, these conversations were particularly important as we had received clear proof that Zionism was just a movement for the right of the Jewish State to exist in the ancestral homeland, not some fictional, sinister international conspiracy to subjugate peoples of the world to the will of '*The Elders of Zion*' as we were taught to believe in the Soviet era.

I also wrote about the most disturbing state of affairs in the Palestinian refugee camps in the West Bank. I was troubled not only by the harsh material and psychological conditions in which many thousands of people lived, although their suffering was impossible to ignore. But what disturbed me even more was the atmosphere of intense hatred that I sensed there. The walls of the camps were covered with virulent graffiti calling for the destruction of Israel and the killing of Jews. The slogan 'Death to Israel!' was everywhere. It became clear to me that the new generation that grew up in those horrible conditions knew nothing else and did not want to know. There was no positive program. Even the idea of their own independent state was secondary; it interested these young people less than the primary purpose, the fervent dream of destroying the Jewish state, wiping it off the face of the earth.

Among the prosperous Arab middle class living in their own well-appointed homes in the West Bank, I met several reasonable individuals with whom we had the opportunity to converse. They told us that their lives had become incomparably better after these territories were brought under Israeli control. It was much worse, they said, when Jordan was in charge there, both materially and in terms of security: the police and the Jordanian *Mukhabarat* would seize a few locals every night. There would never be any trial or investigation, and those people often disappeared forever. Those who had seen a lot, and most importantly, who had been economically successful, understood the inevitability of finding some compromise to create an independent Palestinian state that would exist in parallel with Israel. But those young, down-and-out, destitute dwellers of the camps did not want to hear about it.

I raised this issue with officials at the Israeli Foreign Ministry. I said, 'Look, I understand — you've washed your hands of it, and it's now the UN and other international organisations that oversee the camps. But these places have become breeding grounds for hatred, where an entire generation of terrorist fanatics is clearly being raised. You shouldn't simply stand by and watch this happen. Forget about human rights for a moment and think about your own security.'

But it fell on deaf ears.

Of course, I was not the only one who sounded the alarm. And Israel is not the only party to blame for what followed. The entire Western world was shamefully, even criminally, blind to the rise of jihadism. Other factors also played a role in this, especially the Afghan war that the Kremlin's gerontocrats started pointlessly. But the poisonous seeds grown in those camps with the general connivance of all have yielded their terrible fruits. Hamas took control of the Gaza Strip and became a powerful force in the West Bank as well. It is impossible to reach an agreement with the generation that grew up in those camps.

Why did Arafat give up the Camp David's great compromise at the last moment, missing a real opportunity to establish an independent Palestinian State in most of the territories occupied in 1967? Why hasn't his successor, Abu Mazen, who had a reputation for being a much more accommodating negotiator, lived up to the expectations? The answer to these questions was to be found in those camps. The virus of blind hatred cultivated there infected Palestinian public opinion, causing it to become extremely radicalised and increasingly inclined towards the position of Hamas. The PLO leaders had already lost influence because of their more moderate stance. They believed that any further steps towards Israel could cost them their positions — or their lives; they would be overthrown or removed from power. The result was a stalemate, and I fear that this generation will not see progress in the Middle East conflict. But at the time, in those naïve and optimistic years at the end of the Cold War, everything seemed possible.

The Palestinians did not react to my publications; I'm afraid they were not particularly happy with my writings, and I didn't receive any further invitations from them. In Moscow, there was no official reaction to my articles, but I heard that Alexander Yakovlev, the architect of *Glasnost*, liked them. At the same time, the leader of the Stalinist faction in the CPSU Central Committee, Gennadiy Zyuganov, was irritated with what he saw as my 'pro-Zionist stance'. I don't know what the Soviet (officially Finnish) diplomats in Tel Aviv thought of my effort.

Shortly before we visited the Promised Land, a new, large section opened at the Embassy of Finland in Israel; in fact, it was the Soviet consular group. But their work wasn't confined to visa issues. It was an unofficial mini-embassy of the USSR. When I entered their premises, I almost burst out laughing: it was amusing to see our typical fellow countrymen working and speaking Russian under the Finnish flag and the portrait of the Finnish president. What, I thought, was this comedy for?

How many spies were there among them? Certainly, there were some, as they were always present everywhere and at all times in the Soviet state. After all, this was one of its fundamental characteristics.

Three years were left before the complete restoration of diplomatic relations, which were broken off by the USSR in 1967, ostensibly as a gesture of solidarity with the Arabs. In fact, the main reason for the breakup was the sense of resentment and humiliation felt by the Soviet establishment. In June that year, the Arab countries were preparing to start a war to destroy Israel. The USSR aided and abetted the Arabs, arming them to the teeth and training their military personnel. But Israel managed to strike a pre-emptive blow. During the six-day war, the Arab armies were crushed, and their aircraft and artillery were practically wiped out. It was a terrible blow for the Soviet military. They perceived it as their own defeat and a victory for the 'main adversary' – the United States, which fully supported Israel. The generals were pushing for direct involvement in the war on the side of the Arabs, but Brezhnev would not allow it. As a consolation, the hawks in Moscow were thrown a political bone - the severance of diplomatic relations with Tel Aviv. From the point of view of Soviet political interests, that decision made no sense. Brezhnev instinctively understood it and several times attempted to raise the subject of restoring relations, but encountered serious resistance. Rumours started making the rounds in the Central Committee corridors that the General Secretary had a strange soft spot for the Jews: could it be that he himself had some Jewish ancestry? Then somebody came up with an explanation: it was all about his wife, Victoria Petrovna. Indeed, those who were prepared to stretch their imagination somewhat could discern some possible Semitic features in the appearance of Brezhnev's ageing wife. But it was total hogwash, of course, Brezhnev's feeble attempts to question the wisdom of severing ties with the Jewish state were just the expression of elementary common sense, of which the general secretary wasn't totally devoid. Why deprive yourself of a channel of communication with a very important actor on the international scene?

Brezhnev's power was far from absolute. He did not make any hasty moves and tried not to antagonise the rest of the Politburo members and the security forces, especially the military. He had to be cautious about possible improvements in the Soviet relations with Israel. The General Secretary has managed to press through, though, a directive allowing some clandestine contacts with Israelis through Evgeniy Primakov, who was deemed irreplaceable for such sensitive tasks. Those contacts took place from 1971 to 1977 in Vienna, and Primakov even secretly visited Israel a couple of times. Like so many of Primakov's promising secret missions, this one came to nothing, too — as did his efforts to reconcile the Kurds with Saddam and Damascus with Baghdad. Not because he lacked ability, but because secret diplomacy seldom bears fruit.

When Boris Pankin left for Israel in October 1991, Gorbachev allegedly left the final decision on restoring relations to Pankin's discretion. He was supposed to take into account the reaction of

Arabs, including Palestinians. But it soon became clear from hints dropped by Pankin's entourage that the minister was determined to go down in history as someone who achieved a breakthrough and finally restored full diplomatic ties.

Just think of it: for that to happen, the August putsch had to fail, weakening the iron grip of the KGB, the Central Committee, and the reactionary part of the Foreign Ministry on Soviet policy. Meanwhile, without fully-fledged diplomatic relations with one of the parties to the conflict, Moscow couldn't play a serious role in the search for a settlement. But for many years, nobody dared to correct the idiotic mistake made in 1967. After Primakov's failure, any attempts to re-establish ties with the Israelis ceased for a long time. They did not resume until many years later, under Gorbachev. My old acquaintance, Gennady Tarasov, a councillor of the Soviet Mission to the United Nations, was quietly conducting secret negotiations with Israelis on behalf of Shevardnadze.

It would seem truly bizarre that, while the restoration of relations with Israel was supported by both the head of the Foreign Ministry and Gorbachev's principal adviser, Anatoly Chernyaev, Gorbi still did not dare to take the final step. But why?

Allegedly, he feared a sharply adverse reaction from Arab countries and the PLO. For many years, the Soviet leader had been seeking an opportune moment to 'sell' the restoration of relations with their enemy to the Arabs, ideally timed to coincide with moves that could be presented as a breakthrough in the Middle Eastern settlement. But in reality, it was but a lame excuse and self-deception. The absence of direct contacts with the Israelis, on the contrary, hindered the search for any breakthroughs. Besides, the Arab world 'forgave' Western Europe, Japan, Latin America and many other countries for maintaining relations with Israel, why then wouldn't Moscow have been 'forgiven'? When diplomatic ties were finally restored, the sky did not fall, and nothing much changed in Moscow's relationship with Arab countries either.

In general, the presence of a foreign embassy signifies nothing extraordinary; it is simply a necessary institution of modern civilisation, without which the effective regulation of international affairs would be impossible. The USSR, after all, maintained diplomatic relations with Hitler's Germany and other hostile states in its time — and there was nothing remarkable about that. But Israel's case was indeed special. But why? Why this almost irrational resistance of the 'deep state', which Gorbachev could not or did not dare to overcome for such a long time? How can we explain the strength of this resistance?

I think much had converged in the 'Israeli issue' for the Soviet system. In 1967, Moscow decided to put its stake solely on the Arabs. Together with them, the USSR went all-in, hoping to defeat Israel and harm its strategic ally, the United States. This goal became an obsession for some military and establishment hawks, serving as existential proof of the viability of the Soviet system. Such an achievement would have demonstrated that, despite lagging behind Western economies, the USSR remained a powerful force capable of triumphing against its 'main adversary', as the KGB, GRU, and the Central Committee officially referred to the United States. Billions of roubles and dollars have been spent, thrown into the furnace for this purpose. The money was used to arm Egypt, Syria, Iraq to the teeth, to support and train the military from these countries and Palestinian fighters. For the sake of this confrontation, the quality of life of the Soviet population was sacrificed for decades, as these billions could have been used to raise their living standards. And what, to admit now that all this was in vain? In 1973, after another defeat of the Arabs in the war with Israel, the irritated Brezhnev again returned to this topic, talking about the desirability of restoring relations with the Jewish state. But sensing the hostile reaction from Andrei Gromyko, the military, and the security forces, he chose to remain silent again.

But there was another underlying reason for the endless delays — the deep-rooted, incurable anti-Semitism inherent in the party and security forces of the USSR, which, since Stalin's time, had become an extra gene in the Soviet DNA.

Quite often, pathological hatred of Jews is a sign of a severe mental disorder characterised by bitterness and obsession. I have encountered individuals who are completely consumed by the so-called 'Jewish question', thinking about it constantly, viewing every aspect of the world through this distorted lens. This condition can be found globally. However, in the Soviet Union, anti-Semitism became almost indistinguishable from Soviet patriotism, effectively turning into a kind of ideological creed. Yet, despite its prevalence, it was only ever acknowledged in hushed tones and disguised under the official label of 'anti-Zionism'.

When Pankin was signing an agreement in Tel Aviv to exchange diplomatic representations, I found it hard to believe my own eyes. It was not only a major international event, but also an earthquake, an act of catharsis, a sign that Russia (then still nominally part of the USSR) was finally free from a dark delusion. In a sense, it was the end of Soviet power.

Only in retrospect did it occur to me that all the hints suggesting the issue of signing the agreement had not been settled before Pankin's visit might have been mere camouflage — or perhaps a tactic designed to flatter the Arabs a little. By that time, the USSR had already decided to act as one of the sponsors of the Madrid Peace Conference on the Middle East. It would be absurd to try to play such an important role without having diplomatic relations with one of the parties to the conflict. The conference was due to open at the end of October 1991, and there were only a few days remaining.

I didn't know then that one year later, fate would bring me into contact with Boris Pankin in London, where, after the collapse of the Soviet Union, he would serve as the Russian ambassador. He was an interesting figure: a longtime, successful editor of the daily newspaper Komsomolskaya Pravda who later became the head of the Copyright Protection Agency. There, he came into conflict with the party bureaucracy and the KGB. After that, he was sent into honourable exile to Sweden as an ambassador. Then, when his old pal Gorbachev came to power, he was moved to Prague. That's where he had his hour of glory, gaining world fame for his open, direct condemnation of the putsch in August 1991, which he called an illegal coup d'état. No other Soviet ambassador dared to do so. My friend Sasha Ivanov-Galitsyn was the only Soviet diplomat to denounce the putsch earlier; I have already written about this brave act, which gave me moral support at the most difficult moment. However, Sasha was only a councillor at the Soviet Embassy in London, and his condemnation occurred during a brief, impromptu BBC interview, while Pankin spoke at a specially convened press conference attended by correspondents from all major international media outlets. Generally, an ambassador's word carried much more weight. My father-in-law, who had already retired by that time, was frankly pondering aloud what he would have done if he were in Pankin's place. He self-effacingly admitted that maybe he would not have dared to take such a brave, desperate step, although all his sympathies were, of course, on the side of Gorbachev and Yeltsin. But why, he wondered, did many Soviet ambassadors hurry to support the coup d'état, rushing to appointments with local officials to read them the putschists' statement? 'I would have procrastinated as much as I possibly could under whatever excuse, hoping that Gorbachev would come back and the putsch would be defeated,' my father-in-law was saying.

The fact was that an average Soviet ambassador had no doubts: the new Stalinist regime would hold power for a long time. Only Pankin had the courage and integrity to go against the grain. Moreover, quite a few among the ambassadors were simply delighted with the prospects of restoring 'good old order'.

Together with Pankin, his deputy, Alexander Lebedev also took part in that fateful press conference. Previously, he had held major positions in the Central Committee and was a key figure in the liberal faction, being closely associated with the architect of *Glasnost*, Alexander Yakovlev. It was Lebedev who stunned me one autumn evening of 1988, when he personally phoned me at home and politely asked me if I would mind doing some unofficial work for his department (including a bit of speechwriting). It came out of the blue. I hadn't even met him by then; I was just a special correspondent of *Izvestia,* and he was the deputy head of a very important Central Committee department. It seemed he and his boss, Yakovlev, liked my articles in *Izvestia*. The call and what followed played a significant role in the further zigzags and turns of my life.

After the coup failed, Pankin received a phenomenal reward: he was appointed Minister of Foreign Affairs of the USSR, replacing Alexander Bessmertnykh, who had been dismissed for collaborating with the coup plotters. Lebedev was also rewarded handsomely, becoming the Soviet ambassador to Prague. But it is essential to acknowledge that neither Pankin nor Lebedev could have foreseen how the coup would ultimately unfold. In fact, logic and all previous experience indicated that the conspirators would be victorious. Everything was on their side: the army, the KGB, the police, and the still robust network of party organisations. To this day, their defeat seems to me something of a miracle. Their inability to hold on to the power that was already within their grasp was further evidence of the profound decline and degradation of Soviet institutions. However, from the outside, the arches of the rotten building looked quite solid, and no one could have imagined that they would collapse from a slight push. Those within the system who dared to resist the coup did so not out of self-interest or in the hope of advancing their careers; on the contrary, they did so at considerable personal risk. It was a courageous act, fraught with danger to their lives and freedom.

From Israel, I flew on Pankin's official plane to Paris, then back to Moscow. I was met at Vnukovo-2 Airport by a black limousine sent by *Izvestia,* and the driver handed me a new blue service passport, which was already stamped with a Spanish visa. The next day, I had to fly to Madrid, where a historic international conference on the Middle East was scheduled to open.

Part Four

SPY CHIEFS AT CLOSE QUARTERS

Chapter Thirteen

Fisher of Men

I was settling into my hotel room in Madrid when the phone rang.

'Mr Ostalski, this is Ivan Sergeyev,' said a suave voice. 'I am a member of the Soviet delegation at the Middle East peace conference. Could I, please, ask you to be in your room at seven o'clock precisely this evening?'

'Eh? At seven pm? Well, yes... I suppose so, don't see any problems with that,' I answered somewhat wonderingly. 'But why? Will you, please, explain yourself?'

'I would not like to go into details right now, but I hope we will not cause you any inconvenience if we ask you for such a favour?'

'No,' I said, still puzzled. 'It will not be difficult.'

'That's fine, then, we are very grateful to you,' said Sergeyev and hung up.

'I wonder,' I thought. 'Who are those 'we'? The Soviet delegation?'

In fact, I suspected I knew which specific part of the delegation Mr Sergeyev was referring to.

Exactly at seven pm sharp, the phone rang again in the room. And the same voice said: 'Good evening, Mr Ostalski, will you kindly come down to the reception, please?'

I came down into the hotel's lobby. Near the reception desk, a stranger approached me, smiling and, shaking my hand, said:

'Vyacheslav Ivanovich would like to invite you to dinner at a good restaurant. He hopes you wouldn't mind the short notice.'

I gasped. No, not just gasped, it's an inadequate word. I nearly choked; that is what happened when I immediately understood who exactly Vyacheslav Ivanovich was. Having him suddenly as a dinner host in Spain was quite a twist. A shock, even. Immediately, my superego started screaming inside my head: 'Decline, decline, for God's sake, don't accept this, refuse under any plausible pretext! It's useless, and it's dangerous!'.

But my damned curiosity prevailed. And then I had a plausible excuse to rebuff my over-cautious superego: if someone had explained to me in advance with whom I would be meeting at 7 pm, I could calmly consider the situation and, perhaps, politely decline the invitation. However, the refusal would now have looked extremely rude. I told my superego to shut up and, without giving myself another second to reflect, smiled back at Sergeyev, saying: 'But of course, accepted with pleasure'.

He led me outside the hotel and into the street, where a luxurious limousine with a diplomatic number plate was waiting. The car looked quite ambassadorial to me, but it was not an ambassador waving at me cheerfully from the back seat of that car, but the Soviet Spy-in-Chief himself, Vyacheslav Gurgenov. He held the rank of lieutenant-general in the KGB and, to all intents and purposes, was practically the head of its foreign intelligence service, the so-called First Main Directorate (*Pervoye Glavnoe Upravleniye* - PGU).

A few weeks earlier, Yevgeny Primakov had been officially appointed head of that department, but at the time, no one took the appointment seriously. It was seen as a stopgap measure for the transitional period, resulting from the convulsion of the dying Soviet power, and was considered strictly temporary. It was the time when many such transient figures emerged from nowhere only to disappear into oblivion quickly. Everybody was sure that the president of the new Russia, Boris Yeltsin, who was gaining more power by the day, would never allow Gorbachev's protege, 'the Red Primakov', to lead such an important organisation. Yeltsin was expected either to find his own political appointee or, if opting for some continuity, to leave the acting PGU chief, Gurgenov, a respected professional, in his place, at least for the time being. I heard that Yeltsin's first reaction to Primakov's candidacy was indeed more than sceptical. Then he abruptly changed his mind; sometimes the president of Russia acted so unpredictably, as if he just loved to surprise and confuse everyone, confounding all expectations. Primakov managed to charm Yeltsin somehow. A political 'stepchild', a communist inherited from Gorbachev, would continue to command the foreign intelligence service even as it broke away from the KGB, becoming an independent government agency of the Russian Federation. At the beginning of 1996, Yeltsin promoted him to the even more critical position of Foreign Minister, replacing the known pro-Western liberal Andrei Kozyrev, which legitimately made Western leaders worry about the new direction of Russian foreign policy.

However, all of this would come later; for the time being, it was widely believed that General Gurgenov was effectively calling the shots at the KGB's foreign intelligence service.

It was a strange, unique, crazy time when the main spy of the Soviet Union would wine and dine *Izvestia*'s foreign editor. On the one hand, it was a recognition of my newspaper's growing importance; Pravda had lost its leading position along with the Communist party, and *Izvestia* was definitely the most influential publication in the land, but on the other... On the other hand, it still seemed totally incredible. The dinner invitation was supposed to flatter me. Still, I was totally astonished: is there really nothing more important for the general to do on his Spanish trip than to have dinner with Ostalski?

I was riding in Gurgenov's car, engaged in small talk with him, trying to keep my composure and smile nonchalantly, as if I were totally unfazed. But deep inside, I was undoubtedly nervous, if not freaking out. After all, this handsome, elegantly dressed, and well-mannered gentleman, with sharp but not unpleasant features on his patrician face, was not just a man; he was a function. And what a function it was! This king of the mountain operated a super-powerful giant machine and controlled the thousand-headed octopus, whose tentacles stretched across the globe. The invisible web, which he held in his hands, covered all countries and continents, with the possible exception of Antarctica. Many thousands of specially selected and trained intelligence officers, together with tens of thousands of agents recruited by them, worked day and night, sucking in unimaginable amounts of information like a giant vacuum cleaner, carrying out covert operations, manipulating the weak to use their weakness to steal secrets. One of their former bosses had come up with a breath-takingly cynical description for their weird and frightening profession: *'lovyets chelovyekov'* – 'Fishers of Men', a direct quote from the Bible (in Matthew's Gospel, Chapter 4, verse 19, Jesus says to the brothers James and John: *'I will make you fishers of men.'*). But in the Bible, it is used in a positive sense, meaning capturing souls in the cause of Christ, whereas for somebody whose job it is to snare people, to lead them into a trap, possibly destroying their lives, to compare himself to one of Christ's apostles sounds like sheer mockery and utter arrogance.

For so many years, I had to live and work among such 'fishers of men', surviving next to them. I had to be cunning and always on the alert not to get into one of their traps, dodging them like in a bizarre dance, and do it all with ultimate caution —gently, politely, walking on eggshells, so as not to anger them too much, not to provoke. I looked at them with fear, sometimes with a shudder, but also with a grudging curiosity. The spies I had to meet occupied only modest places in the espionage hierarchy, somewhere in the lower part of the giant pyramid, and now I was suddenly sitting in the back seat of a car next to somebody who stood at the very top of it. How those operatives of all sorts and the chiefs of the stations would envy me, how much they would give to be in my place right now, I thought.

No, it was not an easy moment. It was quite an effort to keep chatting nonchalantly as if the devil himself was my brother, and I shuddered, imagining how the shutters of the hidden cameras belonging to various intelligence and counterintelligence services were clicking all around us, going into overdrive. And I had a mental picture of secret analysts in many different countries bending over the photo image of my humble person, wondering what kind of a super-agent that might be if General Gurgenov himself was going out of his way to please him. 'You must have done a lot of damage to yourself,' I thought with exasperation. 'From now on, you will be suspected of God knows what.' On the other hand, anyone of sound mind would understand that, since this meeting is taking place entirely in the open, in front of everyone, without the slightest attempt at secrecy, it must mean that this has nothing to do with any secret operations. But then the devil only knows what kind of logic drives all those spooks; probably paranoia rather than rational reasoning reigns supreme in their world.

I do not remember at all what I ate there, in that good, expensive restaurant in the centre of Madrid. At the table with us was a Soviet 'diplomat' accredited in one of the Arab countries. It was clear that he was one of Gurgenov's men, and, probably, somebody special, who enjoyed his exceptional confidence for some reason. Leonid Mlechin, the number one expert on Soviet intelligence history, writes that a middle-ranking KGB officer, even an average colonel, most likely never has the chance to visit the office of the chief of the Foreign Intelligence Service. Those colonels could not even dream of being with him at the same table in a foreign restaurant.

The conversation was quite mundane, nothing to do with anything spooky; allegedly, Gurgenov just wanted to know my opinion about the prospects of the Middle East peace conference. I did have something to say about this. I reminisced about that ill-fated night interview in Baghdad, when Arafat first broke the news to me that he was willing to accept autonomy rather than demand full independence. And then I talked about how this idea had been transformed. It seemed that the Palestinian position was changing, becoming more flexible and constructive. I correctly predicted that attempts to torpedo the negotiations, turn the conference into another empty hot-air talk and arena of propaganda war, should be expected to come not from the PLO, but from the Arab states, first of all, Syria. But the Israeli delegation could also become ruffled, fearing it might appear weak to its own public opinion and be accused of making dangerous unilateral concessions. And yet, I said, we are witnessing history in the making, as the conference has established a crucially important precedent. From now on, it will be easier to move forward, especially if Washington and Moscow join forces. And, thank God, we now have an embassy in Israel at last, so we can really begin to play an essential role in the Middle East settlement. Gurgenov listened attentively, but I could not get rid of the feeling that this was all a ruse. That my opinion was of no great consequence for him. Indeed, he had plenty of highly qualified Arabists at his disposal. What does he really need me for, then? I was asking myself.

It's time to tell the story of how I first met General Gurgenov; it's a fascinating tale.

When I unexpectedly found myself in the position of *Izvestia*'s Foreign Editor, I got an excellent, bright and spacious corner office with a spectacular view of Pushkin Square. On my new desk, among other, more ordinary telephones, a pale-yellow contraption with the USSR state emblem was sitting. It was the *vertushka* – the device for secret government communications that I already mentioned earlier in this book. It served as a direct line to the Kremlin telephone exchange (ATS-2). Previously, the purpose of this machine was to provide communist leaders with an instrument to promptly convey the will of the Central Committee and other key government departments to the editors. But now everything had been turned upside down, and this phone had become a magic tool in the hands of journalists, helping them to organise interviews with the big shots and to extract information from them. This idyllic state of *Glasnost* did not last long, though. Quite soon, the high and mighty adapted to the new reality and shut themselves off from the hacks, with the help of assistants who picked up the phones and decided whether to connect callers to their bosses. But in those happy revolutionary days, most of the nomenclature would cheerfully pick up the phone receivers themselves according to the former Soviet order. Top-level officials (ministers and above), though, used a different line - ATS-1. Only the chief editor of our newspaper had that level of access.

That day, Western news agencies reported that Mikhail Butkov, the Trud newspaper's correspondent in Norway who had mysteriously vanished from his office a few months earlier, had now appeared in England and was revealed to be a KGB officer and a defector. In the past, we would not have even dreamed of publishing such a story in our newspaper. Now we were free to do whatever we felt was right. However, simply reproducing the Reuters item wasn't all that interesting; our readers would expect us, like grown-up journalists, to find additional details, put the news into context, and obtain a comment from those in the know.

A small red book accompanied the government communication phone – a secret telephone directory of the Kremlin exchange. It worked as follows: all contacts were listed in strict alphabetical order. Positions and departmental affiliations were not specified; only the surnames, first names, and patronymics were provided. It was assumed that members of the nomenclature should be familiar with the names of the heads of important departments. I was trying to figure out how to contact the KGB, the foreign intelligence service. And then it dawned on me.

I had recently met a man in the corridors of *Izvestia*, who until recently had been in charge of this very service – the First Main Directorate (*Pervoye Glavnoye Upravleniye* – PGU). After the failure of the putsch, he even led the entire KGB for a short while, but suspicions arose that he had been tacitly complicit, if not directly involved, in the August 1991 failed coup. It was alleged that he appeared to be aware of the conspiracy but did nothing to stop it. (He himself categorically denied it). He was sacked and sent into early retirement. He showed up at Izvestia to see his university pal, Vladimir Skosyrev, hoping to get his support and perhaps publish his side of the story in the newspaper to defend his reputation. Skosyrev introduced us fleetingly. I was, of course, curious: what does a man who only yesterday possessed such enormous power look like? There was nothing ostentatiously evil in his face; he looked intelligent enough and had the sad eyes of a clever dog (which is definitely a compliment in my book). I was amazed by his appearance, for I half-expected to see a brute with terrifying eyes, somebody not unlike Saddam Hussein. But no, nothing like that. I remembered the surname of the sacked KGB boss: Shebarshin.

The Red Book of Government Special Communications was periodically updated, but not quickly enough, especially during the mass elite turnover that inevitably followed the coup's failure. You could expect that many of the *vertushka* numbers had not changed, even if their masters had. Thus, I reckoned, under the name of Shebarshin I could hope to find whoever was running the foreign intelligence service of the KGB at the moment. I couldn't be sure of that, though, since such an utterly secretive organisation could easily have altered all the crucial numbers, but I had nothing to lose by trying. I opened the directory at the "Sh". There he was - Shebarshin Leonid Vladimirovich, one and only. I dialled the number listed there, and someone immediately answered; a deep male voice said, 'Gurgenov.'

This was the first time I heard that name. But how to find out who he was? I couldn't just say: 'Tell me, are you by any chance the new chief of the spies, or is it a wrong number?' That would have been dumb. Instead, I introduced myself by giving my name, surname, patronymic, and position.

'Pleased to speak to you,' the man at the other end of the secret connection answered quite courteously. 'I am acting head of the First Main Directorate of the KGB of the USSR, Gurgenov Vyacheslav Ivanovich."

I told him about my incredible request: could he kindly confirm or deny the Reuters story about Mr Butkov's defection?

My interlocutor seemed to have been stunned by my impossible suggestion. After a moment's hesitation, he said:

'I am afraid I will have to consult on this. Can I call you back? Is your number in the directory?'

'No,' I answered. 'Not yet.' And I dictated the number of my predecessor.

About twenty minutes later, Gurgenov called back.

'Alas,' he said, 'it will not work. We cannot help you with this.'

He paused, then astonished me by suggesting that, in this new era of openness, some forms of cooperation between the press and intelligence services can be found. Listening to him, I suddenly had an inspiration to take the general at his word.

'Vyacheslav Ivanovich,' I said. 'Since it's a matter of openness, why don't we meet face to face? I would love to interview you about the changes your organisation is going through. The best option for me would be to visit you at your headquarters. As I understand it, you are located somewhere 'in the woods', as they call it, southwest of Moscow, am I right? However, if this is not possible, we can meet at a neutral location. What do you say?'

'I'll call you back,' said Gurgenov.

This time it took him much longer, about two hours. I nearly gave up on my brazen attempt to penetrate the headquarters of the Soviet foreign intelligence service when '*vertuska*' rang again, and the by now familiar deep voice said, using my patronymic:

'Andrei Vsevolodovich, I invite you to pay us a visit. I'll send a car for you.'

On the appointed day and time, a black Volga limousine pulled up to the *Izvestia* building. Next to the driver in the front seat sat a well-groomed, prim but very polite young man, Gurgenov's aide or assistant. I sat in the back seat, and we set off.

It is now common knowledge that the SVR, the successor to the First Main Directorate of the KGB, is located in Yasenevo, behind the ring road. One of the buildings, of a very ordinary type made of glass and concrete, is perfectly visible from the Moscow ring road. But at that time, even I, who had read all available Western literature on the subject, had a very vague idea about the location of the KGB spies' den. I only knew that they were hidden somewhere outside Moscow, unlike their colleagues from the counterintelligence and secret police whose office was in the very centre of Moscow, in *Lubyanka* (aka *Dzerzhinsky square*). I had an impression that the foreign intelligence was much further from the city, in fact, somewhere in a dense forest. At the 20th kilometre of the southwestern highway (called '*Kievskoye Shosse*'), I spotted a somewhat mysterious left-hand turn with a huge sign forbidding entry. 'That's where they are probably hiding,' I thought (wrongly: I wasn't even close).

I also heard that there was no way to get there by public transport. Employees who had their own cars could come to work independently, while all the others had to gather at the terminal southern metro (subway) stations, from where they would be driven to work by coaches. The building was initially intended for the International Department of the Central Committee of the CPSU. However, the powerful KGB chairman, Yuri Andropov, managed to persuade the Politburo in the early 1970s to allocate it to the First Main Directorate (PGU) of the KGB instead. Before that, the spies were huddled with members of other KGB departments at Lubyanka. That didn't make much sense, of course. After all, it meant that all incoming and outgoing PGU personnel could be easily observed with the naked eye (or camera lenses) and noted. That was a lousy arrangement from the perspective of clandestine security. Interestingly, the GRU, the military intelligence service, is still housed in the heart of Moscow, on *Khoroshevskoye Shosse*, where its operatives can be spotted entering and exiting the vast complex. Recently, for an inexplicable reason, the GRU was renamed the GU, losing the letter 'R' (standing for *Razvedyvatelnoye*, Intelligence) in the process. Why? Did somebody think that this 'R' in its abbreviation was giving it away, and getting rid of that letter would disguise the GRU/GU's activities better? Oh, how very clever.

The KGB spies always despised their military rivals, calling them *Sapogi* ('Boots') behind their backs. The widely used insulting moniker suggested that the GRU spies lacked sophistication and came 'from trenches'. It was true that, at some point in the 1960s, military intelligence was ordered to recruit its cadres exclusively from graduates of military schools, while the KGB was allowed to select its spies from top universities.

But as far as the masking of their secret headquarters went, the KGB didn't beat their competition by much. On the gates of the vast, mysterious complex was a rather silly sign: "Scientific Research Centre". That could sound right only to the illiterates, and all the locals knew what was behind those thick and tall double walls anyway.

In front of the main gate stood a large grocery store, where the spies would shop at the end of their working shifts. Later, I was told that the choice of food there was somewhat better than in the general shops in town, but not by much. When real deficit items, such as high-quality sausage or meat, were occasionally on sale, the queues could be substantial. Around the gates, a huge parking lot was available for staff vehicles; personal cars were not permitted to enter. But our black Volga was waved through instantly. I only managed to catch a glimpse of impressive security: guards with Kalashnikovs, fierce dogs, and barbed wire on the walls, among other things. Our car was hardly examined at all. I wasn't asked to show any ID, which surprised me, and all I was granted was a casual glance from one of the guarding officers.

The stretched-out main building, five or six floors high, built in the typically plain style of the late 1960s, resembled a large hotel rather than a spy headquarters; there was nothing particularly sinister about its appearance. It was designed by a Finnish architect who, of course, didn't have the foggiest idea of its future destiny. Gurgenov's office also struck me as a relatively modest affair; mine at *Izvestia* was probably more impressive.

I was trying hard to concentrate on the forthcoming interview, and it impeded my powers of observation, which I would come to regret. That was a very narrow window of opportunity that would soon close – for good. It felt unreal – the thought that it was history in the making and that I was on the verge of doing something totally unprecedented gave me shivers. But I tried to take it in my stride and pretended that something like that was par for the course in my job.

Of course, it would have been very naïve to expect total frankness from Gurgenov. Successful spies, especially those who have reached such dizzying heights in their careers, are by nature incapable of uttering a single simple word without an ulterior agenda. They are professional actors; this is second nature to them. You have to play a complicated chess game with them, trying to second-guess the meanings, to fill in the omissions, deciding what could be, with some approximation, interpreted as being close to the truth and what should be discarded as white noise. And of course, they have every chance to beat you at this game. But the moment was very special; the spies were panicking, not being sure of their future after the leaders of the KGB got implicated in the failed putsch. That is why I hoped Gurgenov would try to be genuinely sincere and open up as much as he could. And he tried hard. Of course, I couldn't hope to squeeze any big secrets from him. But he certainly looked and sounded plausible and charming. In general, he said what I wanted to hear. I put that message into the title of the series of the two articles I wrote for *Izvestia* as a result of my fantastical trip to the spies' lair: 'Foreign Intelligence is divorcing KPGB'. In this, I was referring to the cult novel *Moscow 2042* by dissident writer Vladimir Voinovich, who devised the hilarious abbreviation for supreme power: the CPSU and the KGB merged into a single governing body, the Communist Party of the State Security (*Kommunisticheskaya Partiya Gosudarstvennoy Bezopasnosti*). It was a dystopian satire, but it did reflect the nature of the Soviet state, the symbiosis of the all-powerful party and its political police as its instrument of repression. In my pieces, I was playing with the writer's quip while also seriously suggesting that there was a chance, a hope, that after the failure of the hard-line putsch and with the prospect of political democratisation in Russia, the foreign intelligence service could start with a clean slate. To do this, spies had to be freed from both the false ideology and totalitarian power of the CPSU, as well as the KGB's horrible historical reputation.

Now I must accept that I have been disabused of my naive hopes. But initially, events seemed to bear out my prognosis: in the early 1990s, the KGB was disbanded, and the former PGU became an independent government agency called SVR (*Sluzhba Vneshney Razvedki* – The Foreign Intelligence Service), which was supposed to be answerable to democratic oversight. Alas, in the end, it made a full circle. Now the SVR is shrouded in total secrecy, not supervised adequately by anybody, and the most worrying thing is that it insists on 'continuity', presenting itself as the downright successor of the GPU-NKVD-KGB and disregarding the horrible role those organisations (or, rather, the same organisation under different names) played in the history of our country and the world. To put it mildly, it is a highly unhealthy and alarming association which doesn't bode well for our future. But at that incredible moment in Russian history when I met Vyacheslav Gurgenov, everything seemed possible. I sincerely believed in the likelihood of the Foreign Intelligence reforming itself, and it seemed to me the general had faith in it, too. Or pretended convincingly.

Comparing my two close encounters with him, I must admit that it was much harder for me in Madrid, on foreign soil. In Yasenevo, it felt like a journalistic scoop. But in a way, it was still a pretty normal situation, a newsman interviewing the head of an important, legitimate, albeit unusual and mysterious department. In Spain, despite the complete innocence of our conversations, I was perturbed by the sense that there was an element of something illicit, forbidden, if not criminal, in our meeting.

Only on the plane home from Madrid did I learn why Gurgenov was going out of his way to be so sweet to me. I am sure he sincerely wanted to maintain a positive contact with the leading newspaper of the new Russia. But there was also a specific question he wanted to ask me in private, and to which, he thought, I might have known the answer. It was, I must admit, a pretty flattering compliment, by the way.

Settling down into my seat in the Aeroflot IL-62, I caught a glimpse of the general who was travelling first class, while I, of course, was sitting in economy. He waved at me, and I waved back.

As the plane gained altitude, a flight attendant approached me and asked if I would mind visiting the first-class cabin.

I hesitated but then decided that it would be impolite to refuse the invitation. Gurgenov offered me the seat next to his and treated me to brandy and some snacks. After engaging in small talk for a while, he then casually, as if in passing, asked the main question, for the first time calling me by my first name:

'Andrei, strictly between us, what will be your advice: Gorbachev or Yeltsin? I now have to make a choice on whom to put the stake on.'

I was stunned but answered without much hesitation:

'Yeltsin, and only Yeltsin. Everything I know suggests that the power is passing to him. And soon.'

'Are you sure?'

'I am, as far as one can be sure of anything in our unpredictable country.'

I realised that the foreign intelligence service was caught between two fires at this surreal time of dual power, and now it was time to make the hard choice: deciding on whom to bet – on the President of the crumbling USSR or the head of the new assertive Russia. It was becoming impossible to continue sitting between the two chairs. Gurgenov thanked me, saying how much he appreciated my advice. But, as I learned later, he didn't follow it. If he did, he probably would have had a chance, however small, to remain at the head of the foreign intelligence. However, when Gorbachev decided to send in Evgeniy Primakov, Gurgenov offered him his full support. A few months later, when Gorbachev resigned and the Soviet Union finally collapsed, Russian President Boris Yeltsin, now the fully-fledged head of state, attended the SVR's governing body meeting to discuss who should run the organisation. He expressed serious doubts about Primakov's candidacy, but Gurgenov delivered an impassioned speech in his defence, which seemed to make all the difference. Yeltsin was so impressed that, in the end, he allowed himself to be persuaded to leave Primakov at the top of the foreign intelligence service.

So, my advice given on board the Aeroflot flight from Madrid to Moscow in the autumn of 1991 was, in the end, wasted, as were all Gurgenov's efforts to court me.

Something similar happened eight years later when Yeltsin's press secretary Dmitry Yakushkin invited me for lunch at a restaurant not very far from the Kremlin and stunned me with his question: who, in my opinion, should succeed ailing Yeltsin as the president of Russia? My advice, for what it was worth, was, of course, totally discarded. I am sure that Yakushkin and his boss, the president's chief of staff, Valentin Yumashev, put the same question to dozens of people at that crucial time, and I doubt very much that many of those asked would have come up with Vladimir Putin's name. As a politician, he was virtually unknown. But it was Boris Berezovsky's opinion that prevailed; Putin was his protégé. Paradoxically, that choice cost the former his freedom to live in his homeland (he had to flee to Britain) and then his very life. As far as I was concerned, in 1999, it didn't occur to me for a moment that Putin could become the next leader. However, if this name had been brought up at that lunch, I would have pleaded with Yakushkin not to go in that direction. As another former KGB general told me in confidence, a highly trained intelligence officer shouldn't ever be a political leader.

These are two very different professions; a spy would forever remain a spy and would always try to substitute policy with the perpetual succession of 'special operations' and clandestine machinations.

'He simply can't help it; his brain is programmed to function in this way,' the general whispered in my ear.

Back in late 1991, no one in Moscow's political circles had even heard of Putin's name. At that time, he was just a little-known assistant to the mayor of St. Petersburg, recently appointed to the position after leaving the KGB with the rank of lieutenant colonel.

On that Aeroflot flight from Madrid to Moscow, the plane was preparing for landing, so I went back to my Economy seat. That is when another phantasmagorical scene unfolded. And this time it was I who had to run to Gurgenov, begging for help.

Izvestia had sent one of its best photo correspondents with me to Spain. His name was Sergei Smirnov, and he was a living legend. He was then seventy and had been snapping excellent photos for the newspaper for many decades. He excelled in all genres. Still, his real forte was artistic photo portraits of the high and mighty and the famous, catching them unawares and shooting from unusual angles, making not only Gagarin and Khrushchev but even Brezhnev look human and likeable. Nevertheless, Sergei never thought it beyond him to produce straightforward photo illustrations of current affairs for the paper. He was an absolute professional who would never let you down. And it was all the more striking given the fact that, as I already knew, Smirnov *'sil'no zakladyvayet za vorotnik'* – was 'laying a lot under his collar'. I am sure you guessed what this Russian colloquialism means. It is no accident, of course, that in Russian there are dozens of synonyms describing this phenomenon. Since I moved to Britain, I have discovered that English is quite rich in that respect as well. *To bend one's elbow, to wet one's whistle, to get hammered or smashed*, the list of appropriate expressions could be very long. Sergei Smirnov drank a lot and regularly. He was probably an alcoholic, but of a special, unusual kind. He was rarely sober, but in some mysterious way, he always managed to do his job impeccably. There were times when he stood unsteadily on his feet, but his hands would still firmly hold the camera at an absolutely right angle with his fingers pressing all the right buttons at the right time as if leading an independent existence.

Legends about Sergey Smirnov were abundant, both regarding his talents and his impressive circle of friends (including the world-famous choreographer Yuri Grigorovich), as well as his incredible ability to consume enormous amounts of alcohol. This is what my good friend and colleague Vasily Zakharko, himself a veteran of Izvestia and its former editor in the 1990s, told me:

'In Soviet times, it was the only way to succeed in that profession. Once, Smirnov and I went to Estonia to cover a big event there. The first thing he did was to pay a visit to the head of the local photo agency and have a good drink with him. As a result, everything worked like clockwork. He drank with the guys from the KGB Ninth Directorate responsible for Kremlin security, so he could always move unhindered anywhere, even if most journalists had restricted access. He was fabulously generous to all his colleagues and working contacts, always carrying with him not only numerous bottles of vodka, but also dozens of cans of caviar.'

On our way to Madrid, I hadn't yet settled into my seat when Smirnov began to show his famous generosity. A stewardess tried to stop him, but to no avail. He managed to bamboozle her with his jokes; he was a real pro in that respect, too. The man who knew how to sway the fierce officers of the Ninth Directorate and the Kremlin celestials couldn't have a problem overcoming the feeble resistance of a kindly flight attendant. Out of his bag, he drew a treasured bottle (the first of several) and a considerable number of appetising snacks, including some smoked fish which looked delicious. At the same time, he was babbling incessantly, telling impressive stories about his adventures, quickly switching from one topic to another in his hoarse, cosy, squeaky voice, calling me familiarly 'Andryusha' (the term of endearment that I don't particularly like) even though previously we barely knew each other. Most importantly, he kept pouring vodka in a small glass he had supplied me with from the very start.

Had I not resisted his hospitality and drunk everything he had intended me to drink, I would have been unable to get off the plane in Madrid.

I once again recalled my experience with alcohol. At the university, Rudolf Dodeltsev, the assistant professor who taught us the history of philosophy and was one of those who strongly defended me against the dean's attacks, repeatedly explained why my prospects for a Soviet career were limited.

'Oh, Andrei,' he would say, 'you have everything going for you, you could have had a fantastic career, but, alas, there is a fatal flaw in you: you do not drink.'

What he really meant was that I couldn't consume large quantities of alcohol, not more than one or two glasses; that was my limit. And whenever I had to force my body to exceed this dose, I felt absolutely terrible, sick. Just so.

Dodeltsev was right. Alcohol was the main lubricant of the Soviet system.

I witnessed this many times myself. However, the most memorable incident occurred in late 1976, when TASS sent me on a short internship to its Ural branch in the city of Sverdlovsk (which has since reverted to its original name, Yekaterinburg). On one occasion, the head of the regional TASS bureau assigned me to cover the opening of a new blast furnace in the nearby city of Nizhniy Tagil. The event itself was dreadfully dull; I quickly produced the usual obligatory piece of propaganda and dictated it over the phone to the TASS stenographers (the internet age was still far in the future). That, of course, was all that was required of me.

All the journalists covering the grand event were then put on a bus and driven to the suburban residence of the first secretary of the Nizhniy Tagil Communist Party Committee. His dacha was large and lavish, on the level of a multi-millionaire's villa somewhere in the 'decadent West', and was sitting in a gorgeous forest with pines and cedars. But we were not given a chance to enjoy the surrounding natural beauty; instead, we were pressed to take seats around a huge oval table in the residence's dining room. On my way, I managed to have a quick peek into a storage room and gasped: it was nearly stacked to the ceiling with dozens of vodka boxes (12 bottles each). At the table, we were seated between party apparatchiks who were closely monitoring us, making sure that no one could shirk from booze. They were shouting 'bottoms up!' after every toast.

Food was abundant and rich, too, but it did not help. One after another, toasts were proposed: to a new blast furnace, to the beloved Communist Party, to Leonid Brezhnev and, personally, to the good health of the first secretary of the Nizhniy Tagil city committee. And then came the turn of those newspapers, news agencies, radio and television stations, which we represented, including my TASS, of course. My good luck was the healthy resistance of my body to alcohol, but that night, my survival was at stake. Despite two local functionaries watching over me from both sides, I succeeded in pouring the contents of a pair of glasses under the table. Then I managed to get to the toilet, where I vomited, which made me feel much better. When, pale and in a cold sweat, I returned to the table, my party supervisors were themselves quite tipsy and in general, the pressure had somewhat eased, and I was able to start slacking off, pretending that I was still drinking. The feast concluded around 2:00 a.m. Not all of the guests were able to move independently. An ambulance had to be called for a colleague, and I have no idea whether he survived in the end. Quite a few of those who could not stand on their feet were carried into the bus. Others were still walking but with enormous difficulty, swinging from side to side, making for a nauseating spectacle. It took our hosts nearly half an hour to herd everyone into the bus, which took us to the railway station. First Secretary accompanied us in his black Volga. The special railway coach we arrived in from Sverdlovsk was waiting for us, but there was nothing to attach it to: apparently, no trains were expected until the morning. But the solution was found.

'Where is the backup locomotive, the one that is to be used in the event of a war?' asked the chief communist of Nizhny Tagil.

He was informed that such a machine was indeed available, but its use was strictly prohibited in peacetime.

'On my responsibility!' he barked, and off we went. On the way, some passengers were singing drunken songs before falling asleep, somebody was crying loudly, and others were puking. As far as I was concerned, I soon fell into deep, unhealthy sleep.

Since then, I have witnessed many other similar episodes, which convinced me of the very special function of alcohol in our state mechanism. After coming to power, Gorbachev made a fatal mistake of starting a campaign of partial prohibition. Perhaps this measure seemed necessary to him when he read terrifying secret reports, prepared by the KGB, on the scale of alcohol abuse and binge drinking in the country. But he shouldn't have started his rule with that campaign, as it had overshadowed entirely his *Perestroika* reforms. All his political capital was spent on it; his credibility was severely damaged, and public goodwill was eroded. For millions, including many in the party apparatus, he immediately became a hate figure. And then all his other reforms were met with hostility.

So yes, they were right, Rudolf Dodeltsev and Vasiliy Zakharko, and many other wise people who were telling me that alcohol was the material that glued everything together in the Soviet system.

Another vivid illustration of this thesis was sitting right next to me on the plane. When we landed in Madrid on our flight from Moscow, Sergei Smirnov moved as though he were walking through a storm. I took him by the arm, helped him off the plane, and together we successfully passed through passport control and customs.

But on our return flight to Moscow, things turned out to be far more complicated. Smirnov had many friends — other photographers, various journalists, and officers of the KGB's Ninth Directorate — all of whom he felt duty-bound to share a drink with. Aside from the official protocol events of the Peace Conference, I saw him only briefly. He would swiftly complete his work and then vanish.

On the sidelines of the Madrid conference, the Soviet–American summit was also taking place. Gorbachev and George Bush Sr. later held a joint press conference. I rather regretted that Smirnov hadn't captured a crucial moment when I was able to ask a question that made Gorbachev visibly angry. I was taken aback — I hadn't intended to provoke him. I just wanted to understand how he and Yeltsin were dividing power between them at that extraordinary historical juncture. His answer confirmed what I had feared: the situation was spiralling out of control.

All I had asked was:

'Mikhail Sergeyevich, could you please tell us who remains at the helm during your absence from Moscow?'

Gorbachev flushed, replied irritably, and seemed momentarily confused. But the essence of his answer was this: nobody. No one was in charge, and there was, he claimed, no need to delegate authority to anyone. To me, his response only reinforced what I already suspected — that power was steadily shifting to Yeltsin, who was busily consolidating his authority while Gorbachev was away.

Perhaps Gorbachev felt personally offended by my question, suspecting me of alluding to the August events, when he had left Moscow for his holiday in Crimea, leaving Vice President Gennady Yanayev in charge, and Yanayev had promptly joined the conspirators, legitimising the attempted coup. Now, officially, Gorbachev had no deputy, yet Yeltsin was de facto performing his duties, preparing to dismantle Soviet power entirely.

Gorbachev was still enjoying the trappings of presidential authority, but his power base had been eroded. Theoretically, he still had a government answering to him, but it had been half-paralysed after Prime Minister Pavlov and many members of his cabinet supported the August putsch and were purged as a result. At the same time, the massive party apparatus, which until recently controlled every city and town in the land, had been practically disbanded. The power was slipping through his fingers. This was Gorbachev's last summit and his last press conference as the head of a great power, which had only a few weeks left to live.

When the press conference ended, I saw Gurgenov from a distance; he nodded and, it seemed to me, even winked. I understood this to mean that he wanted to say, 'your question was good.' But I couldn't be sure; maybe I was imagining things.

The fact that Sergei Smirnov wasn't present at that moment in the hall slightly disappointed me. Gorbachev's answer to my question was an interesting historical detail, and I wouldn't have minded having a photograph of it as a souvenir, something to show to the grandchildren.

But Smirnov was somewhere drinking with friends. He reappeared only on the day of our departure back to Moscow at Madrid airport, at the very last moment. He was tipsy, but that was something to be expected; I was stunned by the sight of the vast number of bags, parcels and packages of various shapes and sizes that surrounded him. There was no way one person could carry them all. A couple of tipsy friends helped to deliver them to the Aeroflot check-in. Mesmerising all around him with his gentle manners, infectious genial laughter, and hilarious jokes, Sergei quickly found volunteers among fellow passengers who helped him drag all the luggage onto the plane. There, we somehow contrived to place all those items on the upper shelves, under the seats, and so on.

'What is it all about, Sergei, gifts to family and friends?' I could not resist asking.

'We must help people,' he answered cryptically.

To my horror, shortly after take-off, he pulled a bottle of vodka out of one of his bags. But at that very moment, I was invited by Gurgenov to join him in the first-class cabin, and I left Smirnov alone with his supply of alcohol. However, as it turned out, he quickly found himself other drinking companions — as he always does.

When I returned to my seat before landing, Sergei was sitting in total silence, wearing a grave, thoughtful expression. That was a worrying sign. 'This is bad!' I thought. But I had no idea just how bad it was.

'Is everything all right?' I asked, though I knew perfectly well it wasn't. Sergei groaned in response; it seemed he couldn't speak.

When the plane stopped at the terminal, it became clear that Sergei couldn't walk either. He struggled desperately to get up from his seat, finally managing it after several failed attempts and with some help from me. But then there was the problem of the enormous hand luggage. Between the two of us, we couldn't carry even half of it.

This time, no one was going to help — the passengers were already hurrying past towards the exit as I struggled to haul

Sergei's limp body upright. Frankly, I panicked. With great effort, I might just have managed to drag him off the plane without attracting the police's attention. Getting him through passport control and customs, however, seemed rather more problematic. Still, I knew I could rely on him to sober up quickly at the first sign of danger. But I had absolutely no idea what to do with those damned bags.

Out of sheer despair, I ran after the first-class passengers and caught sight of Gurgenov's back as he stepped off the plane through the jet bridge and turned into the passageway leading to the VIP lounge.

'Vyacheslav Ivanovich, will you help us out?' I shouted. He turned around and, seeing me in such a distressed state, came back. I quickly explained our predicament.

'No problem,' he said. 'Just get back on board and wait there for a few minutes.'

When I returned, I found Smirnov struggling with his vast collection of hand luggage, unsuccessfully trying to gather it all together. It was quite a spectacle — he kept attempting to hold more and more bags and packages in his hands, only to drop one or two each time and start again.

A few minutes later, several impeccably dressed young men with military bearing appeared on board. Within seconds, they scooped up all the bags and carefully escorted Sergei Smirnov off the plane and into the airport terminal. I could barely keep up with the team and soon lost sight of them altogether. We met again only outside passport control and customs, where a subdued and seemingly almost sober Sergei Ivanovich was patiently waiting for me — all his luggage neatly arranged around him.

It was, I suspect, a unique KGB operation of its kind — and one I couldn't help but admire.

But the most remarkable thing about Sergei Smirnov was that he went on working for many years, taking outstanding photographs while consuming unimaginable quantities of vodka, and somehow managing to wriggle out of every bit of trouble he got himself into. And I have no doubt he continued to stumble into trouble regularly. I often worried about his liver — how could any organ withstand such relentless assault? Yet the endurance of this extraordinary man's body was nothing short of astonishing. He lived to the age of ninety-two and worked almost to the very end, even holding his own photography exhibitions. Truly, some incredible human specimens walk among us mere mortals on this earth.

I never saw Gurgenov again. But recently, I have been reminiscing about him with a very good friend of mine, Vladimir Skosyrev, my mentor and fellow anti-Stalinist at *Izvestia*. Vladimir had known Gurgenov during his student days at the Institute of Oriental Studies, and later met him again in Dhaka. After the war for the independence of Bangladesh, they both found themselves, for a time, lumped together in the same hotel along with other journalists, diplomats, and spies.

Vladimir remembered Gurgenov as a highly sociable, cheerful man — a great wit with a fondness for the occasional practical joke. This description, however, does not match the man I met in 1991. Whether the rapid ascent through the ranks of such an organisation drains all humour and joy from a person, or whether he chose not to reveal a more human side of himself to me, I cannot say. But a strange thought occurred to me: at the time, I felt understandably tense in his presence — yet what if he was equally uneasy around me?

Those were turbulent days, following the defeat of the neo-Stalinist coup, the arrest of his senior superiors, and the dismissal of his immediate boss, Leonid Shebarshin. The rule of the Communist Party had suddenly and dramatically come to an end. The political situation was in complete flux, and the KGB — both its secret police and foreign intelligence divisions — was facing fierce public criticism. The monument to the organisation's founder, Felix Dzerzhinsky, which stood in front of the KGB's main building in *Lubyanka*, was torn down by anti-Soviet revolutionaries without resistance from law enforcement or the government and with the tacit approval of the Russian president.

Gurgenov himself was probably expecting to be dismissed — or worse — at any moment. Everything had become uncertain; the ground beneath his feet was shaking. In the absence of any strong authority, he must have been desperately searching for something — or someone—to cling to. In that situation, a newly promoted upstart, fresh in the role of senior editor at the most influential newspaper in this bewildering, incomprehensible new Russia, may well have seemed like a straw to clutch at.

    Who would have thought then, in the autumn of 1991, that Vyacheslav Gurgenov — so youthful, strong, and athletic in appearance — had less than three years to live? He died before reaching the age of sixty.

Chapter Fourteen

Kidnapping in Mexico

Soon after I returned from Spain, the sacked head of the KGB, Leonid Shebarshin, came to see me in my *Izvestia* office. He was asking for a favour, interceding this time on behalf of the general Yuriy Drozdov. Would I kindly agree to meet him?

I felt that I had had too many KGB generals in my life of late; they had been coming on as if in a shoal. But Drozdov was a special case; I couldn't possibly decline the offer to see this notorious individual with my own eyes. For many years, he had been the head of the most secretive and enigmatic branch of the KGB Foreign Intelligence Service, known as 'The Directorate S.'. That department had been (and probably still is) running deep-cover super-agents, known as 'sleepers' or 'illegals'. They were sent to live abroad with false identities as Western citizens, to win the trust of the decision-makers and solicit or steal sensitive information. The 'illegals' were also acting as cut-outs between agents. In addition, they were (and perhaps still are) expected to plan and even prepare for acts of major sabotage in the event of war breaking out.

Drozdov had recently been fired and, as I could easily guess, was full of resentment against *Perestroika*, Gorbachev, Yeltsin and the idea of an open and democratic Russia in general.

I didn't anticipate meeting a soulmate; on the contrary, I was sure that we would quickly recognise an enemy in each other. Still, I was keen to try and understand what made him tick. After all, in theory, he may well have been the model for *Karla*, the sinister character created by John le Carré and cast in his novels as the mastermind behind Soviet machinations across the globe. I knew that Le Carre's work was an artistic exaggeration, but I was intrigued to see the possible prototype of such an evil genius.

In my imagination, Drozdov should have been handsome in a sinister way, with penetrating, unblinking, steely eyes, graciously greying hair, and a wrinkled face of an old sage who had been through hell and high water. In short, I thought he would look like a Hollywood villain.

The skinny old man who entered my office had a surprisingly narrow, elongated bald skull, small eyes, and a large nose. There was nothing remotely ominous about him. In Gurgenov and Shebarshin, for all their good manners and polished appearance, one could still sense — beneath the veneer of civility — the presence of some deep, dark force. In this man, however, I felt nothing of the sort. Nor did I detect any apparent signs of a powerful intellect. Had I met him in the street, I would have taken him for a quartermaster or the manager of a provincial factory.

Still, appearances, as they say, can be deceptive. I concealed my disappointment, smiled, and invited him to sit down. After all, this was Pavel Sudoplatov — the notorious founder of Directorate S. (its designation derived from the first letter of his surname) — who was supposed to exude an aura of sinister magnetism. He and his henchmen had been engaged in large-scale assassinations and acts of sabotage during Stalin's era. By contrast, Drozdov's subordinates were primarily involved in recruiting 'assets' and acquiring or stealing sensitive information; in the vast majority of cases, they never even handled a weapon.

The 'illegals' had to undergo highly specialised and extremely sophisticated training before being planted, under false identities, into foreign societies. They were required to speak local languages like natives and to behave indistinguishably from the people among whom they lived. While other agents worked undercover — 'under the roof', as the jargon went — in embassies and other foreign missions, these men and women had to live quietly and inconspicuously among the general population, blending in thoroughly.

A highly romanticised image of the 'illegals' has been portrayed in the American television series *The Americans*. It tells the story of a seemingly ordinary American couple, Elizabeth and Philip, who are, in fact, KGB officers Nadia and Misha — Russians through and through. As entertainment, the series works brilliantly, and the acting is entirely convincing, but the characters are constantly shooting and killing. Of course, this bears little resemblance to reality — yet television follows its own rules. No one really wants a faithful depiction of the illegal spy's mundane, monotonous routine; it would be so dull that nobody would watch it.

The institution of 'illegals' is amazing. After getting to know Drozdov and the sensational journalistic investigation that followed, I have been dealing with this topic in London, writing and doing radio essays in both Russian and English. I can't say I have become a true expert in that field, but I learned something and tried to share that knowledge with readers and listeners.

The first question I asked was: Why don't Western countries use 'illegals'? The answer was simple: for precisely the same reason that Western cities have no underground palaces serving as metro stations — unlike Moscow, with its marble walls, soaring ceilings, glittering chandeliers, and ornate mosaics. It is simply too expensive. Only the Stalinist economy, built on the use of slave and semi-slave labour, could afford to construct, at such immense depths, those architectural and engineering masterpieces. Likewise, only the so-called 'socialist' countries, which were not obliged to count their money, could pour vast resources into training their citizens to impersonate foreigners and then implant them convincingly into hostile societies.

One former employee of Directorate S. once boasted that the cost of training and deploying a single 'illegal' was nearly equivalent to that of building a jet aircraft. Perhaps that was an exaggeration, yet there is no doubt that it was an extravagant indulgence. From a pragmatic Western perspective, the game was hardly worth the candle.

Like almost everything else in the Soviet Union, the illegal intelligence network gradually deteriorated. It reached its lowest point with the glamorous Anna Chapman and the rest of her group of ten, who were exchanged for several prisoners held in Russian jails. One fake American couple spoke English with such a heavy accent that even their neighbours suspected them of being spies — and specifically, Russian ones at that.

But the very fact that modern Russia still tries to maintain illegal intelligence operations is itself an aberration; in any normal country, such things would be unthinkable. In our time, it is far more cost-effective to rely on electronic espionage and surveillance, supplemented by the work of "legal" intelligence officers operating under diplomatic cover in embassies. These days, hackers are far more efficient — and far cheaper — than any 'illegals'.

The most famous Soviet 'illegals' of the 20th century were Rudolf Abel (whose real name was William Fisher) and Gordon Lonsdale (Konon Molody). The former played a significant role in stealing American nuclear secrets, while the latter succeeded in spying on British naval institutions. Both were caught and sentenced to long prison terms — in the United States and the United Kingdom, respectively — and both were later pardoned to be exchanged for Westerners apprehended by the Soviets. Abel–Fisher was swapped for the American pilot Gary Powers, whose reconnaissance plane was shot down over the Urals, while Lonsdale–Molody was traded for the British businessman Grenville Wynne, who had served as a liaison with one of the most valuable 'assets' the British had ever recruited within the Soviet military establishment — Colonel Oleg Penkovsky.

It's amusing that I was just two handshakes away from both of them — Fisher and Molody, that is — close to people who had repeatedly shaken hands with them.

In his youth, Abel–Fisher served in a radio unit of the Red Army alongside the future famous actor and later director of the illustrious Maly Theatre, Mikhail Tsaryov. They resumed their friendship after Abel's spying career ended. My father was on friendly terms with Tsaryov, and I had the opportunity to meet him as well. My university mentor, Vladimir Segal, had been a friend of Molody during their student years. After the spy returned from England in 1964, they began socialising again.

A highly popular feature film titled *The Dead Season* was made about Lonsdale–Molody's espionage. Abel–Fisher not only acted as the principal consultant but also appeared on camera, introducing the subject in a preamble.

The talented Lithuanian actor Donatas Banionis delivers an outstanding performance in the leading role. I was told that there was a certain inner resemblance between him and Molody — both the spy and the actor possessed the same captivating, almost hypnotic charm. As for the film's content, there are a few small fragments of truth scattered throughout, but very little overall; most of it is sheer invention, amounting to a somewhat more polished version of anti-Western, anti-British propaganda. A rumour has been circulating in Moscow that the film made a strong impression on the young Vladimir Putin, shaping his career choice and perhaps partly accounting for his enduring hostility towards the United Kingdom.

Steven Spielberg directed a feature film about Abel, and it is a far more truthful work of art. Entitled *Bridge of Spies*, it features the British actor Mark Rylance, who delivers an extraordinary performance portraying the famous — or rather, notorious — Soviet 'illegal' as a highly sophisticated character. Rylance's acting is simply stunning. But the film shows very little of the 'illegals' mundane life and regimen, all that remains behind the scenes.

Neither film offers any real insight into how the two great spies adapted to life in their homeland after returning from the cold. Did they ever harbour doubts about the virtue of the cause they had so loyally served throughout their lives, and for which they had made such extraordinary sacrifices? After all, the life of an illegal agent is harsh; it involves unrelenting psychological strain that inevitably damages both body and soul. One must surely possess an exceptional temperament to condemn oneself to such an unnatural existence. Even the most congenial adventurers, who may find a perverse satisfaction in the adrenaline rush of such exploits, often end up suffering from nervous breakdowns — if not entirely losing their sanity.

In that respect, little is known about Abel–Fisher. He was always cautious, walking on eggshells and keeping his mouth firmly shut. In retirement, he unfailingly toed the official line, supporting orthodox ideology and its accompanying myths. That is hardly surprising, given that he — unlike Molody — had endured Stalin's purges. At one point, he was dismissed, then reinstated, and for many years lived under constant threat of arrest and even execution, helplessly watching as most of his colleagues and former superiors perished one after another in the dungeons of the NKVD (*Narodny Komissariat Vnutrennikh Del*, or People's Commissariat of Internal Affairs).

But Konon Molody proved to be a maverick — an independent spirit who did not easily succumb to primitive orthodoxy.

Vladimir Segal told me some remarkable things about him. The fact that Molody spoke English as his first language was unsurprising, as he had spent his childhood living with his aunt in California. After enrolling at the Institute of Foreign Trade in 1946, he began learning Chinese from scratch — one of the most difficult languages for a European to master. By the time he completed his studies, he had achieved such proficiency that he was able to write a textbook on the subject.

Molody was clearly exceptionally talented in many fields; he was both an economist and a successful businessman. While spying in Britain, he was obliged to conceal his identity as an entrepreneur and, in doing so, amassed a substantial fortune through trading in machinery and jukeboxes. In the end, he became a millionaire, owning a yacht and a fleet of cars — all of which, of course, he had to abandon in Britain.

Segal told me that, after returning from the UK and comparing the reality of life in the USSR with what he had witnessed in the West, the super-spy became virtually a dissident. He was appalled by the inefficiency of the Soviet economy, the bureaucratisation of everyday life, and the pervasive incompetence that seemed to infect every level of the system.

Segal recalls that on one occasion, when Molody was visiting him, he noticed the wretched state of the lift — the dented buttons, the broken handle. 'What on earth is happening to this country?' he asked. 'What kind of system is this, when in the very centre of Moscow, in a building regarded as one of the more respectable ones, such appalling squalor prevails?'

He soon became an irritant to the KGB, as he did not hold back his opinions — even when addressing members of the organisation at meetings. Before long, he realised he was being followed. Molody was outraged. 'I am officially considered a hero, yet they treat me as though they don't trust me. Do they think the Brits turned me while I was in an English prison, or what?' he complained to a friend.

At the KGB clinic, doctors with KGB ranks administered a series of injections, even though he had not reported any illness. The jabs provoked severe headaches. When he protested, he was told to be patient — that his condition might temporarily worsen before improving. Shortly afterwards, he died of a heart attack while gathering mushrooms in a forest near Moscow, at the age of forty-eight. Was he killed — 'eliminated', in the professional jargon of spies? Anything is possible, though we shall never know the truth.

A famous KGB defector, Major Viktor Sheymov, wrote in his memoirs that he decided to break with the organisation and flee to the United States after his closest friend — also a KGB officer — was murdered for openly criticising the Soviet system.

In a sense, the opposite of Molody was another super-spy named Alexander Korotkov. Although not widely known in the West, he became a legend within the intelligence community. Molody was a prodigy, born into a well-educated family — the son of a professor. Korotkov, by contrast, was a proletarian who joined Stalin's secret police (then known as the GPU — *Gosudarstvennoye Politicheskoye Upravleniye*, or the State Political Directorate) without even completing secondary school. Yet he was a curious phenomenon — as if he had been specially created for this creepy profession.

At the GPU, he began as a humble lift operator. But during Stalin's era of relentless purges, when countless secret policemen and spies were imprisoned or executed, there was a constant shortage of personnel. Matters became so dire that even an uneducated lift operator, if considered sufficiently quick-witted, could be transferred to an operational role, on the understanding that he would somehow acquire the necessary training in the course of his work. Probably, in most cases, it is not a good idea to fill important vacancies with the first proletarians that come to hand. But this was indeed an exceptional case.

Korotkov learned quickly, mastering arcane skills and foreign languages, and eventually becoming fluent in both French and German. At one point, he even studied at the Sorbonne, the University of Paris, posing as an Austrian. He possessed a prodigious memory and impressed his superiors with his utter, almost pathological, fearlessness. For instance, after Germany unexpectedly attacked the Soviet Union in June 1941, he somehow managed to break through the Nazi blockade surrounding the Soviet embassy in Berlin — twice — and, using his network of agents, established radio contact with Moscow. He reported in detail on the plight of Soviet citizens trapped in

Germany and received the appropriate instructions in return. This allowed for a complete and unequal exchange of the entire Soviet colony in Germany for German Embassy employees in Moscow, even though the former outnumbered the latter several times over. You can imagine what risks Korotkov took and what the Gestapo would have done to him if he got caught.

On the other hand, he also orchestrated the assassinations of 'traitors' and Trotskyites abroad — and, on occasion, personally carried out the killings of Stalin's enemies. He later oversaw reprisals against the rebellious Hungarians in 1956. Clearly, he was a brute, an absolutely ruthless murderer with a lot of blood on his hands. All in all, he had a spectacular career in Soviet intelligence, eventually commanding a worldwide network of 'illegals' in the 1950s and directing the missions of both Fisher and Molody. And who knows what else? After all, we only learn about clandestine operations when they fail; the successful ones remain hidden from public view. A great deal must have taken place behind the scenes.

Korotkov, however, died quite early and unexpectedly, at the age of just fifty-one. It seems there was a price to pay for leading such a stressful life — or was he also 'liquidated', just in case, because he knew too much?

In summary, if anyone could have served as the real-life prototype for the sinister *Karla*, it was surely Alexander Korotkov.

Until quite recently, the general public in the West had only the vaguest notion of the scale of Soviet espionage — and even less understanding of its intricacies, such as the distinction between 'legal' and 'illegal' intelligence operations. Georgy Agabekov, who defected to the West in 1937, attempted to shed light on this for the public. But, acting on Stalin's orders, Alexander Korotkov trapped and killed Agabekov on the Spanish–French border.

Later came the revelations of Alexander Orlov, who was hiding from Stalin in the United States. Yet his disclosures were more general in nature, limited by a tacit understanding between Orlov and the dictator. If the former refrained from crossing certain red lines, the latter would allow him to live. (It was rumoured that the worst of Stalin's secrets were kept in a safe somewhere, to be made public in the event of Orlov's suspicious death).

In 1954, another KGB officer, Yevgeni Brik, became desperate to tell the world the truth about Soviet 'illegal' intelligence. He phoned the editorial office of the *Montreal Gazette* and solemnly announced, 'I am a Russian spy. Do you want to hear my story?' But Brik's voice did not sound sober, and the journalists refused to believe him. Convinced they were being hoaxed, they hung up the phone. It was a grave mistake. Brik could have provided them with a sensational scoop — with details that no Hollywood producer at the time could have imagined. He might also have revealed to Canada and to the broader world how years of meticulous preparation and vast sums of money spent embedding him in a foreign society were ultimately wasted by the oldest and most human of failings: love for a woman and the unbearable strain of living a double life. He had tried to numb the tension with alcohol, but to no avail.

Canadian journalists could hardly have imagined anything like it. As it happened, Brik's secrets were offered to Canadian counterintelligence, and he began working for them, becoming a so-called 'double agent'. The term, however, is somewhat misleading. In the vast majority of cases, it means that a spy is truly serving one intelligence service while only pretending to work for another.

Evgeni Brik had already inflicted significant damage on Korotkov's department before he himself was betrayed — for a mere five thousand dollars — by another traitor, an employee of the Canadian secret services who was deeply in debt. Korotkov hoped that this somewhat farcical episode would remain an isolated incident. But before long, several other 'illegal' agents were exposed under similar circumstances.

The legendary Fischer-Abel, for example, was betrayed by his assistant, KGB officer Reino Häyhänen, who seemingly could not endure the nerve-racking life of an 'illegal' and broke down. Häyhänen later died in a suspicious car crash in 1961 — most likely 'liquidated' by the KGB as a traitor.

Failures among the 'illegals' became increasingly frequent. Despite their rigorous selection and training, they clearly lacked something their pre-war predecessors had possessed — the ability to withstand immense stress, to improvise skilfully under pressure, and to charm strangers with ease. Almost none of the old guard remained; Stalin had repressed most of them, and others had perished during the war. Entirely different people replaced them.

The quality of new 'assets' — Westerners willing to spy for the Communist state — was also slipping. Those recruited before the Second World War, the 'stars' such as Kim Philby and his fellow Cambridge spies, had delivered Moscow first-rate intelligence — though Stalin often dismissed their reports, with disastrous consequences for Soviet foreign policy. Among the American scientists who built the atomic bomb, there were a few who, on principle, chose to pass nuclear secrets to the Soviet Union. Increasingly, both the KGB and the military intelligence (GRU) had to depend on mercenaries — individuals motivated by greed or personal grievances rather than ideology. Meanwhile, those who still held genuine communist convictions often felt uneasy about being asked to spy on their own countries. Stalin's response was typically ruthless: he said such communists should be 'thrown into a pit'.

The Centre sought to compensate for these weaknesses by increasing spending on intelligence operations and imposing harsher punishments. Yet neither fear nor money could fill the ideological void. The only course left for the heads of the 'illegal' departments was to pretend that these problems were merely temporary setbacks; they could not bring themselves to admit that the golden age of Soviet intelligence in the West had come to an end.

What was happening in the murky world of international espionage was just a symptom of a much wider malaise. The new official representatives of the Soviet Union bore little resemblance to their charismatic predecessors. They were all buttoned up, stilted and unsmiling, always on the look-out for hostile tricks, the product of living in an atmosphere of Stalinist mass terror. Nationalism, anti-Western xenophobia and anti-Semitism had taken the place of Marxist internationalism as the worldview of the Soviet state. In fact, these new Communists knew only an abridged and simplistic version of Marxism dissected and repackaged to serve the primitive propaganda of the day. 'New Soviets' were not encouraged to read the works of Marx and Engels in their original form; some of their articles were practically banned. Only an assortment of useful (to Stalin) quotes and slogans, set out of context, were to be memorised at school or university. Who could those blinkered semi-robots turn into their faith, if faith it was?

'Illegals' were certainly a cut above the average Soviet level, more sophisticated, more gifted and skilled. Still, there was a noticeable decline within their ranks as well. The geniuses of Stalin's espionage, such as Korotkov and Abel, were remnants of former greatness. Molody was one of the rare exceptions that proved the rule. His nonconformism, which ultimately led to his downfall, revealed that he was made of different material—perhaps not entirely Soviet—possibly due to his childhood spent in North America. When he returned to the USSR as a young man, the war had just broken out. He volunteered to fight, blissfully avoiding many of the stifling and mind-numbing aspects of fully developed Stalinism.

The Second World War seemed to end in triumph for the USSR, which had defeated a mighty enemy, albeit at a terrible price. The USSR had greatly expanded its borders and its sphere of influence, establishing satellite states across Eastern Europe. Victory in the war, together with the acquisition of nuclear weapons, had transformed it into a superpower. Yet only many years later, with the benefit of hindsight, did it become clear that the Soviet Union had reached its peak, from which the only direction left to go was down.

The gradual decline in the state's brutal efficiency had, paradoxically, a positive side for the weary and oppressed citizens of the USSR. Although Communist Party rule remained totalitarian and fundamentally based on lies, it became less violent and less bloody. The so-called 'vegetarian times' were approaching. The state of the intelligence services mirrored the condition of society as a whole. Even the appearances of their members reflected this shift. In photographs, Alexander Korotkov's eyes appear frighteningly narrowed, his lips thin and pressed tightly together in anger, almost merging into a single hyphen. Compare this with the way Yuriy Drozdov looked: in contrast to his fearsome predecessor, he seemed harmless—almost homely—nothing like the stereotypical image of a sinister spy chief. Yet, perhaps appearances were once again deceptive, as I had to remind myself.

In defence of Drozdov, I should probably say that from the conversations with his former subordinates, I learned that he was so fluent in German that he could pass for a native speaker. Apparently, he was also an outstanding actor and a man of great personal courage, too. He brilliantly conducted complex operations abroad. At the very start of his career, he successfully impersonated Abel's 'German cousin' and, in that capacity, established contact with him and then helped to organise the exchange on the Glienicke Bridge, depicted in Spielberg's brilliant film. On top of this, he enjoyed a reputation as a fatherly figure within his department, well liked by the rank and file. He was seen as extremely demanding but always fair and caring, protecting his subordinates from any cavils and snipes from outside. But there was a lot to say about him from the prosecution's position at a hypothetical international trial, too. He was one of the organisers of the assault on the palace of Afghan President Hafizullah Amin in December 1979. Dozens were killed there, including the president himself, his guards, servants and most of the family. According to eyewitnesses, the carpets in the palace were literally 'soaked in blood.' Drozdov and his team had no legal or moral right to this massive extrajudicial killing; it was clearly a war crime, as was the entire Soviet adventure in Afghanistan. So, this bald general was not your kindly grandad after all.

In the late autumn of 1991, he was eager 'to tell the truth' about what he claimed was the real story: that the democratic revolution, the failure of the August coup, the dismantling of the KGB, and the emergence of freedom of speech and the press were all 'the result of a CIA conspiracy carried out with the help of traitors — Gorbachev, Yeltsin, and others'.

I offered him to write an opinion piece. But when he submitted it, I was astonished not by its hateful anti-democratic diatribes, which I had fully expected, but by how badly the piece had been written. I had expected that he would concoct something pretty sophisticated, the clever mixture of lies and half-truths, a deft manipulation.

My expectations were proved wrong. What I got was so crude and primitive that I couldn't believe my own eyes. This was the familiar territory of the unrefined Communist Party's propaganda, possibly on a par with the worst examples of this inane genre that I had ever encountered in my life. Hot air, anathemas and insults instead of facts and logical arguments, tired clichés piled one upon another. I was sitting in my office, looking at Yuriy Ivanovich across my desk, trying to decide whether it had been a hoax. But no, Drozdov seemed deadly serious, sitting in his chair with a stubborn expression on his face, his lips tightly pressed together, clearly determined to stand by every word he had written. But what had I to make of the man sitting opposite me, then? That he was a total idiot, or what?

It was the same man who had run Directorate S. for 11 years and, before that, had served as the chief of the most important KGB stations, first in Beijing and then in New York. Surely, I had to allow for the fact that a master spy doesn't necessarily require a literary or even an elementary journalistic talent. But it was still a shocking eye-opener.

I decided to try to outwit the fox.

'Yuriy Ivanovich,' I said, 'I want to propose a deal. I will publish this article of yours exactly as it is, without changing a single word. But it will have to be a trade-off. First, you must write another piece — this time about the incredible adventures of your charges in various countries around the world. If necessary, you may conceal or alter the names of your agents and the nations they operated in. But the essence, the main storylines, must be true. The fact is, here at *Izvestia* we could do with a bit of light reading — something vivid and entertaining to balance our serious coverage of current affairs. And from your perspective, it would serve as excellent publicity for those brilliant and fearless Soviet spies. Would you be interested in such a deal?'

My reasoning went as follows: publishing Drozdov's 'ideological' article might actually prove useful, serving as a kind of self-exposure. Let the readers see for themselves the intellectual poverty and clumsy reasoning of the enemies of democracy. On top of that, I might acquire some genuinely thrilling material as a bonus—something that could even lift the veil of secrecy surrounding illegal espionage. All the Western newspapers, I imagined, would be queuing up to secure reprint rights from us.

Drozdov enthusiastically accepted my proposal. But when he submitted his second piece, it turned out to be remarkably similar to the first. The same frothing denunciations of an alleged CIA conspiracy against Russia and the 'American fifth column' within the country were scattered among vague platitudes about 'heroic Soviet agents' operating behind enemy lines. It contained no specifics, no concrete facts or details — and was, frankly, excruciatingly dull. It was clear that Drozdov either genuinely failed to understand what I had asked for or was pretending not to.

So I came up with another idea: I asked two highly-skilled journalists to sit down with Drozdov for a lengthy, unhurried interview. One was Vladimir Skosyrev, an experienced and versatile feature writer and editor—a consummate professional and a staunch anti-Stalinist. The other was a lively, sharp young reporter named Gennady Charodeyev. The plan was for them to extract as much material as possible from Drozdov, then reshape it into something engaging and readable for our audience. The hope was that the general would approve the final version, allowing it to appear under his byline.

It seemed to work—up to a point. The result was far from brilliant but at least moderately entertaining. However, Drozdov insisted on 'improving' the text, once again trying to 'sharpen it ideologically'. Predictably, the piece deteriorated significantly after his revisions, and he even removed several fascinating details.

By then, I had grown weary of Yuriy Ivanovich Drozdov and regretted ever becoming involved with him. My brief 'flirtation' with the former head of Soviet illegal intelligence appeared to have come to nothing. I was already looking for a tactful way to end our acquaintance when fate unexpectedly intervened. Quite unwittingly, General Drozdov helped us to uncover another, genuinely fascinating story from the shadowy world of illegal espionage.

A letter from Mexico had just landed on my desk. A woman named Angelica Torrago was seeking help in locating her husband—or at least his grave. Her husband, she wrote, was supposedly a Swiss photographer, but in reality, he had turned out to be a Russian spy, a KGB agent. When Angelica discovered the truth, she gave him an ultimatum: he had to choose between his family and his espionage work. After much painful hesitation, he chose his family and resigned. For a time, they were happy; he adored his two daughters. But then, according to Angelica, the KGB kidnapped him and dragged him back to the USSR. What happened to him afterwards remained a mystery. Her appeals—first to Brezhnev, then to Gorbachev, and now to Yeltsin—had all gone unanswered. Perhaps, she hoped, the free press might finally help.

The newly liberated Russian press would indeed have been eager to pursue such a story. Yet I was plagued by doubt. My mentor, Vladimir Segal, had once told me a tale about a distant relative of his who lived somewhere in Soviet Central Asia. The man had managed to convince his wife that he was working for Soviet intelligence, regularly embarking on secret missions into neighbouring Iran. In truth, those 'missions' were brief visits to his lover's home. The deception lasted several months—until the unfortunate 'spy' was spotted by his wife's best friend at the local bazaar.

What if the Mexican story were similar? What if this supposed Russian 'illegal' had abandoned his wife for another woman, spinning a cloak-and-dagger tale to throw her off his scent? Still, the coincidence struck me: I had General Drozdov himself sitting across from me in my office. Of course, that didn't necessarily mean he would tell me the truth—but I thought, *why not give it a try?*

I showed him a translation of the letter. After reading it, the general said:

'I don't recall anything of the sort. But I can ring the current head of my old department and ask him to check. May I use your *vertushka*?'

Ah yes, the *vertushka*—the government's secure telephone line, once the dreaded instrument of Party control—suddenly repurposed as a tool of the free press. The general dialled a number and spoke to someone he referred to as 'Yura' (a diminutive form of Yuriy), who was Drozdov's namesake. He asked whether the department had any record of an illegal agent in Mexico who had tried to resign and might have been abducted. Yura promised to call back.

And he did.

As I waited, I sat at my desk in disbelief, thinking: 'Am I dreaming? How can it be that the former head of Soviet illegal operations abroad is phoning his successor, using *my* telephone, and, at *my* request, is trying to obtain sensitive information?'

Ten minutes later, the second Yura called back and categorically assured Drozdov that nothing resembling the kidnapping story had ever happened to any member of Directorate S. staff in Mexico.

For some reason, I believed the two Yurys—though, of course, they might have been leading me up the garden path. I picked up the letter, ready to toss it into the wastebasket. But Drozdov stopped me.

'Wait a second,' he said. 'Have you checked with 'the Distant Neighbours'? Maybe it's their case?'

I was taken aback. 'But do *they* also use 'illegals'? I asked.

'You bet!' said Drozdov.

A brief digression into Soviet topography is called for. In Stalin's time, the Soviet Foreign Ministry occupied a building on *Kuznetskiy Most* Street—just a five-minute walk from *Lubyanka*, the headquarters of the NKVD, later renamed the KGB. (Today, that same building houses the Russian secret police, the FSB). So, when Soviet diplomats wished to refer to the NKVD–KGB spies in coded correspondence or private conversation, they used a euphemism: *Blizhniye Sosedi*—'the Near Neighbours.' Meanwhile, the headquarters of the military intelligence agency, the GRU, was located farther away, so its employees were referred to as 'The Distant Neighbours'.

Over time, even the spies themselves adopted these informal labels. I have already mentioned the far more irreverent and derogatory nickname that KGB officers used for their GRU counterparts: *Sapogi*, meaning 'Boots'. It reflected both the rivalry between the two secret services and the KGB's professional snobbery. Its spooks always felt superior and despised the military intelligence operatives.

A KGB officer once told me that after the war, Stalin had taken illegal espionage away from the *Sapogi*, making this costly and risky enterprise the exclusive domain of the more 'refined' KGB. I accepted that version at face value—it sounded plausible enough. But now Drozdov shattered my naïve belief, insisting that I had been misinformed and that the GRU had never ceased engaging in illegal intelligence operations.

Looking back now, I suspect that the general may have been playing me from the start. He probably knew the truth about the Mexican story all along, but didn't want to be seen as openly betraying his former rivals to a journalist. Instead, he preferred that I stumble upon the truth myself. It's quite possible that the conversation between the two Yurys on my *vertushka* was staged—or that the new head of Directorate S. simply confirmed what Drozdov already knew: that the story of the kidnapped Soviet illegal in Mexico was genuine.

The spy in question was, in fact, an officer of the military intelligence service, the GRU, not the KGB, as his wife had believed. (She probably had no idea there was a difference between the two). It was only when Drozdov saw that I was about to throw away her letter that he decided to intervene, blurting out the fateful words that revealed the involvement of the 'Distant Neighbours'.

So, which of the two of us was the fool remains open to debate. Perhaps both—each in his own way.

I thanked the general, though my gratitude would have been far more profound if I realised that he had just steered me towards one of the biggest scoops of my journalistic career. The very next day, I summoned our military correspondent, Nikolai Burbyga, who had extensive contacts within the General Staff and even the GRU itself, and I filled him in on the story. He was sceptical at first, but promised to use his connections to find out more.

I will not recount all the trials, twists, and turns of that investigation—nor attempt to tally the number of hours Nikolai spent in Russian steam baths or the bottles of fine whisky he had to share with senior officers and other well-informed sources. Suffice it to say that, a few weeks later, he returned with results:

he had discovered both the name of the kidnapped spy and the place to which he had been taken after his abduction.

In Mexico, he had been known as a Swiss photographer named Maurice Bronelier, but his real name was Oleg Skoryi. He had served as an 'illegal resident' for many years, operating primarily against the United States and American interests. His work had been considered so successful that he was awarded a high military decoration and promoted to the rank of lieutenant colonel.

Thus, his 'resignation' came as a complete shock to the generals in Moscow. It was utterly unprecedented, and they had no idea how to deal with it. At first, his control officer tried to reason with him, but Skoryi stood firm. As far as he was concerned, his spying days were over. He made it clear that he would remain silent, would never betray his comrades, and that none of the GRU's secrets would be exposed. But, he insisted, there would be no more espionage for him—thank you very much.

The leadership could not accept this. A decision was made to lure him to Peru, abduct him there, and 'evacuate' him to Moscow via Havana.

Oleg Skoryi had created a serious problem for the GRU: how could they explain such an extraordinary situation to the Central Committee? The Soviet secret services were accustomed to the occasional defection—these were as inevitable as rain or snow—but this was something entirely different. This was not a case of a spy turning traitor for financial gain or ideological reasons. Here was a loyal and accomplished operative who wanted to resign purely for personal reasons. Such a thing was unheard of.

Some clever rationalisation was required that would assuage the Central Committee's wrath. So, someone in the GRU came up with an ingenious idea – to explain away Skoryi's weird behaviour by mental illness. It was presented as a case of an abrupt onset of a medical condition rather than an act of gross subordination. The Central Committee chose to believe this version, especially as Skoryi was indeed in a state of nervous breakdown – who wouldn't be after all he had to go through? He faced the totally impossible choice, torn between the family he loved so much and his sense of duty.

The medical explanation suited everybody. No one was punished, and even Skoryi got away lightly: he received an honourable discharge for health reasons, allowing him to keep his medals and receive the military pension. It was decided to hide him away in his native Kyiv, under the scrutiny of local military spooks. Nobody could have guessed that only a few years later, Ukraine would become an independent country and the GRU would lose all control over Skoryi's life. That's why we at *Izvestia* were able to find him and establish contact.

Everything turned out to be a bit more complicated in real life than in Angelica's letter. Apparently, the Mexican wife of Oleg Skoryi was a daughter of a senior official called Ernesto Torrago, who, according to the GRU sources, had himself been an old collaborator of the Soviet military intelligence. If this is true, it means that the marriage of Oleg and Angelica was not an accident; the GRU had probably arranged it. I am not sure that Angelica's protestations of her total innocence were genuine. However, it does happen that even in arranged marriages, people sometimes genuinely fall in love – a feeling that can never be fully compatible with the creepy rules of the espionage world. That is when the situation may slip beyond the spooks' control. According to a semi-official version available from GRU-friendly journalists (which does not necessarily mean it is entirely accurate), once she was informed of his clandestine work, Angelica agreed to assist Oleg in his covert activities, drawing on her journalistic contacts. She allegedly visited Moscow twice at the invitation of the GRU. However, in her letter, she insisted that from the very beginning, she had tried to persuade her husband to end his double life. She clearly didn't realise that a 'resignation' of an active officer-spy is impossible, that the GRU would not allow it under any circumstances.

It is puzzling that Skoryi himself showed such incredible naïveté; how could he, even for a moment, believe that he could get away with it? Apparently, he had settled into the role of a Swiss photographer too well and certainly loved his wife and daughters. And the mind's plasticity has its limits: the human in him outweighed the professional, proving that 'illegals' are not machines.

I think Oleg was lucky in that he was just kidnapped and not killed. I am sure that the latter option was also on the cards. Had the kidnapping failed for any reason, Oleg would have been most certainly 'liquidated'.

We at *Izvestia* initiated and helped to organise an unbelievable reunion: Angelica came to Kiev with her two daughters to see Oleg again. The emotions experienced by the participants of that meeting are beyond my ability to put into words.

We, of course, ran this sensational story in our pages with all the incredible details. It was undoubtedly a huge scoop, but it didn't get the attention it deserved because, at the beginning of 1992, Russia was experiencing an economic and social convulsion, undergoing a tectonic transformation of unprecedented proportions. The all-powerful state abruptly crumbled, and there was suddenly so much freedom that it bordered on anarchy. Millions instantly lost their incomes and savings as shop prices skyrocketed and the rouble was drastically devalued. People were electrified, yet confused and frightened by the rapid changes in their lives. At times, it felt as if the country was on the verge of a new bloody civil war. In this situation, the amazing story of love and espionage was relegated to the margins of public attention, maybe noted but then quickly forgotten.

The story, meanwhile, had a rather sad but logical ending. Arriving in Kiev, Angelica was shocked to discover that Oleg Skoryi had another wife there. He married her after his return from Mexico, certain that there was no chance in the world he would ever see his beloved family again. The fact that also raises an interesting question: can 'illegals' be accused of the crime of bigamy? I don't know if it is possible to apply any legal norms to individuals who are compelled by their country to maintain two distinct personalities.

At the end of that whole sorrowful saga, I was left with a lingering sense of incompleteness. Perhaps that is why, many years later, I wrote a novel titled *Жена Нелегала* (*The Sleeper's Wife*), which was published in 2010 in St. Petersburg. In it, I tried to offer some answers to the mysteries of that baffling story, questions that continue to haunt me to this day. I do not mean the cryptic details of the clandestine operations, or the technical aspects of espionage, compelling though they are in their own way. What drew me in far more deeply was the psychological struggle—the impossible choice forced upon the protagonists.

I was captivated by the power of raw human emotion when pitted against an artificial, contrived world that seeks to suppress or deny it. And for what purpose, ultimately? To serve the fleeting interests of a few decrepit old men in the Kremlin?

I couldn't get off this subject. A few years later, I wrote a dystopian novel titled *Синдром Л.* (*Syndrome L.*), published by EKSMO in Moscow in 2014. It tells the story of a fiery, passionate and obsessive love affair between two people. The relationship is conceived and orchestrated by a security service for its own dubious ends, but, in an unexpected twist, it brings about a most unpleasant outcome for the spy chiefs who engineered it.

Epilogue

'My life, I'm reading with disgust,' wrote Alexander Pushkin, Russia's foremost literary genius, in one of his most celebrated poems, *Remembrances*. I do not for a moment pretend to be anywhere near Pushkin's league, but there are times when I cannot help feeling something akin to revulsion as I leaf through the pages of my own life story. There have been too many wrong decisions, too many words I wish I had never uttered, and too many moments when life seemed unbearably unfair.

On the brighter side, there were, without doubt, many happy moments as well. I have known the joy of requited love. I have also had the good fortune to meet an array of remarkable and fascinating people—from Mikhail Gorbachev and the great Russian reformer Yegor Gaidar, to former British Prime Minister Tony Blair and the late Princess Diana, among others. I even came to know several Russian billionaires personally—the kind the Western press rather loosely and unscientifically refers to as 'oligarchs'. Observing them at close range proved both intriguing and illuminating, though not always pleasant. In the end, I concluded that this peculiar species of humans is best left to associate exclusively with its own kind—or with its subordinates and hangers-on. I belonged to neither group.

I count myself lucky that the work I devoted most of my life to was both absorbing and stimulating, offering intellectual satisfaction and a sense of purpose. The pinnacle of my career—and of my professional fulfilment—undoubtedly came in the late 1980s and early 1990s, when Mother Russia was undergoing an awe-inspiring transformation through the bold reforms of *Perestroika*. It truly felt as though the ground was trembling beneath our feet. The sense of being personally involved, of actively participating in those momentous changes, was exhilarating and unforgettable. As the monolithic power of the Communist Party began to crumble, I rose through the ranks at *Izvestia*, eventually becoming, at the end of 1991, its Foreign Editor responsible for overseeing all international news coverage.

At that time, *Izvestia* was, in my view, the best workplace any Russian journalist could dream of. Today, the Russian authorities have all but destroyed the newspaper, turning it into a contemptible propaganda sheet despised by all thinking people.

I was also extraordinarily fortunate to have had the opportunity to work alongside the highly professional journalists of the *Financial Times* in London for nearly two years. Later, in 2000, I went on to represent the *FT* in their new Russian venture—an ambitious collaboration with their chief rival, *The Wall Street Journal*. The project didn't quite work out for me personally, but the newspaper, *Vedomosti*, was a resounding success, becoming the most respected and influential publication in Russia. Alas, as a Western-backed project, it was ultimately doomed. The dramatic shift in Russian politics meant that Vladimir Putin would not tolerate such a prominent Western presence in the Russian media landscape.

My fifteen years at the BBC were far less satisfying. One decision I deeply regret was accepting the position of Editor of the BBC Russian Service in 2001. I had naively believed that, in this new managerial role, I would be able to apply the practical experience I had gained from successfully reforming *Izvestia*'s Foreign Desk. In Moscow, my most significant accomplishment was a little *Perestroika* of my own — reshaping the desk's working methods to make the most effective use of each journalist's individual strengths.

At the BBC, however, this proved utterly impossible. The Russian Service had its share of talented and interesting individuals, but, as a whole, it remained trapped in old habits, incapable of innovation or transformation along the lines of the English BBC. My attempts at modernisation met with resistance, and before long, I had made several mortal enemies within the service. They retaliated in the time-honoured Russian fashion: through backroom intrigues and anonymous denunciations. It was all carried out in the most underhanded way—no one ever confronted me directly or dared to say a word to my face, yet wild, malicious accusations were circulated widely.

At the same time, I had little doubt that there were moles within the Russian Service. A colleague from the BBC's Moscow bureau once told me how he had been aggressively approached by the FSB—the successor to the KGB—who had tried to recruit him as an informant and agent of influence. I also knew of another colleague who had faced a similar attempt. Both were courageous enough to resist, despite the psychological pressure and threats they endured. But how many others had given in, losing their nerve and succumbing to coercion? I could only speculate.

I had reason to believe that some of our employees in London were also working for Russian intelligence, while others appeared to be currying favour with the exiled billionaire Boris Berezovsky—Vladimir Putin's sworn enemy—who later died in suspicious circumstances, almost certainly murdered on the Kremlin's orders. There was little I could do to change this troubling situation; I lacked concrete evidence of deliberate wrongdoing. Matters only worsened once Moscow adopted an openly anti-Western stance and began tightening the screws on its own people at home.

The real turning point came with the murder in London of Alexander Litvinenko, the former KGB officer who had defected to Britain and was working for Berezovsky. Russian–British relations deteriorated sharply thereafter. The BBC's ethos of impartiality was increasingly rejected by the Russian public—largely brainwashed by state propaganda—except for a relatively small group of intellectuals. For Putin and his entourage, simply reporting the truth had become an act of subversion and sabotage, as it clashed directly with their web of lies. In the best KGB tradition, propaganda was seen as a legitimate instrument of psychological warfare.

But against whom was this war being waged? As the liberal politician Grigory Yavlinsky observed, 'It seems as though the Russian state is at war with its own population, which, like an enemy in wartime, must be constantly misinformed and deceived.'

That internal war—against Russia's most enlightened citizens, against its own culture and conscience—has now erupted into open aggression against Ukraine and its people, the Russians' closest kin and fellow Orthodox Christians. This war now threatens to engulf the whole of Europe. Back in the late

2000s, such a development still seemed unimaginable. Yet even then, within Russia itself, the post-truth era had already begun.

Meanwhile, the BBC Russian service, in its previous form, was dying. In a desperate search for budget cuts, the World Service decided to end Russian-language radio broadcasting. The Service became exclusively internet-based, and I felt there was no longer a place for me there. I volunteered for redundancy, which was probably my wisest career move at the BBC.

And that, I suppose, brings me to the end of my personal *Jeremiad*. There is a popular Russian proverb: *'There was no luck until misfortune came to help.'* The English equivalent would be *'a blessing in disguise'* or *'every cloud has a silver lining'*. For me, that silver lining was that, upon retiring, I was finally free to pursue what I had always dreamed of—writing books. I might have been a contented soul if not for the relentless torrent of horrifying news from Russia that continues to reach me each day.

My beloved motherland fills me with dread, a feeling that burrows under my skin and stays there. Many thousands of innocent people languish in prisons and labour camps, condemned by corrupt police and venal judges. At the same time, thieves and opportunists thrive through sycophantic devotion to the Kremlin and its master, accompanied by grotesque outbursts of hateful jingoism. Those who dare to speak the truth risk imprisonment, torture, or death. The level of political repression under Khrushchev or Brezhnev now seems mild by comparison with Putin's police-state regime, which bears a chilling resemblance to Stalin's purges. It is no coincidence that new monuments to Stalin—the worst tyrant and mass murderer in Russian history—are being erected across the country.

With around 80 per cent of the population now brainwashed into supporting Putin's crude nationalism and his war, modern Russia has come to believe that might is right, and that true power rests solely on brute force and amoral cunning. This belief did not emerge from nowhere. Its roots lie deep in the culture of ruthlessness and xenophobia cultivated under Stalin, particularly within the KGB and the other secret services of the Soviet empire.

Gorbachev and Yeltsin made a fatal mistake by allowing these sinister institutions to survive intact. As a result, they stepped into the ideological vacuum left by the collapse of communism, filling it with their own paranoid, conspiratorial worldview. Once, the Communist Party ruled the USSR, and its spy agencies served as its instruments of power. But when the master disappeared, the instrument became the master.

The high point came at the end of 1999 and the beginning of 2000, when the question of President Yeltsin's successor loomed large. My good friend Igor Malashenko was first offered the position of Chief of the Presidential Administration, and then that of Prime Minister of Russia—appointments that would have placed him directly in line to succeed Yeltsin. He categorically declined both offers. Nevertheless, Igor remained an influential adviser within the Kremlin and invited me to witness some of his conversations with key figures when Vladimir Putin's candidacy was first proposed.

Malashenko viewed the prospect with deep misgivings, troubled by Putin's KGB background and his characteristic worldview. In later years, Igor confessed that turning down the opportunity to take a leading political role had been 'the greatest mistake of his life'. He blamed himself for squandering a genuine chance to prevent Russia's reversion to a police state and to avert the mounting hostility between Russia and the democratic world. This sense of guilt weighed heavily on his conscience and may have contributed to his tragic decision to take his own life.

Yet, to understand Putinism fully, one must see it within the broader sweep of Russian history. The country appears trapped in a recurring cycle, shaped by its geography and its position on the border between Europe and Asia—forever suspended between two continents, two civilisations, and two epochs. Having endured centuries under the rule of the Mongol Horde, the early Russian state gradually absorbed and adapted its conqueror's governing methods, becoming, in effect, a continuation of them in a new form. Despite its European façade, the Russian Empire remained oriental at its core — an heir to the traditions of Tatar-Mongol despotism.

When slavery—known as serfdom—was finally abolished by Alexander II in 1861, the reform was resented by nearly every social class, unprepared as they were for such freedom. At the first opportunity, the Bolsheviks succeeded in re-establishing serfdom in another form, through the collectivised farms known as *kolkhozes*. In all other respects, Soviet Russia became a tyranny even more absolute than that of the tsars. This neo-feudal economic system was hopelessly incompatible with the twentieth century, but the half-hearted attempts to liberalise it after Stalin's death only accelerated its decline. Then came a brief decade of freedom in the 1990s. It is difficult to resist the temptation to see it as nothing more than a glitch, an accident, a historical hiccup. When it ended, much of the population welcomed its demise, embracing the emergence of a new paternal figure—a new tsar—as a comforting return to 'normality'. Once again, it appears that the Russian people — or at least the great majority — were not ready for freedom. The question remains: will they ever be?

As for spies, the conclusion suggests itself: ultimately, every nation gets the spies it deserves.

Some names have been changed.

ACKNOWLEDGEMENTS

I am deeply grateful to Jenny Brown for her invaluable help in editing and refining the text of this book; without her expertise, it would scarcely have come to fruition. My heartfelt thanks also go to my old friend and kindred spirit, Daniel Wolf, for his encouragement and support throughout this journey. I would love to thank some of my friends in Russia, but for obvious reasons, I will refrain from doing so, as their safety comes first.